Greek Theatre
in Context

Eric Dugdale

CAMBRIDGE
UNIVERSITY PRESS

CAMBRIDGE UNIVERSITY PRESS
Cambridge, New York, Melbourne, Madrid, Cape Town, Singapore, São Paulo, Delhi

Cambridge University Press
The Edinburgh Building, Cambridge CB2 8RU, UK

www.cambridge.org
Information on this title: www.cambridge.org/9780521689427

First published 2008

Printed in the United Kingdom at the University Press, Cambridge

A catalogue record for this publication is available from the British Library

ISBN   978-0-521-68942-7 paperback

ACKNOWLEDGEMENTS
Cover, pp.63, 115, 129 Martin von Wagner Museum der Universität Würzburg, photo
K Oehrlein; p.3 Department of Classical and Near Eastern Antiquities, National Museum
of Denmark, inv. no. 13817; p.10 Perseus Digital Library Project, Tufts University; p.14
detail, Apulian Red-figure Bell Krater, Name Vase of the Choregos Painter, The J. Paul
Getty Museum, Villa Collection, Malibu, California; p.17 Louvre, Paris, Peter Willi/
The Bridgeman Art Library; pp.19, 60, 94, 139, 163 © copyright The Trustees of the
British Museum; p.20 Photo RMN/© Hervé Lewandowski; p.22 Giovanni Lattanzi; p.24
Soprintendenza per i Beni Archeologici della Toscana – Firenze; pp.30, 44 Epigraphical
Museum, Athens © Hellenic Ministry of Culture, Archaeological Receipts Fund, inv. nos.
EM 13262 & EM8225; p.33 en.wikipedia.org; pp.47, 54 Kyle Dugdale; pp.49, 52 © King's
College, London; p.51 original drawings from Fiechter *Dionysostheater*, figs. 30 & 31 in
Margarete Bieber *The History of the Greek and Roman Theatre*, Princeton University
Press, 1961; p.55 Eric Dugdale; p.57*t* Parktheater GmbH, photo Martin Kunzmann;
p.57*b* from Graham Ley *The Theatricality of Greek Theatre: Playing Space and Chorus*,
University of Chicago Press; p.61 original drawing by E. Gilliéron, fig. 202 in Margarete
Bieber *The History of the Greek and Roman Theatre*, Princeton University Press, 1961;
p.86 Antikenmuseum Basel und Sammlung Ludwig, inv. BS415, photo Andreas F. Voegelin;
pp.88, 125 photograph © Museum of Fine Arts, Boston; pp.97, 118 The Nicholson Museum
© The University of Sydney; p.98 bpk/Antikensammlung, SMB/Johannes Laurentius; p.122
Archaeological Museum Kavala; p.140 William K. Freiert; p.148 The Metropolitan Museum
of Art, Rogers Fund, 1951 (51.11.2) image © The Metropolitan Museum of Art; pp.158, 177
Museo Capitolino, Rome, Italy/The Bridgeman Art Library; p.169 © Museum of Classical
Archaeology, Cambridge; p.190 Bruce M. White © photo Trustees of Princeton University.

Every effort has been made to reach copyright holders. The publishers would be glad to
hear from anyone whose rights they have unknowingly infringed.

Contents

Introduction

Greek drama continues to speak powerfully to ever wider audiences. The works of great playwrights such as Sophocles, Euripides and Aristophanes are studied in classrooms and lecture halls around the globe; they are performed in small community theatres and on Broadway; and they inspire a proliferation of adaptations and new works. In 2007 at the National School of Drama in New Delhi, India, for example, a collaborative venture by Indian director Abhilash Pillai, Iranian director Mohammad Aghebati, and Uzbekistan's Ovlyakuli Khojakuli staged a new dramatic interpretation of the tragic characters Medea, Jocasta and Clytemnestra. And a version of Sophocles' *Electra* by internationally acclaimed Japanese director Tadashi Suzuki is about to take to the stage in Moscow.

Many who read and study Greek drama, however, do so in a virtual vacuum. Often the only set texts in courses on ancient theatre are the plays themselves. Written 2,500 years ago, they raise many intriguing questions for which we must look elsewhere for answers. What did an ancient performance look like? Why did Athens allow its comic poets to ridicule its leaders? Do the powerful female characters of Athenian tragedy in any way reflect the reality of Athenian society? The evidence gathered and evaluated in this book helps answer these and other questions. A wide range of ancient authors along with vase-paintings and other material evidence provide important clues that help set the plays in their context. A lot of our evidence comes from incidental remarks in works on non-dramatic subjects (Athenian lawcourt speeches, philosophical treatises and many other genres). This shows the centrality of theatre in Athenian society – it frequently serves as a point of reference in other discussions, a cultural signifier such as perhaps the cinema is today. A benefit of this is that the reader will learn about many other facets of Athenian life in the process of examining these sources. Not everything that ancient authors say, however, can be taken at face value. Some write many centuries later and make highly speculative claims; others indulge their own peculiar interests and prejudices. Each source, therefore, must also be understood within its own historical context.

The evidence collected in this book has a strong focus on Athenian drama of the fifth, fourth and early third centuries BC. This is intentional, since a primary purpose of this book is to enhance the reader's understanding and appreciation of the surviving plays, all of which were composed by Athenians for performance in the theatre at Athens during this period. It is also a natural consequence of the fact that the bulk of the information that has come down to us is about Athenian theatre. It is clear that other Greek cities had flourishing theatrical traditions, but we know relatively little about them. Already in ancient times, the plays of Athenian playwrights such as Euripides and Menander were acknowledged as masterpieces and re-performed across the Greek-speaking world.

This book generally uses the more familiar Latinized spellings of Greek names instead of transliterating the Greek: thus it has Aeschylus rather than Aischylos and Sophocles instead of Sophokles. The intention is to make it easier for the student to consult reference works such as the *Oxford Classical Dictionary*, which tend to use Latinized spelling. For minor figures (e.g. Sosippos or Autokles mentioned in the inscription at **2.2**) I have preserved the Greek spelling. Greek terms such as *mēchanē* or *kōmos* are italicized. Words that appear in bold are defined in the glossary. Macrons (long marks) are included the first time a Greek word appears and also in the glossary. Primary sources are numbered by chapter (**1.1**, **1.2** etc.) for easier cross-referencing. Square brackets [ ] within translated sources enclose editorial comments added for clarification. For details of ancient sources and abbreviations not specified in full in the text, please see the *Oxford Classical Dictionary* (3rd edn). Dates are frequently cited in the form 456/55 BC; this is because an Athenian year begins in autumn and ends in summer, thus spanning two modern years. All dates are BC unless otherwise stated.

Acknowledgements

In writing this book, I owe a debt of gratitude to earlier works, especially A. W. Pickard-Cambridge's *The Dramatic Festivals of Athens* (Oxford, revised edn 1968) and Eric Csapo and William Slater's *The Context of Ancient Drama* (Ann Arbor, 1994). Both offer valuable collections of ancient sources (see Recommended reading); the latter also includes sources on Roman drama. Without their trail-blazing work, writing this book would have been much harder.

I would like to thank Cambridge University Press and Judith Affleck and John Harrison, editors of the Cambridge Translations from Greek Drama series, for permission to use the following excerpts from translations in their series:

Translations from Aeschylus' *Agamemnon* by Philip de May (2003)
Translations from Euripides' *Bacchae* by David Franklin (2000)
Translations from Euripides' *Medea* by John Harrison (2000)
Translations from Sophocles' *Antigone* by David Franklin (2003)
Translations from Sophocles' *Electra* by Eric Dugdale (2008)
Translations from Sophocles' *Philoctetes* by Judith Affleck (2001)
Translations from Sophocles' *Oedipus the King* by Ian McAuslan (2003)

All other translations of sources are mine.

There are many whose help, advice and support in writing this book I would like to acknowledge, including Kyle Dugdale, Mario Erasmo, Stewart Flory, William Freiert, Alan Hughes, Tobias Jenkins, Mireille Lee, Kathie Martin and the staff at the Interlibrary Loan desk, Matthew Panciera, Jonathan Peasley, Mary Sturgeon, William West and Bronwen Wickkiser. I am especially grateful to James Morwood for his valuable suggestions, editorial advice and encouragement at every step. The mistakes and shortcomings of this book are exclusively mine. I would also like to thank Gustavus Adolphus College for an RSC grant, Corpus Christi College, Oxford, for hosting me while conducting research, and our publisher, Matthew Winson at Cambridge University Press. I dedicate this book to my wonderful wife Brooke.

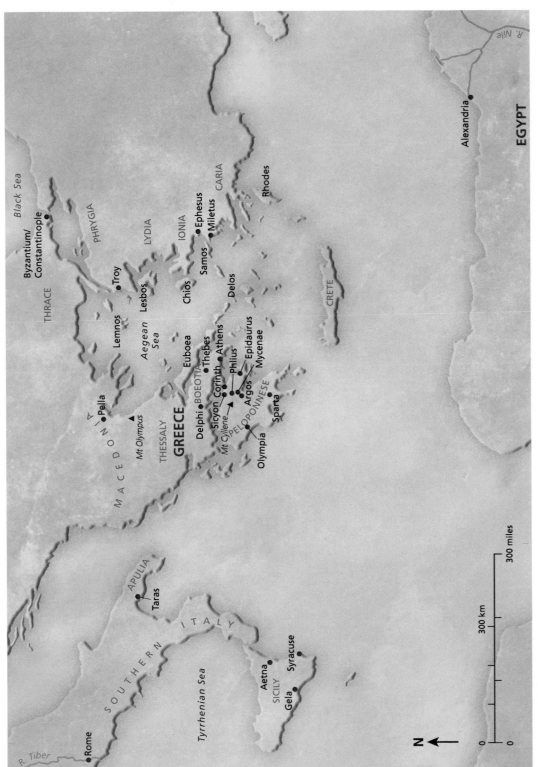

The eastern Mediterranean.

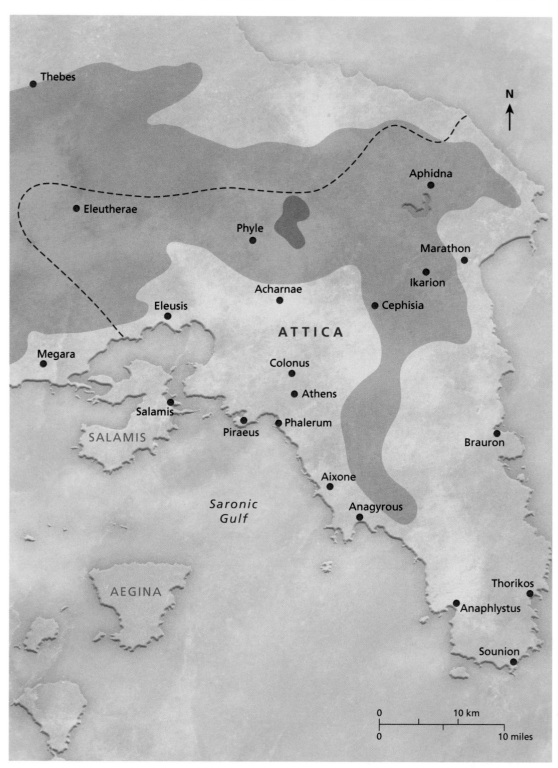

Attica (adapted from Pomeroy *et al.* (2004: 177)).

1 The genres of performance

A spectator at the **City Dionysia** festival at Athens in the fifth century BC could enjoy an extravaganza of entertainment with all the magnetism of a Woodstock or a Glastonbury festival. Everything from dithyrambs to satyr-plays played to an enthusiastic audience of thousands, and the atmosphere was by all accounts electric. Add to this the fact that in any given year you could see tragedies and comedies by great playwrights such as Sophocles, Euripides and Aristophanes, and it is easy to see why Athenians were obsessed with the theatre. Centuries later, these plays are still admired as unsurpassed masterpieces, and their skilful artistry and raw emotion play to packed houses all over the world.

How did we get to this point? And how did Athenian drama come to exert such an influence on western theatre from Shakespeare to Stoppard? Not only the vocabulary of the stage (words like protagonist, episode and scenery) but the very way we think about character, plot and artistic originality is the legacy of the remarkable artistic creativity of Athenian society.

In all, four different types of performance were put on in the theatre at Athens: dithyrambs, tragedies, satyr-plays and comedies. Of these genres, tragedies have come down to us in the greatest number (33); next come comedies, of which 18 have survived entirely or in large part. Of satyr-plays, we only have Euripides' *Cyclops* and portions of Sophocles' *Trackers*; no actual dithyramb survives in full, although its influence may be felt in certain tragic choruses and in the poems of the fifth-century lyric poet Bacchylides.

Dithyramb

Little is known for certain about **dithyrambs** – not even what the word actually means. We know that they were hymns sung and danced in honour of Dionysus. They were not plays as we would think of them, with individuals acting out parts, but rather large-scale choral performances of song and dance. In the City Dionysia festival at Athens, dithyrambic performances took place on the first day and were the 'show opener'. The renowned lyric poets Simonides, Bacchylides and Pindar are all known to have entered the dithyrambic competitions at the City Dionysia. Although our best evidence comes from Athens, dithyrambs were also performed at rural festivals in Attica (the area around Athens), in the Peloponnese and in the Aegean islands.

The following description is given by an ancient **scholiast** (commentator) on Aeschines' (lived *c.* 397 to *c.* 322 BC) lawcourt speech *Against Timarchus* 10, explaining a reference in the speech to 'circular choruses'. In the speech itself, Aeschines explains that Athenian lawgivers have set up measures to protect young boys from unwelcome attention; for example, they have stipulated that those sponsoring dithyrambic choruses be over forty years old to ensure that the education of Athenian youth be entrusted to individuals old enough to act responsibly.

1.1 By custom the Athenians put on choruses of fifty boys **or** fifty men per tribe; so there are ten choruses, since there are ten tribes. They compete with each other in the dithyramb, and each sponsor provides for the needs of his chorus. The winning chorus receives a tripod, which it dedicates to Dionysus. The dithyrambic choruses are called '**circular choruses**'.

The following fragment of a poem by Archilochus, preserved in Athenaeus' *Deipnosophistai* or *Learned Banqueters* (628a–b), dates to the seventh century BC, indicating that the dithyramb went far back.

1.2 Since I know how to **lead off** the lovely song of Lord Dionysus, the dithyramb, when my **wits have been blitzed by wine** ...

The painting on a krater (a large vessel used for mixing water with wine) dating to *c.* 425 BC depicts a choral performance, as is clear from the central figure playing the double-pipe, who is typically included to indicate a live

or   each Athenian tribe entered both a chorus of fifty boys *and* one of fifty men. Thus, the ten choruses of 50 boys and ten choruses of 50 men totalled 1,000 competitors, a sizeable proportion of the population. It would be fair to say that in the fifth century a lot of Athenian males would have had experience performing and would have therefore been a well-informed audience.

circular choruses   (Greek *kyklios choros*) this common description of the dithyramb recalls earlier descriptions in Homer of choruses dancing in circular movements around a floor of beaten earth to the accompaniment of the double-pipe and lyre (e.g. *Odyssey* 8.260–5; *Iliad* 18.484–5, 569–72, 590–606).

lead off   this refers to the role of chorus-leader (Greek *exarchos*). Tragedy also had a chorus-leader (the *koryphaios*) who in addition to leading the chorus in unison singing and in dancing also had individual spoken lines and conversed with the characters in the play. It is likely that in the dithyramb the chorus-leader also sang a separate part (as the officiating priest exchanges alternating responses with the congregation in some liturgies nowadays) and that dithyrambs drew their subject-matter from myth, especially myths about Dionysus.

wits have been blitzed by wine   Archilochus describes the effect of wine using a verb that literally means 'blasted by a thunder-bolt'.

performance. The five men who flank him are mature adults with beards, dressed ornately and crowned with wreaths of ivy, a plant associated with Dionysus. The central figure looks out towards the viewer – thus his frontal representation distinguishes him from the four figures flanking him, who appear to be singing. In the centre of the field is a pole embedded in a stand and entwined with ivy.

This scene is interpreted as a representation of a dithyrambic chorus of men, and the frontal figure is identified variously as the chorus-leader, the poet, or the sponsor of the performance. That five chorus-members are represented rather than the full complement of ten need not concern us since vase-paintings frequently economize like this owing to the constraints of space. The dithyrambic chorus – unlike the choruses of tragedy, satyr-play and comedy – did not wear masks, and there is no trace of a mask on any of the characters in this painting. Each figure is identified by name; the name of the figure facing outwards, Phrynichus, is that of a well-known comic poet. It is possible that this Phrynichus also wrote or performed dithyrambs and is being celebrated on this vase, though the name is a relatively common one.

1.3

1   What might be the function of the ivy-clad pole in the centre?
2   What modern-day performances could you compare to dithyrambic choruses?

Tragedy

Tragedy was performed by an all-male cast which, in its final form, consisted of fifteen chorus-members and three character actors who, between the three of them, played all the speaking parts, male and female alike. The structure of the plays was highly formalized. Almost always, a brief prologue setting the scene was followed by the entry of the chorus (the *parodos*); they remained on stage for the remainder of the play, which consisted of sung choral odes alternating with episodes. Most of the plot developments of the play occurred in the **episodes** (the technical term referring to scenes), which were spoken by the main characters.

Tragedy almost always drew its subject-matter from mythology. Even plays that staged recent historical events, such as Aeschylus' *Persians*, did so in a mythologized form. The Persian invader Xerxes is a victim of destructive *atē* (a blind madness sent by the gods), and the play uses mythological patterns such as the unheeded prophecy, uttered by the ghost of King Darius. Although the general subject-matter was usually familiar to the audience, playwrights had the freedom to develop it in innovative ways.

Tragedy was the most prestigious of the dramatic genres. Tragedies were performed at the City Dionysia and **Lenaea** festivals in Athens; they were also performed in the **Rural Dionysia**, local festivals in communities throughout Attica. At all three events, playwrights competed for prizes.

> Aristotle's *Poetics*, a treatise written in the late fourth century BC, is perhaps the single work that has had the greatest influence on interpretations of Greek tragedy down the centuries. Although Aristotle lived soon after the heyday of tragedy and is therefore a valuable source, his statements are sometimes idiosyncratic and speculative, and his theories have often been misinterpreted. In this extract (1449a), Aristotle traces the origins and development of different genres of poetry, especially tragedy.

1.4   When tragedy and comedy had both come to light, people were drawn to each **according to their natural inclination**. Some became **composers** of comedies

---

according to their natural inclination   surviving records corroborate the picture that we get here that playwrights composed tragedies or comedies but not both.

composers   the Greek word *poiētēs* literally means 'maker' of comedies – this same word gives us our word 'poet'; it stresses the creative element of art (a playwright 'makes' his artistic piece just as a sculptor would) over the written script, which was not at all important in a culture where poetry was primarily transmitted orally. This is reflected in the word translated 'producers of tragedies' which literally means 'teachers of tragedies', indicating the key role played by the poet in teaching his play to the cast.

instead of **iambic poems**, while others became producers of tragedies instead of epics, since these forms [i.e. comedy and tragedy] are greater and more noble than the others [i.e. iambic and epic]. Now to consider whether tragedy is already developed enough in its elements or not, and to critique it in itself and in relation to its audience, that is a separate subject. But since tragedy came into being **from an origin in improvisation** (this was the case with both tragedy and comedy, the former **from those who led off the dithyrambs**, the latter from those who led off the phallic performances, which, even now, continue to be customary in many cities) tragedy grew little by little as people developed every element that was invented; after undergoing many changes, it stopped when it had **attained its own form. Aeschylus** was the first to raise the number of actors from one to two; he **reduced the part of the chorus** and gave the leading role to spoken dialogue. Sophocles introduced three actors and **painted scenery**. Now as to the greatness

---

iambic poems short poems that often included obscene language and lampooned individuals.

from an origin in improvisation, from those who led off the dithyrambs it is wise to be suspicious of Aristotle's explanation of the origins of tragedy. Despite his authoritative tone, it is unlikely that, living in a culture with very few written records, he had any clear evidence on which to base his assertions of what had happened centuries earlier. Nothing that we know about dithyrambic poetry, which appears to have consisted of carefully composed matching sets of verses, suggests that it was improvised. Furthermore, it is strange that dithyrambs were performed alongside tragedy if the former evolved into the latter. The word tragedy seems to mean 'goat-song' – though what exactly goats have to do with tragedy is not at all clear. Perhaps the best explanation is that the word refers to choral songs performed at the sacrifice of a goat (another suggestion is that a goat was the prize for the winning tragic chorus).

attained its own form Aristotle is perhaps influenced by his own interests in the natural world, where he was a keen observer of the different stages of animal development, and by his philosophical belief that everything in the natural world has its own inherent form. His belief in a static mature phase in the development of tragedy seems a little odd: the surviving plays show that playwrights continued to experiment.

Aeschylus … reduced the part of the chorus the Greeks tended to attribute every advancement to a specific inventor: Prometheus was said to have invented metalwork, mining and a multitude of other technologies, while Arion, a poet living in Corinth around 600 BC, was credited with having invented both the dithyramb and tragedy. The innovations that Aristotle here ascribes to Aeschylus and Sophocles could, however, quite plausibly have been made by these influential playwrights. What Aristotle says about the increased prominence of spoken parts and the decline in the role of the chorus (whose odes were sung) can be statistically documented in the surviving tragedies whose date is known.

painted scenery since each of the four plays put on by a tragedian at the City Dionysia might have a different setting, such scenery must have been either generic or easily removable. The surviving plays use the words of the characters to paint the scene in the mind's eye (see p. 65).

of tragedy, which developed from small plots and ridiculous wording, it is only lately that it has become dignified – **since it developed out of satyr-performance** – and the metre has changed from tetrameter to iambic. At first they used the tetrameter because its poetry was appropriate for satyrs and more suitable for dancing; but after speaking was introduced, **nature herself** discovered the proper verse form. For of all the metres, the iambic is the most like speech.

Metres

Tragedy employs a multitude of metres, but Aristotle mentions two by name: the trochaic tetrameter (tetrameter: consisting of four feet to the line), which he believes to have been the original metre of tragic dialogue (and which does appear more frequently in the early plays of Aeschylus), and the iambic trimeter (trimeter: consisting of three feet to the line), which is the main metre of dialogue in both tragedy and comedy. The basic unit of the trochaic tetrameter is the trochee, a long syllable followed by a short. This is the metre used by Longfellow in his *Song of Hiawatha* (By the shores of Gitche Gumee / By the shining Big-Sea-Water). The iambic trimeter, on the other hand, is built up of iambs, which consist of a short followed by a long. This is the metre used in Shakespearean blank verse ('But soft! What light through yonder window breaks?' in *Romeo and Juliet*). Anapaests are also common in tragedy, used by the chorus, especially when they make their entrances and exits. They consist of two shorts followed by a long: you may be most familiar with them in Clement Clark Moore's Christmas poem ('Twas the night before Christmas, when all through the house / Not a creature was stirring, not even a mouse). Unlike English verse, however, which is stress-based, Greek metre is quantitative (i.e. based on syllable length). While the chorus in tragedy sings in a variety of lyric metres, the characters speak predominantly in the iambic metre, said to reflect the rhythms of normal conversation.

---

since it developed out of satyr-performance this comment, included as an aside, is perplexing and seems to contradict what Aristotle writes a few lines earlier about tragedy originating in the dithyramb. We have no convincing evidence that tragedy developed from satyr-play, which seems to arrive later as a dramatic genre.

nature herself in arguing that tragedy's adoption of the iambic metre was a spontaneous adaptation of nature to the introduction of spoken dialogue, Aristotle introduces an important motif of his analysis of drama – that art is imitation or *mimēsis* of reality (in the case of tragedy, Aristotle says earlier in the *Poetics*, what is being imitated are people's actions). For Aristotle, the theatre-goer experiences pleasure in drama precisely because of its mimetic quality – for, as he argues, 'the human differs from all other animals in this respect: that it is the most mimetic' (*Poetics* 1448b). See **6.20**, where the intellectual pleasure of *mimesis* and *Poetics* 1448b are discussed at greater length.

1. What aspects of Aristotle's account of the development of the dramatic genres strike you as most idiosyncratic and least credible?

2. What appear to be Aristotle's main interests in analysing the development of different dramatic forms?

3. 'The purpose of playing', said Hamlet (3.2), is 'to hold as 'twere the mirror up to nature.' Do you believe that theatre does serve as a mirror of real life, or is it inherently deceptive?

The following extract is taken from the work of Diogenes Laertius (3.56), probably writing in the third century AD; his compendium of the lives and doctrines of philosophers collects information gleaned from earlier writers.

1.5   But just as long ago in tragedy at first only the chorus performed, then later **Thespis** devised a single actor in order to give the chorus an intermission, then Aeschylus introduced the second actor, and Sophocles the third, thus bringing tragedy to its complete form – **so too philosophy** at first was of just one type, namely physics, then Socrates added the second type, ethics, and Plato the third, dialectics, thereby completing philosophy.

1. Modern-day audiences tend to see the episodes played by the actors as being the core of Greek tragedy and view the choral odes as intermissions. What evidence do ancient sources such as Aristotle and Diogenes Laertius offer to suggest that this attitude is misguided?

2. What interests and attitudes do these two authors share?

3. What reasons might there be for the introduction of the actor other than the explanation given by Diogenes Laertius – that he was invented in order to give the chorus a breather?

4. What dramatic possibilities were opened up by introducing a second actor?

5. Thespis is still remembered today in the word 'thespian'. How is this word used today?

Thespis Thespis (active in the late sixth century and said to come from Ikarion, a village with close ties to Dionysus) was credited with many different theatrical inventions, including the mask and the invention of tragedy itself. Here he is said to have invented the actor. The Greek word for actor (*hypokritēs*) literally means 'answerer' (though it can also mean 'interpreter' or 'expounder'). One possible explanation for the word is that it reflects the origins of the single actor, who emerged from the chorus and was given spoken lines that responded to the songs of his fellow-dancers.

so too philosophy tragedy is frequently compared to other performance genres, especially philosophy, rhetoric and epic. Like tragic actors, philosophers, rhetoricians and rhapsodes also addressed large audiences, and frequently used the theatre as their venue.

Satyr-play

Satyric drama seems to have been a relatively late addition to the theatrical repertoire; according to tradition, it made its debut at the City Dionysia around 500 BC. However, the tradition of impersonating dancing satyrs seems to go back much further, judging from the pictorial evidence. These early representations portray satyrs as part-human, part-animal (they have the basic figure of a human, with the ears and tail of a horse and a permanently erect **phallus**) and they often accompany Dionysus. Athenians seem to have dressed up as satyrs for the springtime **Anthesteria** festival that celebrated the arrival of Dionysus and of the new wine.

Satyr-plays seem to have shared certain elements, though our direct knowledge of their content is limited, since sizeable portions of only two satyr-plays have survived – part of Sophocles' *Trackers* and all of Euripides' *Cyclops*. They sported a chorus of satyrs, accompanied by an elderly satyr called Silenus (the Athenian word for a satyr) or Papposilenus ('Daddy-Silenus'). These satyrs behaved badly, flouting many of the inhibitions of civilized society. They indulged their appetites to an extreme, eating and drinking without restraint and seeking sexual gratification wherever they could find it. At the City Dionysia during the fifth century BC, each tragic playwright put on a satyr-play after his three tragedies; its subject-matter might or might not be related to that of the preceding three plays. After the intensity of tragedy, whose stage action often exposed the dire consequences of making the wrong choice, the hilarity of a satyr-play must have come as light relief, like the jig at the end of an Elizabethan tragedy. It also might have contributed to what anthropologists identify as one of the key functions of festival, which is to serve as a release for society, a socially sanctioned temporary reversal of societal norms. Like tragedy, it drew its subject-matter from myth; but it took the heroic world of tragedy and epic and subverted it through parody. Written by the same playwrights as the preceding tragedies and employing the same cast, they were clearly an integral part of the ensemble at the City Dionysia festival, though they did not feature among the performances at the Lenaea festival.

A famous vase (**1.6**) dating to *c.* 400 BC offers us a unique look at the cast of a satyr-play. The figures are arranged schematically, with chorus-members (**choreuts**) occupying the flanks, main characters taking up the centre of the upper field, two musicians displayed prominently in the middle of the lower field, and the poet seated to their left. Most are identified by name.

The choreuts are shown in a state of relaxation. Several appear to be conversing; the two outermost figures in the upper field are surveying the scene. One choreut is shown in full swing, performing the *sikinnis*, the vigorous dance of satyr-play.

This snapshot gives us an excellent view, from various angles, of satyr costume. Unlike the actors in other dramatic genres, members of the satyr chorus wore very little clothing. Their costume consisted of a pair of shaggy breeches, representing the hairy body of a satyr, to which were attached a horse-tail and phallus, and a full head mask, with the snub nose, straggly beard and elongated ears characteristic of satyrs. Most of the choreuts are holding their masks, and some appear to be scrutinizing them. The second figure from the right in the lower field is wearing an elaborate sleeveless *chitōn* (tunic) and a *himation* (cloak). That he is playing the part of a satyr is indicated by his mask – perhaps his costume distinguishes him as the leader of the chorus, or perhaps he is wearing the robes that he wore in the victory procession. All the choreuts appear to be in the prime of their youth. The names that appear above their heads are generally ordinary Athenian names and reflect the names of the performers rather than of their characters.

The figures seated on the couch are not actors: two of them are women, and women were not allowed to act. The reclining male figure is labelled as Dionysus. He wears a tiara, his wavy hair falls down onto his bare chest, and he holds his characteristic ivy-topped **thyrsus** staff; to his left grows a vine. He shares the couch and footstool with a female figure (probably his consort Ariadne) whom he clasps in an embrace. Neither one carries a mask; they are not characters in the play but are probably included because of Dionysus' association with the festival. Perched on the end of the couch is a woman holding a female mask. She may be a personification (e.g. the Muse of tragedy, or the personification of satyr-play) or she may represent a female part played by one of the three male actors. The high headdress on her mask might suggest that she is an oriental queen. She is attended by a small winged figure labelled Himeros ('desire'), so perhaps she represents the love-interest of one of the male characters.

Flanking this central tableau are the three actors of the play. They are all mature men with full beards. To the left of Dionysus stands an actor carrying a mask with full beard. His mask and his elaborate costume with its rich embroidery suggest that he might be playing the part of a king. To the right of centre stands the actor playing Heracles, wearing trademark lion-skin, club and lion-head mask. His *chiton*, *himation* and high boots are all elaborately decorated and he wears a breastplate that accentuates his physique. Like the actor to Dionysus' left, his face bears a curious resemblance to his mask, so that it almost looks as if he has become the character he is impersonating. Facing him to his right stands the actor who played Papposilenus. The white beard and hair of his mask, which is crowned with an ivy-wreathed diadem, and his full-body woolly tights, dappled with white tufts, characterize him as the patriarch of the satyrs. He carries a staff and a leopard skin.

The vase is called the Pronomos Vase after the piper seated at the centre of the lower field. We know of a famous Theban piper named Pronomos from this time period, so this could well be the same person. It is interesting that the piper and lyre-player are given such prominent positions in the painting, more so even than the young playwright Demetrios, shown to their left holding a scroll and with a lyre beside him that reminds us that the dramatist composed the play's music as well as its script. The vase shows a winning cast, many of whom are wearing their victory-wreaths, and was probably commissioned to celebrate their victory. Tripods such as the one shown at upper left and the tripod atop a columnar monument in the right field were given as prizes to sponsors of successful productions at the City Dionysia, and were then erected by the sponsor as a victory monument such as the one shown.

1.6

1   Why might the vase-painter have chosen to represent the cast at rest rather than performing?

2   What conclusions might be drawn from the fact that chorus-members are labelled with the names of the actors while those playing the main parts bear the names of their characters?

3   This victorious cast had also performed in the three tragedies that preceded the satyr-play. Why might the Pronomos Vase show them costumed for the satyr-play rather than for their tragic roles?

4   In what ways was a Greek playwright involved in the production of his play? Are modern playwrights typically involved in the staging of their plays?

Comedy

Comedy was the latest genre to be incorporated into the dramatic competitions of the City Dionysia (in 486 BC); five playwrights entered single plays into a separate competition, though the number may have been cut to three during the Peloponnesian War. Shortly before 440 BC, comedy was also included in the Lenaea festival, and it featured in Rural Dionysia festivals at least by the fourth century BC.

The origins of comedy seem to go back to at least the sixth century BC. Our scant information about this early period, however, comes from vase-paintings and the theories of later writers such as Aristotle (see **1.4**), whose historical value is open to doubt. Vase-paintings from this period show dancing comic figures known as komasts or 'revellers' (see **1.8**); they also show men participating in animal choruses (see **4.14**). What is not clear is how these performances are connected to Athenian comedy. Comedy is also seen as having been influenced by traditions of formal abuse – the genre of abuse poetry (some of which still survives), and the custom of festival participants trading insults with onlookers, which seems to have been an element of certain festivals (as it is in other cultures). The word 'comedy' was derived by the ancients (cf. Aristotle, *Poetics* 1448a) from either *kōmē* (village) or *kōmos* (revel).

What has survived of Athenian comedy belongs almost exclusively to two playwrights, Aristophanes (career 427 to *c.* 386 BC) and Menander (career *c.* 321 to *c.* 291 BC). Even in ancient times they were recognized as the greatest comic playwrights of their generations. Although we must acknowledge that what we recognize as the hallmarks of their surviving works may not necessarily be typical of comedy in general, it is safe to say that fifth-century comedy differed radically from that of the late fourth century, and it is these changes that led ancient commentators to divide comedy into the periods that are still used for reference today. Although the way in which the periods were divided varied, with some writers referring to an 'earliest' period (i.e. from the introduction of comedy into the City Dionysia in 486 BC to the mid-fifth century), the most common division is into Old, Middle and New Comedy.

Old Comedy	*c.* 486–386 BC (including the period of Aristophanes)
Middle Comedy	*c.* 386–321 BC (the period between Aristophanes and Menander)
New Comedy	*c.* 321–263 BC (the period of Menander and after)

- The Romans had their *Fescennini*, improvised songs of abuse sung at weddings, generals' triumphs and other occasions; Scots of the sixteenth century had their flytings; and African-Americans had a tradition of 'playing the dozens', in which two competitors would take turns exchanging insults. Can you think of modern-day contexts in which trading insults is an accepted and integral part of a performance genre? Or can you think more broadly of types of performance in which the normal rules of socially acceptable behaviour are temporarily suspended?

Old Comedy

Unlike tragedy, which favours settings such as the Thebes, Argos or Troy of a bygone age, Aristophanes sets his plays in Athens and deals with contemporary Athenian issues – even plays that take us to Mt Olympus (*Peace*), the never-never setting of Cloudcuckooland (*Birds*) and Hades (*Frogs*) end up bringing to these places Athenian concerns and Athenian characters. Fragments and titles of the plays of other poets of Old Comedy such as Cratinus and especially Eupolis suggest that at least some of their plays offered the kind of topical and personal satire that abounds in Aristophanes' plays, though others chose mythological themes.

In Aristophanes' comedies, obscure individuals and prominent politicians (e.g. Cleon in *Knights, Wasps*) alike take a pounding, and tragedians (e.g. Euripides in *Women at the Thesmophoria, Frogs*), philosophers (e.g. Socrates in *Clouds*) and even gods (e.g. the delegation of gods in *Birds*) are subject to parody. Social norms are turned on their head in these plays – women line up in battle formation, defend the Acropolis and debate in political assembly (*Lysistrata*), a man dresses up as a woman and sneaks into a women-only festival (*Women at the Thesmophoria*), and a slave gets a god to carry his luggage for him (*Frogs*). This role reversal is seen as a key element of festival, with its temporary suspension of social hierarchy, while the public humiliation of powerful figures is an exercise of democratic freedom of speech and a check on the dominance of powerful figures, analogous to the practice of ostracism.

The chorus played a central role in Old Comedy, and many plays get their names from their chorus. With 24 members, it was larger than the chorus of tragedy, and often played an active role in the plot. Some of Aristophanes' plays even have a second chorus (e.g. *Lysistrata, Frogs*). Several of the plays of Aristophanes and his rivals featured animal choruses (e.g. *Birds, Frogs*). Other choruses were personifications (e.g. Cratinus' *Seasons*, Eupolis' *Cities* and *Demes*), while in Aristophanes' *Clouds*, the chorus play clouds in the costume of women!

The surviving plays of Old Comedy usually have a larger number of characters than we see in tragedy. Their plot structure is episodic; over the course of the play, the main characters encounter – and often come into conflict with – a string of minor characters. If the three-actor rule applied to Old Comedy, the third actor would have had to change character with ridiculous frequency (five times within 130 lines or so, at one point in *Acharnians*), and some costume changes would have had to have been executed in the space of a few lines. If this were the case, the mad pace at which the character would have had to dash off the stage and back on again may have been deliberately accentuated to contribute to the humour. It is just as possible, however, that several different actors played the minor roles.

The costumes of Old Comedy were designed to make their wearers look ludicrous. Actors playing male characters wore a limp leather phallus sewn to their tights, a feature frequently referred to in the explicit sexual comments that were a mainstay of the humour of Old Comedy. In general, the characters of Old Comedy use the vulgarities of vernacular language, but some also indulge in clever word-play, using puns and coining new words at every turn.

A painting on a red-figure vase from Taras (modern Taranto in southern Italy) dating to *c.* 380 BC (**1.7**) offers an intriguing representation of a comic performance. Four actors occupy a low wooden stage. On the far left is Aegisthus, the figure from myth who seduced Clytemnestra while her husband Agamemnon led the Greek expedition to Troy, then murdered him on his return. The figure standing on the upturned basket is named Pyrrhias, a name meaning 'fiery' that was often given to slaves for their red hair (Greeks tended to have dark hair). The figures on either side of him are both labelled ***chorēgos***. This identifies them as the sponsors responsible for financing and training a chorus. Each wears a *himation* whose trailing end is gathered up and draped over his left arm. This item of clothing is not typical of the comic costume and perhaps identifies these as wealthy citizens such as would sponsor a chorus.

In all other respects, the three figures on the right wear the costume and masks of comedy. Their masks are larger than life size and have comically distorted features; each wears a tunic short enough to reveal the dangling leather phallus; underneath they wear body padding to accentuate their buttocks and bellies. They wear body tights on their arms and legs, representing naked skin.

In contrast, the figure on the left wears the costume of tragedy: a long, elaborately decorated tunic, with a bordered ***chlamys*** (a cloak often worn by messengers and soldiers) tied at the neck with a brooch. The tragic costume is completed by decorative sleeves extending down to the wrists (theatrical costumes tended to cover up the arms and legs – this must have helped a hairy male actor pull off a female role), a ***pilos*** or conical traveller's hat and the high-laced ***kothornoi*** or 'buskins' that distinguish tragic actors from comic actors, who are usually barefoot. He carries two spears and appears to have just come on stage through the half-open door of the stage-building.

What is going on in this scene? It probably belongs to a lost play from Athenian Old or Middle Comedy. A number of plays have titles that suggest that their plot may have been about drama itself: Aristophanes wrote a *Plays* (*Dramata*) and a *Pre-contest* (*Proagōn*), Cratinus a *Productions* (*Didaskaliai*), Phrynichus a *Tragedians* (*Tragōidoi*). That a comedy might put a character from tragedy on stage should not surprise us since, in Aristophanes' *Frogs*, Dionysus, the god of theatre, goes down to the Underworld and hosts a contest between the tragedians Aeschylus and Euripides. Throughout the play, their tragic art is the butt of Aristophanes' humour: Aeschylus is satirized for his pomposity, Euripides for his egalitarianism and both of them for their dramatic mannerisms – and the play draws much of its humour from putting these grand masters of tragedy on the comic stage.

In this scene, then, the figure labelled Aegisthus may be representative of tragedy in general, a character whose elaborate regal costume and set of spears cast him as a figure from the age of heroes and make him look out of place on the comic stage. His face and his pose are also telling. Unlike the comic characters, he does not wear the oversized and distorted mask of comedy; his face shows the neutral and life-like features typical of tragic masks, but it does not have the open mouth characteristic of masks. Is he even wearing a mask? Is he perhaps a non-speaking, walk-on part representing tragedy? The way he holds his head may express the feeling of bewilderment of a tragic character who has just walked in on a comedy.

1.7

The differing stances and gestures of the three characters are perhaps our main clues to decoding this scene. The *choregos* on the left of the trio faces the tragic character, and his upraised hand may acknowledge his entry, perhaps even in greeting, while the *choregos* on the right is looking at him askance. Since the presence of two *choregoi* must imply that they are responsible for two different, presumably competing, productions, it could be that the white-bearded *choregos* sponsors a play that includes Aegisthus as a character, and that the other *choregos* expresses his disdain for his rival's play.

The figure labelled Pyrrhias uses an upturned basket as a podium, and his outstretched arm probably indicates that he is in mid-speech; certainly his face turned out towards the viewer clamours for attention. Perhaps he has been enlisted as an *ad hoc* arbiter in a dispute between the two *choregoi*, just as Dionysus served as judge in the contest between Aeschylus and Euripides in Aristophanes' *Frogs*. In that play, the contest was between the older type of drama espoused by Aeschylus and the more modern style championed by Euripides; in this vase-painting too, as Oliver Taplin notes (1993: 57), there is a clear age gap between the white-bearded *choregos* on the left, who seems to favour the presence of the tragic character, and the younger *choregos* on the right, who seems to oppose him. That a slave-character called Pyrrhias should occupy such a leading role is very typical of Old Comedy, in which the normal social hierarchy is frequently reversed and women behave like men and slaves like masters. It is worth noting that Pyrrhias' costume is more ornate than is typical of a slave's clothing, so that he may be 'dressing up', as slaves tend to do in Aristophanic comedy when they are playing other people's roles.

This vase-painting raises many questions and allows few sure answers, and scholars have interpreted the scene in a number of different ways. A. D. Trendall (1991: 8), for example, interprets the label *choregos* as meaning 'chorus-leader'; each of the two figures labelled *choregos*, according to this view, leads his own semi-chorus. Oliver Taplin interprets *choregos* in its more normal sense of 'sponsor', but suggests that the two figures represent a whole chorus made up of sponsors of performances, half of whom would have been young, half old; furthermore, he argues that Pyrrhias is representative of comedy just as Aegisthus represents tragedy, and that this scene illustrates the opposition of comedy and tragedy and comedy's tendency to make reference to itself.

> • The surviving texts of ancient plays give us the bare script. Vase-paintings, in contrast, offer us a glimpse into the visual world of the theatre, though they often depict a scene whose script has since been lost. What can we learn from vase-paintings like the Choregos Vase that we could not know from the texts?

Middle Comedy

The term Middle Comedy is used to describe plays that belonged to the period between Aristophanes and Menander (i.e. roughly 386–321 BC). Like the terms Old Comedy and New Comedy, it was coined by ancient scholars. However, since no complete plays survive from this period, it is difficult to make any definite statements about Middle Comedy. Many see in the later plays of Aristophanes a shift in subject-matter and structure, marking a transition to a new type of comedy (see **7.14**). So, for example, his *Wealth*, performed in 388 BC, has as its main plot line the fantasy of giving Ploutos (Wealth) back his sight so that he can become the most powerful god. Its subject-matter is mythological, like that of three of the four plays it competed against (Aristomenes' *Admetus*, Nicophon's *Adonis*, Alcaeus' *Pasiphae*) if we can judge from the titles of these plays alone. It features prominently the impudent and crafty slave that will become a mainstay of New Comedy (it is the slave Cario and his master Chremylus who conspire to carry out the plan). And the part of its chorus has been greatly reduced: only one choral song is included in the manuscripts. Elsewhere choral song is merely indicated with the word *chorou*: '(performance) of the chorus'; it has been demoted from cornerstone to mere episode-divider. The multitude of often loosely related episodes typical of most Aristophanic comedies has given way to a tighter sequence of extended conversations, which all take place in front of the house of Chremylus. Even the cast of walk-on characters has been reduced. Its critique of the unjust distribution of wealth through the life-story of Ploutos may herald the moralizing and increasingly sympathetic portrayal of the lower classes that is typical of later comedy. And for the most part social parody has replaced political vitriol. It is hard not to relate this change in focus to historical developments in Athens: with its decisive defeat in the Peloponnesian War (404 BC), Athens lost her status as the leading superpower and her drama no longer showed the same preoccupation with her political leaders, her civic institutions and her relations with other states.

What survives of the plays of Middle Comedy are a substantial number of excerpts quoted by later authors such as Stobaeus and especially Athenaeus. His *Learned Banqueters*, a work of fiction in which erudite guests at a banquet quote from ancient authors (see **1.2**), gives the impression that Middle Comedy was obsessed with food and drink, but this impression reflects the subject-matter of his work as much as anything. It seems as if no single playwright dominated Middle Comedy as Aristophanes and Menander did with Old and New Comedy respectively. Many playwrights – including many non-Athenians – shared the limelight, though a few names (Alexis, Anaxandrides, Antiphanes, Eubulus, Platon, Timocles) are mentioned more than others.

The surviving list of over eight hundred titles of plays is revealing. It suggests a wide range of types of plays being performed during this period. Some plays deal with contemporary political figures (e.g. Eubulus' *Dionysius*, Mnesimachus' *Philip*). Many deal with mythological themes (Araros, Philiscus and Antiphanes all produced an *Adonis*, for example, and there are many other plays with titles such as *Calypso*, *Circe*, *Galatea*, *Ganymede* and *Nausicaa*) and seem to offer a burlesque treatment of them, or a parody of tragedies. But we also see the rise of plays which deal with everyday life and which present character types, with titles such as *The Farmer* (*Agroikos*), *The Doctor* (*Iatros*), *The Parasite* (*Parasitos*), *The Pimp* (*Pornoboskos*), *The Grumbler* (*Mempsimoiros*); these types become the mainstay of New Comedy. Several plays are named after the figure of the courtesan, who became a key character in many plays of New Comedy; they have titles such as *Young Chick* (*Neottis*), *Honey* (*Melitta*), *Soft Girl* (*Malthakē*) and *Bad Girl* (*Ponēra*).

The visual evidence for Middle Comedy shows actors wearing the costumes of Old Comedy but now also playing characters such as the old nurse and the cunning slave characteristic of New Comedy.

Characters in Middle (?) Comedy – terracotta figurines dating to c. 375–350 BC wearing the body padding, short chitons and masks with exaggerated facial features of comedic actors. The figure on the right wears a pilos or traveller's hat. At some point during this period, the dangling phallus worn by all male characters in Old Comedy was discontinued. Similar figurines are found all over the Greek-speaking Mediterranean.

New Comedy

New Comedy is the term given to comedy written from the time of Menander's debut in *c.* 321 BC until Athenian comedy loses its star playwrights and its stature in the first half of the third century BC (Philemon died last, *c.* 263). The most famous playwrights of the period were Menander, Diphilus and Philemon. Of the three, Menander (lived *c.* 344/43 to 292/91 BC), though not the most successful during his lifetime, was soon singled out as the greatest. Thanks to exciting rediscoveries of papyri texts (see pp. 183–4), we now have a virtually complete text of one Menander play (*Old Cantankerous*, Greek *Dyskolos*) and substantial portions of several others. Papyrus fragments and quotations in other authors also preserve excerpts from other playwrights of New Comedy.

New Comedy differs radically from Old Comedy. It chooses as its subject-matter situations from everyday life, including the at times thorny relationships between father and son, master and slave, young man and girl next door. The action typically takes place outside two neighbouring houses, and the plot often centres on a young couple in love. Their relationship is bedevilled by a host of obstacles, which complicate the plot but are eventually surmounted. The complications frequently arise through misunderstanding or a case of mistaken identity; one mistake leads to another, threatening to derail the plot. But, in due time, these mistakes are resolved by a combination of creative thinking and good fortune. These comedies of error and their resolution rely heavily on coincidences of time and place; they are a key element of the humour of New Comedy. It is a subtler and less rambunctious humour than that of Old Comedy, and frequently takes the form of situation comedy. Thus Greek New Comedy is the ancestor of a long tradition of situation comedy, from Shakespeare to P. G. Wodehouse to the popular TV show *Seinfeld*.

New Comedy developed a set of stock situations, such as the rediscovery of long-lost children, typically born of a one-night stand at a festival. Its plots may have been far-fetched (this was, in fact, a deliberate part of their humour), but they were also intricately constructed, with one plot development leading to the next. The chorus now played a minimal part; its chief function seems to have been to separate the play's episodes, which were now divided into five acts.

New Comedy also developed a set of stock characters – that is, types of characters who appear in many plays and generally behave in certain ways. The professional chef tends to be fussy and chatty and likes to boast and boss people around; the grumpy old man hates everybody and is an utter killjoy; the love-struck young man is wide-eyed and impractical. These stock characters, which had already begun to appear in Middle Comedy, were easily recognizable by their mask and their costume.

A professional chef sets the table in a New Comedy (krater from Taras, mid fourth century).

Drama outside Athens

Early performances

Athens was undoubtedly a mecca of theatre. But it certainly wasn't the only place in the Greek world where one could catch a dramatic performance. In fact, the ancients gave all four genres origins outside Athens. Among the figures credited by different sources with 'inventing' early forms of dithyramb and tragedy are Arion of Methymna and Epigenes of Sicyon; both are said to have worked in the early fifth century BC, the former in Corinth, the latter in Sicyon, a city near Corinth. And Pratinas of Phlius, another nearby town (see map, p. vii) was supposed to have either invented satyr-play or introduced it to Athens in the early fifth century. The ancients, it seemed, believed that this region of the northern Peloponnese developed a dramatic tradition that then spread to Athens. This is not implausible, since this area was a centre of commerce and had a vibrant artistic culture during the sixth century. Corinthian vases from the early sixth century show scenes of dancing; in some, the dancers are wearing padded costumes and are performing a narrative scene (see **1.8**). Comedy is also said to have Doric origins, and in particular a connection to the town of Megara, located between Athens and Corinth. The trouble is that there is not a shred of reliable evidence that these other dramatic traditions directly influenced the forms of drama that developed in Athens over the course of the fifth century. Certainly there were non-Athenians who entered their plays into the competitions at Athens; but the most prominent playwrights – names like Aeschylus and Aristophanes – were home-grown talent.

A Corinthian krater (a bowl used for mixing wine with water) dated to *c.* 600–575 BC shows dancers engaged in an energetic dance. They wear a skin-tight costume with padding to the stomach and buttocks like that later worn by characters in Athenian Old Comedy. The figure third from left is named *Komios* (reveller). The word **kōmos**, which Aristotle saw as the origin for the term comedy (meaning '*kōmos*-song'), refers to a group of men who are revelling (i.e. singing and drinking in a festive manner). The other figures also have names suggestive of a festival context (e.g. the one second from left is named Paichnios, which may well be derived from *paignion* meaning 'jest', or 'comic performance'), though their etymologies are hard to ascertain.

1.8

Sicily and southern Italy

There is clear evidence, on the other hand, that Athenian drama began exerting its influence elsewhere. Hieron I, the rich tyrant of Syracuse, commissioned Aeschylus to write a tragedy (the *Women of Aetna*) to celebrate his founding of the city of Aetna, and the playwright also reperformed his *Persians* in the theatre of Syracuse. Plutarch (*Nicias* 29), describing the failed Athenian expedition to Sicily, says that those among the captured Athenian soldiers who could recite from memory lines from Euripides' plays won their freedom. This anecdote suggests the popularity that Athenian drama had gained in Sicily by the end of the fifth century, though it perhaps also implies that locals did not have access to the latest plays to have hit the Athenian stage. Sicily and the region of southern Italy known as **Magna Graecia** (Great Greece) because of the many Greek colonies that were established along its coasts have produced an astonishing quantity of vases depicting theatrical scenes dating from the fourth and third centuries BC (as well as other theatre-related artefacts such as terracotta masks and figurines). Some of the scenes that can be identified on these vases depict plays originally put on at Athens in the fifth century and apparently reperformed in Magna Graecia. This trend seems to have been widespread, with touring troupes of actors putting on performances of **Attic** drama in many locations. With the spread of Greek culture in the wake of Alexander the Great's conquests, open-air theatres built out of stone sprang up all over the Greek-speaking world.

Although these structures, hundreds of which still dot landscapes from Spain to Syria, bear testimony to the importance of theatre to the civic life of a Greek *polis* in the **Hellenistic** world, we know little about what kinds of plays were performed in these theatres. Not all of what was staged was imported from Athens. There were certainly local theatrical traditions in a number of cities. The most notable example was Syracuse. It already had a sizeable theatre and an established comedic tradition in the early fifth century, when drama at Athens was still in its infancy. In fact, Aristotle claims that the practice of composing plots originally came from Sicily (*Poetics* 1449b), perhaps referring to the first use of a set script. A prominent comic playwright putting on plays at Syracuse in the early fifth century was Epicharmus. A number of fragments of his plays survive; they show a developed style that uses a variety of metres and is written in the Sicilian form of the Doric dialect. He seems to have had a liking for mythological burlesque featuring characters such as Heracles and Odysseus, but his repertoire appears to have been very broad. We are told that Socrates considered Epicharmus to be the best comic poet (Plato, *Theaetetus* 152e), winning out even over Athenian playwrights such as Aristophanes.

The Romans in turn embraced Greek theatre, with Sicily and southern Italy as their main points of contact. The earliest performances of plays that we know of in Rome were translations of Greek tragedies and comedies by Livius Andronicus put on in 240 BC; the most famous Roman comedy-writers, Plautus (writing *c.* 205–184 BC) and Terence (writing in 160s BC), owed much to Greek New Comedy in their plots and stock characters. And the Campanian towns of Pompeii and Herculaneum, buried and preserved by the volcanic eruption of Vesuvius in AD 79, show that theatrical scenes continued to be in vogue in all manner of home decor – everything from wall-paintings to floor mosaics and oil lamps.

Roman comedy borrowed wholesale from Greek New Comedy; in the prologues to a number of their plays, Plautus and especially Terence acknowledge that they are using plays by Attic playwrights such as Menander and Diphilus, but claim to be putting a new spin on the Greek originals.

In a scene from Roman comedy in a wall-painting from Pompeii (first century AD – see **1.9**), a young couple (the young man who is the protagonist of many comedies, and his girl, probably a courtesan) stands side by side and listens to a slave, distinguishable by the padding of his belly and the wide-open mouth and bulging eyes of his mask. He is looking sideways, perhaps to warn the couple of the arrival of someone who may discover the secret lovers together, and is perhaps suggesting a cunning plan to deal with the situation. The expressions of the couple register their alarm.

1.9

Other genres of performance

The following is a brief overview of other Greek genres of performance with affinities to drama.

Epic

Like drama, epic poetry was composed for live performance, originally sung by a bard while accompanying himself on the lyre. The two great poems attributed to Homer, the *Iliad* and *Odyssey*, were soon recognized as masterpieces and were frequently recited from memory by performers known as rhapsodes. These rhapsodes competed for prizes for the best performance at festivals such as the Panathenaea at Athens. They were, in essence, live entertainers, and their performances predate the development of drama.

Tragedy especially shows signs of the influence of epic poetry. Like epic, it compresses all action into a short time-span and focuses on a few pivotal crises. Tragedies were often set in the heroic world of epic and peopled with the same characters, but seem to have deliberately avoided covering the same subject-matter, perhaps out of respect for the great masterpieces (of the more than a dozen surviving tragedies which deal with the story of the Trojan War, only *Rhesus* describes an event also narrated by Homer).

Improvisation

We have already read Aristotle's puzzling remark (**1.4**) that both tragedy and comedy 'came into being from an origin in improvisation'. Although this and most other references to impromptu performances are very hard to interpret, it does appear that there were many occasions at which an ancient Greek could participate in unscripted performance of one sort or other. Vase-paintings show scenes of costumed performers that don't have any apparent connection to the theatre. Athenians seem to have worn satyr costumes to accompany the Dionysiac procession at the Anthesteria festival. Women joined in ritual laments at the death of a family member. And in Plato's *Symposium*, we get an account of a dinner-party hosted by the tragic poet Agathon at which each guest (and the guests included such celebrities as Aristophanes and Socrates) was asked to make up and deliver a speech in praise of Love. Among the forms of improvisation that ancient sources mention is the practice of ritual abuse, perhaps intended as an apotropaic practice (i.e. to ward off the jealousy of evil spirits). The genre of iambic poetry, out of which Aristotle claims that comedy developed (see **1.4**) and which was practised in various parts of Greece, combined satirical abuse of individuals with obscene comments; it was written for public performance, often in a festival context.

Oratory

Athens was famous for its public speakers. Orators such as Demosthenes and Lysias wrote and delivered speeches both for the political assembly and for the lawcourts. In fact, the ability to persuade your fellow-citizens was the key to success in a participatory democracy such as Athens.

There are many parallels that can be drawn between the assembly (*ekklēsia*) and the theatre. Both drew large audiences (certain important resolutions brought before the assembly required a quorum of 6,000 citizens). Policies were decided through debate; speakers would respond to points made by previous speakers. Like the theatre, the assembly's open-air meeting ground at the Pnyx (similar to the theatre in general shape, though somewhat smaller) called for a powerful voice, persuasive arguments and the ability to win over the hearts and minds of the audience. It is not surprising that a number of famous actors also taught public speaking, which shared the same repertoire of gestures and range of intonations as theatre. The close affinity between the assembly and the theatre was put to good dramatic effect in Aristophanes' *Knights*, in which two slaves, the Paphlagonian and the Sausage-seller Agoracritus, are cast as rival demagogues (populist politicians) engaging in debate and trying to win over the favour of *Dēmos* (the People), personified as a cantankerous old man. Much of the action takes place at the Pnyx, but mirrors the attempts in the theatre by comic poets such as Aristophanes to win over their audience and defeat their rivals.

Like the theatre and the assembly, the lawcourts were a male domain. The jury was chosen by lot (as were the judges for the theatrical competitions) to prevent bribery. The prosecution and the defence each had one speech to make its case; from the lawcourt speeches that survive, we see that the defence responded to allegations made in the prosecution's speech. Many tragedies include a scene in which two characters engage each other in a formal debate (called an *agōn* or 'contest') in which each in turn lays out his case.

2 The festivals

The Greeks loved their festivals. Since their calendar wasn't broken up into weeks as ours is, it was these festivals, sprinkled across the year, which provided the break from everyday work that we now get from weekends. Even at the height of war, warring states would observe a temporary truce in order to allow participation in festivals such as the Olympic Games.

Festivals provided important occasions for members of a community to come together. At Athens, a number of festivals in honour of Dionysus occurred in the winter and early spring. Dionysus was a god of fertility and rebirth as well as god of wine and the theatre; these festivals to the god were held at a time when the natural world was about to emerge from its winter hibernation and crops would begin to germinate.

Rural Dionysia

The Rural Dionysia were held in the month of Posideon (roughly our December). They were local festivals put on by individual **demes** throughout Attica (most of these communities were only the size of villages). Although we know less about them, these rural festivals seem to have predated the larger Dionysia festival at Athens, which was called the 'City Dionysia' or 'Great Dionysia' to distinguish it from the Rural Dionysia. Different communities put on their Dionysia at different times; though it is unlikely that this was due to concerted planning, Plato (*Republic* 475d) speaks of people going from one festival to the next. In his time (fourth century BC), a number of demes included dramatic performances as part of the festivities, though they were on a smaller scale than at the City Dionysia

Attic vase-painting showing a giant phallus-pole and mannequin carried aloft by festival participants.

and sometimes specialized in just one genre. Still, the records show that even great playwrights like Euripides competed at the Dionysia in Piraeus, the harbour town for Athens.

What went on at the Rural Dionysia in the early days is far from certain, but it seems that a core component from the start was a procession of the whole community accompanying a phallus-pole, a giant fertility symbol (a representation of such a pole appears on an Attic cup from the mid-sixth century, shown on p. 24).

City Dionysia

Ancient sources credited the Athenian tyrant Pisistratus (in power *c.* 546–527) with instituting this festival. Although in later times Athens was a radical democracy, for periods during the sixth century it was ruled by tyrants, who at times used strong-arm tactics to maintain their supremacy. If the City Dionysia did in fact go back to the time of Pisistratus, then he may well have used the City Dionysia as a way to centralize political power under his leadership and to reduce the influence of local aristocrats, who would have been the main organizers and sponsors of the Rural Dionysia. These he now eclipsed with his own festival on a much grander scale. Although the tyrants were ousted in 510, the City Dionysia continued as a major festival that drew participants from all over Attica and created a sense of 'national' Athenian identity. It probably adopted practices from the Rural Dionysia (e.g. the procession into the city with the phallus-pole), but later on the Rural Dionysia were in turn borrowing certain elements from the City Dionysia. These probably included the dramatic competitions, apparently part of the City Dionysia from its outset (*c.* 533) but for which there is no early evidence at the Rural Dionysia.

The two main festivals at which dramatic performances were held were the City Dionysia and the Lenaea. Of the two, the Lenaea came first in the year: it occurred in late January in the month of Gamelion, while the City Dionysia occurred in late March or early April during the month of Elaphebolion. Like other festivals of Dionysus (the Rural Dionysia in December and the Anthesteria or 'Flower festival' in late February), both came during a lull in the agricultural calendar – the seed had already been sown and the farmer now had to wait for the spring crops to grow. But late March marked the beginning of the sailing season, and so the City Dionysia, unlike the Lenaea, was a festival that drew an audience from beyond Attica. As Athens grew to be a superpower over the course of the 450s and 440s and headed an alliance of smaller states that increasingly became an Athenian empire, she required allied states to send a delegation to the City Dionysia along with their yearly tribute, which was put on display in the theatre. So the City Dionysia was a chance for Athens to put on her public face and impress her allies with a show of culture, wealth, power and public spirit as well as an occasion at which to honour foreign dignitaries. A comparable modern event would be the Olympic Games. These too allow the host nation to parade its culture and have, on occasion, taken on a political dimension: Hitler's grandstanding during the 1936 Berlin Olympics, the boycott of the 1980 Moscow Olympics by the United States and others at the height of the Cold War, and the 2008 Beijing Olympics showcasing China's rapid modernization – these are three of the most notable examples.

Preparations

The amount of planning that went into the festivals was remarkable. In the case of the City Dionysia, preparations began nine months beforehand (see **2.1**) and overall responsibility was put in the hands of one of the highest officials, the eponymous *archōn* (see **2.1n**) who, soon after the festival, was subject to a formal investigation to determine whether he had successfully discharged his responsibilities. Demosthenes (*Philippic* 1.35–6) contrasts Athens' track record of success in organizing its big festivals with recent military failures and attributes the difference to two things: funding and planning (nothing is left to chance in festival planning, he says, since everything has been prescribed by law).

The degree of state involvement in festivals throughout Attica is reflected in the many pieces of legislation that have survived in the form of inscriptions. One such inscription (*IG* II² 380) relating to the Rural Dionysia in Piraeus orders local officials to repair the main streets on the route along which the procession will pass. Much of the financial burden was passed on by the state to *chorēgoi* (singular *chorēgos*), sponsors who took on the costs of financing a production as a form of special taxation of the wealthiest citizens known as a **liturgy** (Greek *leitourgia* – the word literally meant 'the work of the people', i.e. public service; the word 'liturgy' means something very different nowadays). There were the occasional complaints that these liturgies threatened to bankrupt an individual (then again, who doesn't complain about taxes!) but, for the most part, it seems that many enjoyed the prestige of a duty that fell exclusively to the super-rich, and basked in their prominence at the festival.

Festival events

The festival proper lasted for five days (see p. 27); during this time, everyday business was suspended, it was illegal to prosecute or arrest anybody, and prisoners were even temporarily released on bail, as we learn from Demosthenes (*Against Meidias* 10; *Against Androtion* 68 and **scholion**). Several important events occurred in the run-up to the festival. The *choregoi* presented the cast and poet of the production they were sponsoring at an event called the **proagōn** (literally 'pre-contest'), a preview of the coming events not unlike the trailers that precede a film release. On the evening prior to the festival, in a ritual procession called the **eisagōgē** (literally 'bringing-in'), the statue of Dionysus, which had earlier been taken to a temple outside the city walls on the road to Eleutherae (see map of Attica), was escorted back into the city by ephebes (young men doing military service) in a torchlit procession and placed in the theatre. Ancient authors explain this as a ritual re-enactment of the original introduction of the cult of Dionysus to Athens: the god is welcomed into the city and given a home (the theatre was adjacent to the sanctuary of Dionysus Eleuthereus). Some modern scholars see this as a ritual that commemorates Pisistratus' transferral of the cult of Dionysus to Athens from its earlier cultic centre at Eleutherae.

The *eisagoge* was separate from the **pompē**, the procession that began the festival proper. The whole community joined in this procession to the sanctuary of Dionysus. The ritual paraphernalia carried in the procession included baskets, loaves, wine-skins, mixing-bowls and water; many bulls accompanied the procession, destined for sacrifice in the sanctuary of Dionysus. The Parthenon frieze, though depicting a different Athenian festival (the Panathenaea), gives a good idea of the pageantry of such a procession and includes similar ceremonial objects. One element of the Dionysia procession, however – the large phalluses – appears to have been peculiar to Dionysiac ritual. An inscription dating to *c.* 446/45 BC (*IG* I³ 46) instructs the Athenian colony of Brea in Thrace to bring an ox and a panoply (a set of armour) to the Great Panathenaea and a phallus to the Dionysia. An off-hand remark by the orator Demosthenes (*On the False Embassy* 287) accusing Aeschines' brother-in-law of revelling in festival processions without wearing a mask may indicate that participants in the procession wore masks.

Probable schedule of events at the City Dionysia

Run-up to festival

8th day of Elaphebolion month *Proagon*

9th day of Elaphebolion month *Eisagoge* or 'bringing in' of cult statue of Dionysus

Festival proper

Day 1	10th of Elaphebolion	*Pompe*: procession to sanctuary of Dionysus
		Contests of 10 boys' dithyrambs and 10 men's dithyrambs
Day 2	11th of Elaphebolion	Contest of comedies (5 poets, 1 comedy each)
Day 3	12th of Elaphebolion	Contest of tragedies (1st poet stages 3 tragedies + satyr-play)
Day 4	13th of Elaphebolion	Contest of tragedies (2nd poet stages 3 tragedies + satyr-play)
Day 5	14th of Elaphebolion	Contest of tragedies (3rd poet stages 3 tragedies + satyr-play)

Ritual

Ritual has largely disappeared from everyday life in the west, so it is hard for many of us to understand it and easy for us to get a wrong impression. Modern-day rituals are by and large solemn affairs – the swearing-in of a president, the taking of wedding vows, the receiving of the eucharist or the ceremony of the Bar Mitzvah. In most modern-day rituals, the public at large is a mere onlooker rather than a participant. In ancient Greece, many rituals occurred in the context of lively and colourful festivals that were anything but sober; sacrifices were followed by feasting, poured libations by drinking. In religious festivals such as the Dionysia, there was no clear boundary between 'religious' and 'secular' components – the whole event was put on in honour of Dionysus. Hundreds of male citizens participated every year in the performances, but *everyone* – male or female, young or old, citizen or slave – could participate in the procession.

On the other hand, there is a danger in seeing ritual meaning behind every act. The plays, though performed in honour of Dionysus, were not intrinsically connected with him in subject-matter. In fact, the expression 'nothing to do with Dionysus' appears to have been used as something of a proverb in reference to the plays. Perhaps a useful modern equivalent is the carnival: festivities such as the *Carnevale* in Rio de Janeiro or Mardi Gras in New Orleans owe their existence to the religious calendar, but their main events are not in themselves overtly religious.

> 1 Have you attended a major festival? If so, how would you describe your experience? You might first think in practical terms (what you saw, heard etc.), and then try to think as a cultural anthropologist and analyse the function of this festival within the community.
>
> 2 What elements of the City Dionysia do you think are still present in large-scale public gatherings today?

Lenaea

The Lenaea was another festival of Dionysus that included dramatic contests. Its derivation is uncertain (a connection with *lēnai*, maenads or female worshippers of Dionysus, is more likely on etymological grounds than a derivation from *lēnos*, the wine-vat in which wine was pressed). It was by all accounts an old festival common to Ionian Greeks (Greeks who lived on the coast of modern Turkey and nearby islands), to which dramatic performances were added *c.* 440 BC, considerably later than at the City Dionysia. In fact, the month in which it occurred – known as Gamelion in Athens – seems to have been called Lenaion by the Ionians. Only tragedies and comedies were performed at this festival (i.e. no dithyrambic choruses or satyr-plays); though the evidence is conflicting, it seems that only two tragedians competed, putting on two tragedies each. For comedy, it seems that five poets competed as in the City Dionysia, but that the number was cut back to three during the Peloponnesian War.

Organizing the performances

> The following is an extract from a work titled *Athenian Constitution* (56.3). It dates from the 320s and was attributed to Aristotle but may well have been written by one of his pupils. After a historical survey of the development of the constitution, the author outlines the current duties of the various Athenian officials.

2.1   Immediately on taking up office, the [eponymous] *archōn* first proclaims that everyone shall hold and retain until the end of his term of office all the property that he held at the start of his term. Then he appoints for the tragedies three *choregoi*, selecting the richest of all the Athenians. In the past he also appointed five *choregoi* for the comedies, but now the tribes choose these. Afterwards he receives the *choregoi* nominated by the tribes for the men's and boys' dithyramb and the comedies at the Dionysia and for the men's and boys' dithyramb at the **Thargelia** (at the Dionysia they are appointed one to each tribe; at the Thargelia one to two tribes, with the two tribes taking turns to provide the *choregos*). The archon handles the **exchanges of property** and processes the **exemptions** in cases where the person claims to have performed that same liturgy in the past, or to be exempt because the period of exemption following another liturgy he performed has not yet expired, or because he is not of the right age (the *choregoi* for the boys' dithyrambs must be forty or older).

> Numerous inscriptions exist recording the honours conferred upon public officials or *choregoi* who contributed to a successful festival. The following inscription from the deme of Aixone probably dates to 313/12 BC (*SEG* 36.186). It was inscribed on a marble stele or slab. Such stelai (Greek *stēlai*, plural of *stēlē*) were displayed in prominent public places and offered enduring fame to those being commemorated in this way. In a society that wasn't saturated with billboards and other text media, the very act of writing something down (quite apart from the considerable expense incurred through the cost of the stone and the stonemason) marked it out as noteworthy.

archōn   an annually appointed officer with a wide range of duties which included organizing a number of festivals. He was responsible for selecting which playwrights would enter the competitions as well as appointing *choregoi* who would fund and train the choruses. He is referred to as the eponymous archon because his name was used to date the particular year in which he held office, and so the year was 'named after' him. The archon was appointed at the beginning of the Athenian year (our July/August), so he had plenty of time to prepare for the City Dionysia in spring (our March/April).

Thargelia   a festival of Apollo celebrated in the month of Thargelion (late May) to mark the beginning of the harvest season. Like the Dionysia and Lenaea, it included a procession and a dithyrambic competition, but only five dithyrambic choruses competed, each representing two tribes.

exchanges of property   if an individual was selected to perform a liturgy and didn't want to do it or didn't have the necessary resources, he could propose another person to replace him whom he judged was in a better position to take on the financial burden. The person nominated would either have to accept the liturgy or, if he preferred, could exchange property with the person originally selected, who would then have to perform it.

exemptions   performing a liturgy was a considerable expense (see **2.6**), so regulations were introduced exempting a person from performing the same liturgy twice (he could still be asked to perform a different liturgy) and from performing one in two consecutive years.

As well as the text of the decree, the monument shows a series of five comic masks in the entablature at the top; below them a young satyr approaches a seated Dionysus, who holds in his outstretched right hand a kantharos, the wine-cup that is his trademark. Below the inscription, two crowns are incised, representing the golden crowns awarded to the two winning *choregoi*, but these are not visible in this photograph.

2.2   Glaukides, son of Sosippos proposed: since the **choregoi** Auteas son of Autokles and Philoxenides son of Philippos performed their duties as *choregoi* well and **ambitiously**, the deme has decided to crown each of them with a **crown of gold** worth one hundred drachmas in the theatre during the comedies that will be put

Top half of the
Aixone stele.

choregoi   two *choregoi* have paired up to share the costs and responsibilities of sponsoring a chorus. Judging from surviving inscriptions, teaming up to share the office was common in the Rural Dionysia (a practice referred to as *synchorēgia*), though there is little evidence of it happening regularly at the City Dionysia or Lenaea (people did split other liturgies such as paying the operational costs of a trireme for a year).

ambitiously   the word literally means 'in an honour-loving way' (Greek *philotīmōs*). Greek society was very competitive, and it viewed honour (Greek *tīmē*) as the supreme good. By putting on such a spectacular show, the *choregoi* had brought honour on themselves and, by extension, on their fellow demesmen. A poor showing, on the other hand, could make the *choregos* a target of criticism, as we see in Isaeus' lawcourt speech against Dicaeogenes (*On the Estate of Dicaeogenes* 36), where the speaker uses Dicaeogenes' poor results (his choruses placed fourth in the dithyrambic competition and last in the tragedies and the Pyrrhic dance) to accuse him of stinginess.

crown of gold   a particularly lavish prize. Sometimes the prize is a crown of ivy (a plant sacred to Dionysus).

on **in the year following** the archonship of Theophrastos, so that other *choregoi* will in the future also perform their duties with ambition; also that the **demarch** Hegesileon and the treasurers give them ten drachmas for a sacrifice, and that the treasurers inscribe this on a stone stele and set it up in the theatre, so that the people of Aixone always put on the finest possible Dionysia.

> 1 Why do you think the victory stele includes images as well as the text of the decree?
>
> 2 Can you make out which stock character each mask represents? They include a young man, an older man, a girl, an older woman, and a slave; these five characters are typical of the romantic plots of New Comedy: the young lover and his stern father, the girl whom the young man loves, her mother, and the slave who serves as the young man's stooge.

Festivals provided a public occasion for the community to recognize individuals who had made special contributions. If you were a rich citizen who had helped fund a public building or were a foreigner who had served the deme's interests, you could be granted the privilege of *prohedria* (right to a front-row seat) or might even be presented with a crown in the ceremonies leading up to the performances. Similarly, those who organized a successful competition were also publicly recognized. Greeks did not see self-effacing modesty as a virtue. Victory in competition was a way to win honour – and this honour was only meaningful if it was celebrated publicly.

> The following inscription commemorating a victory in the Dionysia was found near Anagyrous, a deme on the south-west coast of Attica (*IG* II² 3101). It dates from the second half of the fourth century BC and is written in dactylic hexameter.

2.3   After winning the Dionysia with my sweetly laughing chorus, I set up this gift to the god as a monument to my victory, an ornament for my deme, and an honour to my ivy-clad father. I won the garland-bearing contest even before him.

> Fittingly for a monument celebrating victory in a poetic competition, this dedicatory inscription uses the graceful language and rhythms of poetry; yet

---

in the year following   since the next year's archon had not yet been chosen, the decree has to use this roundabout way to refer to the following year (see **2.1n**). The presentation of the prizes during the performance of the comedies indicates that the *choregoi* were victorious in this category.

demarch   the **demarch** was the chief official of a deme (Greek *dēmos*), the word given to a village or township, its surrounding land and its inhabitants. There were over a hundred demes in Attica, but we don't know exactly how many of them put on their own theatrical competitions. Often the demarch would be honoured with a crown along with the *choregoi*.

we can still sense the intense spirit of competition that underlies it. The victor himself commissioned the inscription to commemorate his victory in the Dionysia (that he doesn't specify which Dionysia may indicate that it was the Rural Dionysia rather than the more prestigious City Dionysia). It seems that his father was also a victorious *choregos*, but that the son won his victory first. The victory dedication was an ornament to the town not only in the sense of adorning its public space with an elegant monument but also in bringing it honour. A garland of ivy was worn by the winning *choregos* and his cast.

Demosthenes lived a century after the 'golden age' of the Athenian theatre of Sophocles, Euripides and Aristophanes; however, his lawcourt speeches offer us a wealth of information about the theatre of his day and clearly indicate its continued importance in Athenian society. In this speech (which was never delivered because the defendant settled out of court), Demosthenes brings charges against his enemy Meidias for assaulting him during a performance at the City Dionysia. In this portion (*Against Meidias* 13–14), he establishes his own public-mindedness in order to later contrast it with Meidias' outrageous behaviour during the festival (see **2.7**).

2.4   When two years ago the tribe Pandionis had failed to appoint its *choregos* and when, at the meeting of the assembly at which the law requires the archon to allot pipers to the choruses, a heated discussion and exchange of insults broke out, with the archon blaming the **overseers of the tribe**, and the overseers blaming the archon, I came forward and volunteered to serve as *choregos*; then when the lots were drawn and I got the first pick of a piper, you, men of Athens, all welcomed these two events – my announcement and my stroke of good luck – with the utmost enthusiasm, and clapped and cheered loudly so as to express your admiration and your share in my joy. **All of you**, that is, except Meidias here, who seems to have been the only one who was upset, and who plagued me throughout my liturgy by continually offending me in matters both great and small.

overseers of the tribe   each tribe appointed three 'overseers' or 'caretakers' (*epimelētai*), officers who were appointed for a year to carry out a wide range of financial, religious and legal duties. These included representing the tribe's interests before the state, as they do in this case in which the archon accuses the tribe of failing to nominate their *choregos* for the dithyrambic competition.

All of you   Demosthenes reminds the assembled jury (there were usually upwards of 200 jurors) of its past goodwill towards him. Having volunteered to perform a major public service and bankrolled a tribe's chorus, it is likely that at least some of the jurors would have felt indebted to him and might thus be naturally sympathetic to his case. Plutarch said of Nicias' rise to political prominence in the 420s (*Nicias* 3): 'he won over the people by becoming the sponsor for choruses, for athletic teams, and other such lavish displays of public munificence, which surpassed those of all his predecessors and contemporaries in extravagance and elegance'.

Choregic monuments

On top of all his other expenses, a *choregos* was expected to set up a monument celebrating his victory, paid from his own funds. These ranged from an inscribed stone stele mounted on a base (see **2.2**) to much larger and more elaborate architectural structures, often capped by the bronze tripod that was awarded as the prize for victory such as the one shown below. In fact, the street leading from the Agora or main market-place to the theatre of Dionysus was known as the 'Street of Tripods' because of the large number of victory monuments that lined its way.

Such magnificent monuments were viewed as natural ways to express the ambition that the Greeks admired (see **2.2**). Theophrastus (*Characters* 22) begins his description of the stingy man with the following example: 'The stingy man is the kind of man who, when he wins the tragedy competition, dedicates to Dionysus a plank of wood with only his own name inscribed on it.' By failing to provide a suitable monument and by omitting mention of the winning poet, actors and tribe, the stingy man shirks his responsibilities towards his community.

Monument erected by a choregos *named Lysicrates to commemorate his victory in 335 or 334 BC.*

Detail of the frieze of the Lysicrates monument showing scenes from the satyr-play (top), with commemorative tripods (below).

A more sceptical assessment of the expenses involved in theatrical productions appears in Plutarch's *Moralia* 348d–349b.

2.5   Looking at this [i.e. the expenses], **a Spartan once said**, quite fittingly, that the Athenians were making a big mistake in wasting their energy on amusements – that is to say, by lavishing on the theatre the costs of equipping large fleets and the provisions that would supply whole armies in the field. If one were to calculate the **production costs** of each tragedy, it would be apparent that the Athenian people have spent more on productions of *Bacchae*, *Phoenician Women*, *Oedipus*, *Antigone* and on the misfortunes of Medea and Electra than on fighting for their **supremacy** and fighting for their liberty against the Persians. For the generals often ordered their men to bring along uncooked rations when they led them off to battle. And I swear that the naval captains would provide for their oarsmen barley-meal with a relish of onions and cheese and then march them onto the triremes. But the *choregoi* set before their chorus-members eels and lettuce and joints of meat and marrow, and **fed them sumptuously** for a long time while they were training their voices and living in luxury. And in return, those of the *choregoi* who lost earned abuse and became a laughing-stock, while those who won were granted a tripod – which, as Demetrius said, is not so much a monument to victory as a last libation poured in honour of a wasted livelihood, a cenotaph to a lost estate.

---

a Spartan once said   it is quite fitting that this critique of the Athenians is put into the mouth of a Spartan: Spartans were their long-standing rivals and, in contrast to the Athenians, were known for their frugality and lack of ostentation.

production costs   the speaker is clearly exaggerating for the sake of effect, but it is true that the expenses incurred in discharging a liturgy could be astronomical (see **2.6**).

supremacy   during the Peloponnesian War and the years leading up to it, when Athens fought to maintain her position as leader of the allied states in what amounted to an Athenian empire.

fed them sumptuously   it is hardly fair to compare the fare of soldiers on the battlefield or sailors mid-voyage to the fresh delicacies available to chorus-members rehearsing. But since funding a trireme and funding a chorus were two of the most common liturgies, it is not surprising that the expenses involved are compared head to head in this way.

A speech delivered by an Athenian who was defending himself against charges of bribery (Lysias, *Defence against a Charge of Taking Bribes* 1–5) gives us the stated costs of each of the many liturgies that he fulfilled over the period 411/10–402 BC (shown as a table on p. 36), during which time Athens was busy fighting the Peloponnesian War. The total expenses incurred by this particular Athenian in performing various liturgies over a period of approximately ten years amount to 63,300 drachmas (see table). One drachma was roughly one day's wages for a skilled labourer.

The statistics make interesting reading: the cost of funding a dithyrambic chorus at the City Dionysia could amount to 5,000 drachmas – almost as much as the cost of funding the operation of a warship for a year (36,000 drachmas over seven years comes to an average of 5,143 drachmas)! And we have to remember that nine other *choregoi* were funding their own choruses in the men's dithyrambic competition alone – not to mention the ten choruses entering the boys' dithyrambic competition, the three tragic choruses and three (or perhaps five) comic choruses. And we are still only talking about the expenses incurred by *choregoi* in one festival (the City Dionysia). Once we add on the costs borne by *choregoi* at other festivals such as the Lenaea and Rural Dionysia, and the additional expenses incurred by the state or deme, then it becomes clear that the Athenians invested a huge amount of capital in theatre. To give this expense a point of comparison, the Athenian navy that sailed against Sicily, described by Thucydides as the largest force ever to set sail, consisted of 134 triremes. Eric Csapo and William Slater (1994: 141) estimate that the figures given in this Lysias speech suggest total costs for the City Dionysia amounting to approximately one-tenth of the total annual expenditure on its navy. That the Athenians continued to put on the festival throughout the Peloponnesian War is in itself remarkable (by contrast, the modern-day Olympic Games were suspended during the First and Second World Wars).

Around 310 BC, Demetrius of Phalerum abolished the system of funding choruses through *choregoi*; an official called the **agōnothetēs** was appointed to organize the festivals. Although the *demos* (the body of citizens) was now officially listed as *choregos*, it appears that the *agonothetes* was usually a wealthy citizen who invested quite a bit of his own money in addition to the money he received from the state.

2.6

Event	Festival	Cost in drachmas	Remarks
Tragedy	City Dionysia	3,000	
Dithyramb (men's event)	Thargelia	2,000	A less prestigious event than the Dionysia with lower funding costs. This was a winning production.
Pyrrhic dance	Panathenaea	800	An armed dance performed by a chorus.
Dithyramb	City Dionysia	5,000	The most expensive event, probably because of the large size of the chorus (50 choreuts); the total also includes the price of the victory monument. This production won first prize.
Dithyramb	Lesser Panathenaea	300	An annual Athenian summer festival: three out of four years it was termed 'lesser'; once every four years a 'greater' Panathenaea was put on.
Trierarchy		36,000 over 7 years	Seven consecutive years funding a trireme (i.e. 5,143 drachmas per year).
Special tax		3,000	Direct taxation of individuals was not the norm in ancient Greece; this was an emergency property tax levied to help fund the war effort.
Special tax		4,000	
Gymnasiarchy	Prometheia	1,200	Funding athletes to compete in the games at the Prometheia festival in honour of Prometheus.
Dithyramb (boys' event)	Unspecified	More than 1,500	The boys' dithyrambic chorus cost less than the more prestigious men's competition.
Comedy	City Dionysia	1,600	Each comic playwright entered only one play (the tragic competition consisted of 3 tragedies + 1 satyr-play). This production won first prize. The figure included the cost of masks, the usual victory dedication in comedy.
Pyrrhic dance (youths)	Lesser Panathenaea	700	
Boat race	Sounion	1,500	
Other contributions		3,000	The speaker ends by listing miscellaneous contributions such as paying the expenses of a sacred embassy and contributing to the Arrephoria festival (held in honour of Athena in the run-up to the Panathenaea).

The following extract from Demosthenes' speech (*Against Meidias* 14–18) picks up where the previous one (**2.4**) left off and describes the various ways in which Meidias attempted to sabotage Demosthenes' liturgy.

2.7   Meidias here, who ... plagued me throughout my liturgy by continually offending me in matters both great and small. Now as for the trouble he caused me by opposing **exemption from military service** for my choreuts and by putting his name forward and urging that he be elected overseer of the Dionysia, these and all similar machinations I will pass over ... [they were frustrating, he goes on to argue, but not grounds for prosecution]. It is his extreme subsequent behaviour that I intend to talk about. And indeed, I would not have ventured to denounce him even now if I had not previously convicted him **in the assembly** immediately afterwards. He planned to destroy the **sacred garments** – for everything that is provided for the festival I regard as sacred until after it has been used – as well as the golden crowns that I had commissioned as ornaments for the chorus by breaking and entering the house of the goldsmith by night. And he did destroy them – though not all of them, because **he wasn't able to**. No one has ever heard of anyone attempting or perpetrating such a crime as this in our city. But he was not

---

exemption from military service   young men at Athens had to do two years of compulsory military service. Since a chorus was in training for several months and was largely composed of young men in their physical prime, chorus-members had to seek an official exemption from military service.

in the assembly   a special meeting of the assembly following the festival to evaluate its organization and investigate any alleged irregularities.

sacred garments   in an attempt to raise the indignation of the jury, Demosthenes characterizes Meidias as someone who is desecrating what is sacrosanct since the costumes are being used in the festival of Dionysus: that theatrical paraphernalia would not normally have been considered sacred in this way is clear from his aside ('for everything...').

he wasn't able to   later a sworn statement by the goldsmith is read out describing how he caught Meidias breaking into his premises at night and prevented him from destroying the golden crowns, which he said were for wearing in the procession. Crowns or wreaths were symbols of celebration, worn at joyful occasions such as festivals and parties. We are told (*Life of Euripides* 20) that when he heard the news of Euripides' death, Sophocles brought on his chorus and actors at the *proagon* without the customary wreaths as a sign of mourning.

content with just that; instead, he bribed my **chorus-trainer**! And if Telephanes, the piper, had not then proved himself such an excellent friend – noticed what he was up to, driven the man away and felt it his duty to drill and direct the chorus himself – we could not have entered the competition, men of Athens, for the chorus would have come on untrained and we would have suffered the ultimate disgrace. But his outrageous audacity did not stop there. He had it in such profusion that he bribed the crowned archon himself, led the *choregoi* against me, and stood by the judges **as they took their oaths**, shouting and threatening. And he blocked the **wings** of the theatre building – a private citizen nailing up private property! – and never stopped causing me indescribable trouble and harm.

---

1 What can we learn indirectly from this passage about the rehearsal process?

2 What does this passage tell us about potential risks faced by a *choregos*?

3 Demosthenes goes on to say that Meidias was responsible for snatching victory away from his chorus when it was on the point of winning (quite how he knows that his chorus was winning and how Meidias prevented this he does not specify). What other claims that Demosthenes makes strike you as far-fetched?

---

chorus-trainer the chorus-trainer or **chorodidaskalos** (literally 'teacher of the chorus') oversaw the training of the chorus and was responsible for the artistic aspects of the production. Often the playwright himself served as *chorodidaskalos* (also referred to as **didaskalos**).

as they took their oaths the judges selected by lot to adjudicate the contests swore an oath in front of the assembled audience that they would be impartial. In the second **hypothesis** (introductory summary) to this speech, the commentator adds a vivid if speculative elaboration of this scene: as the judges were taking their oath to award the prize to the best performance, he says Meidias kept adding 'except Demosthenes'.

wings the projecting wings of the *skēnē* or theatre building (pl. *paraskēnia*, sing. *paraskēnion*); each had a side-door used for entrances and exits onto the stage in dramatic performances (see p. 52).

Rehearsals

> The following speech (Antiphon, *On the Choreut* 11–12) was written for an unknown Athenian, a *choregos* who was accused (in 419 BC) of unintentional homicide in the death of a member of his chorus who died while rehearsing for the boys' dithyrambic competition at the Thargelia festival. The boy died from a medicine that was administered while he was in training at the *choregos'* house, though the *choregos* explains that he wasn't present at the time of death, having delegated the responsibilities of looking after the chorus.

2.8   When I was appointed *choregos* for the **Thargelia festival** and was allotted the poet Pantakles and the tribe Kekropis as well as my own, I served as *choregos* to the best of my abilities and in the fairest possible way. First of all, I equipped the most suitable room in my house as a training room – the same room that I had used for training when I was *choregos* for the Dionysia. Next I brought together the best chorus I could muster **without fining anyone**, or making anyone provide surety, or making enemies with anyone; instead I did everything in a way that was most agreeable and suitable for both parties – I making my requests and entreaties, they sending their sons freely and readily.

> 1   Why do you think the speaker mentions that he had already trained a chorus for the Dionysia?
>
> 2   Why do you think he specifies that he avoided making enemies?
>
> 3   What do we learn about the rehearsal process from this passage?

The *proagon*

Socrates' remarks (see **2.9**) and the dimensions of the **Odeon** (see **2.10n**) suggest that a large crowd attended the *proagon*, or preview of the plays. Playwrights composed new plays every time they entered a competition (and so tragedians seem to have competed roughly once every two years, allowing them time in between to write their next set of plays). Thus no one in the audience would have previously seen the plays, especially since rehearsals seem to have happened behind closed doors. The *proagon*, therefore, gave the audience a preview of what the plays would be about, and provided an occasion at which to publicly celebrate the poets, casts and *choregoi*. After the performances, only the winning cast would have enjoyed the limelight.

Thargelia festival   see note on **2.1**.

without fining anyone   the *choregos* was entitled to co-opt boys to serve in his chorus; failure to enlist could result in a fine for the father of the boy. In cases in which a boy excused himself, the father was required to post surety – which would be forfeited if the grounds for exemption proved invalid.

2.9　'You want to cast a spell on me, Socrates,' said Agathon, 'hoping that I will become flustered by being conscious of my audience's high expectations of a great speech.' 'How forgetful that would be of me,' said Socrates, 'after I witnessed the courage and great presence of mind with which you climbed up onto the platform with your actors, and saw how you looked out at such a huge audience as you introduced your plays without being thrown off in the slightest, if I now thought that you would be flustered by a small audience like us.'

2.10　There occurred a few days before the Great Dionysia, in the building called the **Odeon**, a contest [*agon*] of the tragedians and a display of the plays with which they intended to compete in the theatre – this is why it is **rightly called a *proagon***. And the actors enter **without their masks and costumes.**

Odeon　a covered concert-hall abutting the theatre of Dionysus, built by Pericles (see p. 50) in 446–442 BC. Its scale, magnificence and architectural innovation (this square building measured some sixty metres across and would have required a forest of columns to support its roof) would have amazed the visitor; in fact, according to the first-century BC Roman architect Vitruvius (*On Architecture* 5.9), it incorporated into its structure masts from Persian ships defeated at the battle of Salamis (480 BC). Whether or not this tradition is true, it does suggest that the building was regarded as a monument to Athens' pre-eminence, a position that the city justified on the basis of the leading role that it played in the Persian Wars.

rightly called a *proagon*　the word *proagon* literally means 'pre-contest' or 'before the contest' – the **scholiast**, or commentator, is pointing out the fact that its name reflects its function – an event leading up to the competition proper. It is not clear what the scholiast meant in describing the *proagon* as a contest between the tragedians – perhaps this was the point at which the order of performance was decided.

without their masks and costumes　that the actors were presented out of costume perhaps suggests that the purpose of the *proagon* was to recognize the citizens who had dedicated themselves for so many weeks to rehearsing for the plays; with their masks on, they would not have been identifiable.

Judges

In this passage (*Trapeziticus* 33–4, a speech written by Isocrates in *c.* 393 BC on behalf of a young man prosecuting the banker Pasion on charges of misappropriating his money), Isocrates is trying to add weight to his claim that Pasion falsified a memorandum, by demonstrating that he associates with other well-known crooks.

2.11   Which of you does not know that Pythodorus, the chap known as the travelling salesman (who will say and do anything on behalf of Pasion) last year opened the urns and took out the ballots with the judges' names on them that the council had deposited? Why then should it surprise you when a man, who to gain a small advantage and at the risk of his life dared secretly to open urns that had been stamped by the co-presidents of the council, sealed by the *choregoi*, guarded by the treasurers, and stored on the Acropolis, why then should it surprise you when men like these falsify a mere written agreement in the custody of a foreigner when they stand to gain such a profit?

Here Isocrates describes some of the measures taken by the state to avoid corruption in the judging of plays. The names of candidates eligible to serve as judges were submitted for vetting by the chief executive council (the **boulē**), composed of five hundred members, fifty from each tribe. The names were then deposited into large urns (actually water-jars) that were sealed by the *choregoi*, thereby certifying that they believed the process to be fair. The jars were deposited for safe keeping on the Acropolis (the Parthenon served as the state treasury), and then brought to the theatre on the day of the performance where, in full public view, the archon pulled out the names of those chosen to serve as judges. Perhaps there were ten jars, one for each tribe, and one name was selected from each, though this is not certain. This randomization of the selection process was intended to prevent bribery: if a *choregos* wanted to bribe the judges, he would have to pay off hundreds and perhaps even thousands of citizens whose names had been deposited in the jars. However, even this system wasn't foolproof, as is clear from this passage and other sources.

The extent to which state officials were involved in running the City Dionysia is remarkable; the *polis* clearly took the whole process very seriously, and fraud of the kind alleged against Pythodorus seems to have carried the death penalty.

In the closing scene of Aristophanes' *Assembly-Women* (1136–62), Praxagoras' maid comes on and invites her mistress's husband Blepyrus – and the audience and judges – to the party to celebrate their play's victory. The chorus follow this with a lively dance while singing the mouthwatering menu for their victory-feast. They close the play with a series of shouts of celebration (1180–3).

2.12 MAID   By Aphrodite, you'll be the very last one to arrive at the party. Still, I have instructions from your wife to pick you up and take you there – along with these gals of yours. There's still some Chian wine left over and other tidbits, so hurry up! And any of you spectators who favour us, and any of you judges who isn't **looking somewhere else**, come with us: we'll supply everything.   1140

BLEPYRUS   Why not be a dear and invite them all; don't leave anyone out! Be generous! Invite the old man, the boy, the infant: there's dinner prepared for every single one of them – if they go back home! As for me, I'm heading to dinner right now, and I have this nice little flame to go with me!   1145

1150

CHORUS-LEADER   No point in wasting time, then. Take your girls and off you go! And while you're heading on down, I'll sing you a little aperitif. But first I should like to offer a small suggestion to the judges: those of you who are clever, remember the clever parts and vote for me; those who enjoy a laugh, remember the funny parts and vote for me; in fact, I'm asking pretty much everyone to vote for me. And don't let the **luck of the draw** – that they picked my show to go first – be to my disadvantage. Keep all this in mind and don't break your oath, but always judge the choruses fairly! Don't behave like bad **courtesans**, who only remember the last guy they have been with! …   1155

1160

---

looking somewhere else   looking to cast his vote for a different production.

luck of the draw   the order in which the plays were put on was decided by lot. To the ancients, the use of lots did not constitute blind chance but put the decision in the hands of the gods (*Tychē* or 'Chance' was a daughter of Zeus). Nowadays citizens are still selected at random for jury duty, a practice designed to ensure a fair trial and to allow the full citizen body to participate in an important democratic institution. The possibility that the first production could be eclipsed by those that followed would have been more acute in the tragedy competition, which was spread over a period of three days.

courtesans   there is no exact equivalent to the courtesan (Greek *hetaira*) in our culture today: she offered sexual favours in return for gain, but often had a long-term relationship with her male companion and accompanied him at drinking-parties (which were off limits to a respectable married woman). Courtesans could become rich and influential, and did not carry the stigma borne by prostitutes in modern society. The word *hetaira* literally means 'companion' and is closer to 'escort' or even 'girlfriend' than to 'prostitute'. In New Comedy, the courtesan was frequently the love interest of the young man.

CHORUS   Pick up those legs – iai, euai!
We're off to dinner – euoi, euai!
Euai – to celebrate victory:
Euai, euai, euai, euai!

> - What might be the purpose of these direct references to the judges and audience? Do you think that the playwright intends them to be taken seriously?

It is typical in comedy for the playwrights to make humorous appeals to the judges to vote for their plays and to predict that theirs will be the winning production. That this was a frequent ploy suggests that it wasn't penalized as being improper. It is also common to appeal to the audience for support. Why is this? Among the many references to the at times rambunctious audience, there are several that suggest that the judges were influenced by audience response. That this should happen is hardly surprising – in sports, it is a well-known fact that the reaction of the fans has an effect on the decisions of the referees (a big part of the 'home-team advantage').

> In the following section of his *Varia Historia* (2.13), Aelian describes the audience's enthusiastic response to Aristophanes' *Clouds* at the City Dionysia in 423 BC (though in this particular case the play was placed third).

2.13   [The Athenian public] felt that the *Clouds* was a delightful piece; they applauded the poet as never before and shouted for him to win and ordered the judges from up above to **write down no other name** but Aristophanes.

> Although Aelian is writing much later, in the late second or early third century AD, references in earlier authors suggest that the influence of the audience on the judges was a long-standing concern. For example, Plato (*Laws* 659b–c) complains bitterly at how the roar of the crowd exerts an undue influence on the judges in favour of plays that are 'pleasurable but improper'; this in turn, he argues, corrupts the poets 'who adapt their works to suit the low tastes of the judges, resulting in the spectators becoming the teachers of the poets' (the poet was supposed to be the teacher of his audience).

---

write down no other name   judges wrote down their vote on a tablet and deposited it in an urn. Then, in a process that has been variously reconstructed by scholars, five or more tablets were drawn out at random until a clear winner was established.

1   Plato was an advocate of censorship of unsuitable material. Do you think
    that censorship is appropriate in certain cases, or do you think that an artist
    should be allowed freedom to express even what is socially unacceptable? If
    censorship is appropriate, who should do the censoring?

2   Athenian playwrights composed their plays for competition. To what extent
    do you think this influenced the type of plays they produced?

Victor lists

Much of what we know about the dates of performance of surviving plays comes either from internal evidence (clues within the plays themselves) or from remarks by the ancient commentator writing the introductory note (the *hypothesis*) that accompanied the play's text. However, we are fortunate that the Greeks also had what has been described as an 'epigraphical habit' – they liked to inscribe important events on durable materials, especially stone. A number of inscriptions survive in fragmentary form that record the winners at the City Dionysia.

One such record, dating to the fourth century, may well have been the official record displayed publicly to commemorate the victors. Modern scholars refer to it as the *Fasti*. Most of the fragments were found on the northern slope of the Acropolis, so the inscription may have been displayed in the Agora. The photograph below shows one fragment; a transcription and accompanying translation of the entry it preserves for the year 458 BC is given on p. 45 (**2.14**).

2.14   9   [ἐπὶ Φιλο]κλέου[ς]

[Οἰν]ηῒς παίδων
Δημόδοκος ἐχορήγει

12   Ἱπποθωντὶς ἀνδρῶν
Εὐκτήμων Ἐλευ:(σίνιος) ἐχορή(γει)

κωμωιδῶν
15   Εὐρυκλείδης ἐχορήγει
Εὐφρόνιος ἐδίδασκε

τραγωιδῶν
18   Ξενοκλῆς Ἀφιδνα(ῖος) ἐχορή(γει)
Αἰσχύλος ἐδίδασκεν

9   In (the year of) Philokles [i.e. when Philokles was eponymous archon]

Oineïs (won the dithyrambic competition) of boys [Oineïs was the name of the winning tribe]
Demodokos was the *choregos* [i.e. sponsor of the winning tribe in the boys' competition]

12   Hippothontis (won the dithyrambic competition) of men [Hippothontis was the name of the winning tribe]
Euktemon of Eleusis was the *choregos* [i.e. sponsor of the winning tribe in the men's competition]

In the comedies
15   Eurykleides was the *choregos* [i.e. sponsor of the winning comedy]
Euphronios was the *didaskalos* [i.e. director – this was often but not always the poet]

In the tragedies
18   Xenokles of Aphidna was the *choregos* [i.e. sponsor of the winning tragedies]
Aeschylus was the *didaskalos* [i.e. director of the winning tragedies – the plays in question were Aeschylus' *Oresteia* trilogy and his satyr-play *Proteus*]

Note that Greek inscriptions use only capital letters and do not contain spaces between words. In the transcription at the top of the page, square brackets enclose portions of the text that are missing but have been reconstructed, while round brackets indicate where abbreviations have been expanded (the inscription indicates some of its abbreviations with a mark like a colon). You may be able to make out the name Demodokos (line 11) in the first fully preserved line at the top of the second column.

The inscription (IG II² 2318) was a continuous record of the winners in all the competitions. Judging from its fragmentary heading, it purports to begin from the time when 'komoi to Dionysus were first ...', but it is not clear what is meant by komoi ('revels') in this context. What survive are fragments from quite a few years – the earliest dates to 472 and mentions Aeschylus (his *Persians* from this year has survived), the last to 328 BC. The bulk of the record appears to have been inscribed by a single hand shortly after 346 BC, after which later records were added by other hands.

The order in which events and names were recorded is the same for every year, except that from 447 BC the name of the victorious lead actor in the tragedies category starts being added after the name of the playwright, reflecting the increased prominence that star actors enjoyed. The photograph shows that the text was divided into columns: the right-hand portion of one column and most of another are preserved in this piece.

---

1   What can you deduce from the way in which the information in this inscription is arranged? Why, for example, is the boys' dithyrambic competition mentioned first? Does anything surprise you about what is mentioned and what is not?

2   Athens celebrated those who had contributed to winning performances by inscribing their names in stone. In what ways does modern society recognize artistic excellence?

Another set of inscriptions, known as the *Didaskaliai* (IG II² 2319–23), offers more detailed information for both the City Dionysia *and* the Lenaea: the names of the runners-up are included as well, and the titles of plays are listed. It probably originally dates to the third century BC; by this time, there were separate competitions at the City Dionysia for 'old tragedies' and 'old comedies' (i.e. re-performances of earlier plays). Interestingly, there is no mention of dithyrambic winners (new tribes started to be added to honour certain rulers, and this may have weakened the earlier tribal rivalry and made the dithyrambic contests less meaningful). *Choregoi* no longer appear; instead the names of the principal actor for each production are included as well as the winner of the prize for best actor.

3 The theatre

The best-known Greek theatre today is the beautifully proportioned theatre at Epidaurus (see pp. 54–5). But it is not representative of the kind of theatre in which playwrights such as Aeschylus and Aristophanes put on their plays, since it was built a century later. The fifth-century theatre was a far more rudimentary structure, though it is hard to ascertain its exact form since theatres were often remodelled just as modern sports stadiums undergo periodic reconstruction.

The Greek theatre in its earliest form was not a building but an open-air acting space. Theatres were usually located in a natural bowl on the lower slopes of a hill, so that spectators sat on an incline for optimal viewing; the contours of the bowl also served as a sounding-board so that the voices of the actors didn't get lost in the great wide open. Unlike the later Roman theatres, which tended to be completely enclosed – man-made structures built up with massive amounts of brick and concrete – Greek theatres were open spaces engaging with their surroundings, often providing wonderful views over the stage-building.

There are four main elements to a Greek theatre (see diagram below). The *theātron* (giving us the word 'theatre', literally 'viewing place') is where the audience sat. Originally it was simply a grassy bank, perhaps with temporary wooden seating, but later stone seating was added. The *orchēstra* was the acting space. It means 'dancing place', an indication of the importance of dance and the chorus to Greek drama. In its original form, it was a level space of beaten earth, partially enclosed by the *theatron*, though eventually its surface was covered with stone paving. Although later Greek *orchestras* are perfectly circular, their early forms may often have been irregular and varied in shape. The *skēnē* was the building that formed the backdrop for the *orchestra*. The word literally means 'tent' or 'hut' and it may originally have been a temporary pavilion used by the actors for costume changes. By the middle of the fifth century, the *skene* was a long wooden building abutting the *orchestra*. It often played an important role in the plot of a play (e.g. representing the royal palace in many tragedies), and characters entered and exited the acting space through its central doorway. Finally, there were broad side approaches on either side of the *orchestra*. These are the *eisodoi*; the chorus and actors entered the *orchestra* along one or other *eisodos* (singular), and the audience also used them to enter and leave the theatre. They are also referred to as *parodoi*: _parodoi_ means 'paths on the side' (i.e. side-entrances), while _eisodoi_ means 'paths in' (i.e. entrances).

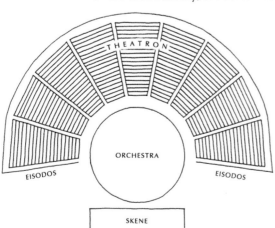

The Theatre of Dionysus at Athens

Since most of the surviving plays were written for performance at the Theatre of Dionysus at Athens, it is worth examining this theatre in greatest detail, tracing its development over time (see diagram below). Its remains are reasonably well preserved, though most belong to later phases of construction.

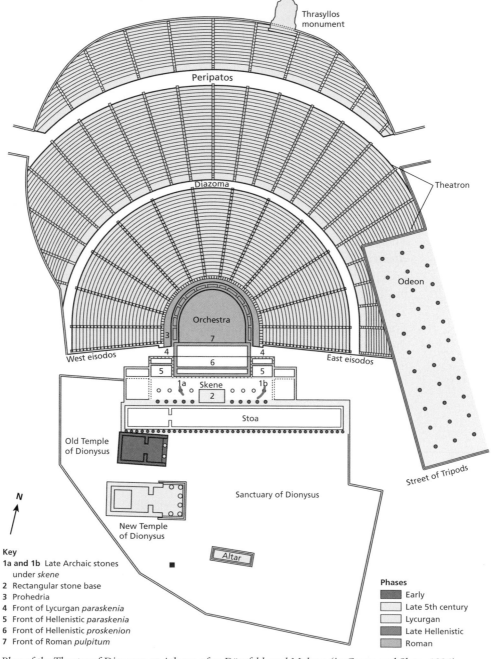

Key
1a and 1b Late Archaic stones under *skene*
2 Rectangular stone base
3 Prohedria
4 Front of Lycurgan *paraskenia*
5 Front of Hellenistic *paraskenia*
6 Front of Hellenistic *proskenion*
7 Front of Roman *pulpitum*

Phases
Early
Late 5th century
Lycurgan
Late Hellenistic
Roman

Plan of the Theatre of Dionysus at Athens, after Dörpfeld, and Malyon (in Csapo and Slater 1994).

Phase 1: the early theatrical space

According to our ancient sources, theatrical performances at Athens first took place in the Agora. Around the beginning of the fifth century, however, they began to be held on a site on the south-east slopes of the Acropolis that became the Theatre of Dionysus. It was situated adjacent to a small temple to Dionysus, and it is tempting to believe that this site was chosen for the theatre because of its proximity to the sanctuary of the god in whose honour the City Dionysia festival was held. Unlike the Agora, where wooden benches had to be built up to create tiered seating, the sloping ground provided an incline naturally suited for watching the plays.

In its first phase during the first half of the fifth century BC, the theatre of Dionysus was probably little more than an open space, with audience members seated on the ground, or on wooden benches, on the lower slopes of the Acropolis to watch performances taking place on the built-up level terrace below them (see reconstruction below). The only surviving archaeological trace of this first phase is a line of stones (marked 1a and 1b on the plan) excavated by the German archaeologist Wilhelm Dörpfeld in the 1880s. He identified these stones as belonging to the retaining wall marking the perimeter of the original *orchestra* of beaten earth, which he calculated (by extrapolating from the curvature of the arc of the stones) to have been approximately 26 metres in diameter. Although scholars have questioned his conclusions and even challenged the notion that the original *orchestra* was round, it remains a distinct possibility given the theatre's form in later phases and the fact that a circular performance space is ideally suited to dances such as those of the dithyramb. Of course, the benches of the early *theatron* would not have described the perfect arc of the later stone seating, since wooden planking is naturally rectilinear.

At some point a *skene* was added; the earliest surviving play that requires a solid *skene* structure is Aeschylus' *Oresteia*, performed in 458 BC; thus this date provides a *terminus ante quem*, 'a limit before which' the *skene* must have been added.

Reconstruction of the earliest form of the Theatre of Dionysus at Athens, with the retaining wall of the orchestra *and the temple of Dionysus in the foreground.*

Phase 2: the Periclean theatre

During the 440s and 430s, Athens enjoyed a period of great prosperity and influence under the leadership of Pericles, who initiated an ambitious building programme that included such architectural wonders as the Parthenon and the Propylaea, the monumental gateway to the Acropolis, and which made Athens the envy of all. His projects included the construction in the 440s of an odeon, a roofed hall that was used for the official presentation of the playwrights and their casts in the *proagon* (see **2.9–10**, esp. **2.10n**) as well as for musical performances. This large square building jutted into the space occupied by the *theatron* and was built at an oblique angle to it. The Odeon's orientation lends further support to the impression that at this time the area occupied by the spectators still comprised a general seating area rather than fixed seating and that its shape didn't involve the perfect symmetry of later theatres, since otherwise the layout of the Odeon is hard to explain. The encroachment of the Odeon probably explains why the *orchestra* was apparently reduced in size and shifted a few metres to the northwest of its original location. Thus the Periclean rebuilding of the theatre is best understood as part of the same redevelopment project that included the construction of the Odeon and so probably dates to the 440s.

The second half of the fifth century, considered the golden age of Athens, was also the period when many of the tragedies of Sophocles and Euripides and the comedies of Aristophanes were composed and performed in Athens; thus this phase of the theatre is of particular interest as we consider the staging of these plays.

Aristophanes' *Women at the Thesmophoria*, performed in 411, describes the audience as seated on benches (see **6.3**), and descriptions of early performances in the Agora also refer to this kind of seating, so that makeshift seating was probably the norm until the fourth century. Some scholars explain away these references to 'benches', suggesting that the term may have lost its original literal force (just as in the sport of broomball the stick is still referred to as a broom, even though the broom has since been superseded by more modern equipment), and believe that the Periclean theatre already comprised stone seating. If the *skene* in its earliest form was a tent or other temporary structure, by now it was a substantial wooden stage-building with a flat roof that was accessible to the actors, who made occasional use of it, especially when playing the part of gods (for which it was called the **theologeion**). The rectanglular stone base marked 2 seems to be a surviving element of this building. Its facade was probably long and flat, broken in the centre by double doors from which characters entered the acting space. Whether during this period the central doorway was flanked by side doors and projecting porches is a matter of debate.

Another topic of debate is whether the Periclean theatre had an elevated stage. Some scholars posit a long stage running the length of the *skene*, low and narrow. Others question the existence of a stage at this point (see reconstruction on p. 51). Some scenes from this period might naturally lend themselves to the use of a raised stage. But these are the exception, and the evidence of the plays suggests that, for most scenes, actors and chorus interacted in the shared space of the *orchestra*.

Renderings of the Theatre of Dionysus at Athens during its Periclean phase.

At some point, a stoa or colonnade was constructed behind the *skene*; it ran parallel to it and shared its foundations (see plan on p. 48). Thus the ensemble of Periclean *skene* and stoa behind it now permanently enclosed the theatre on the south side. Similarly, access to the theatre now seems to have been gained through a gateway (Andocides, *On the Mysteries* 38), so that the theatre has become more clearly delimited by architectural structures.

Phase 3: the Lycurgan reconstruction

Between 338 and 326, the Theatre of Dionysus at Athens was rebuilt by the Athenian statesman and orator Lycurgus who, like Pericles before him, undertook an ambitious building programme. It is this Lycurgan theatre that witnessed the plays of Menander. Lycurgus equipped the theatre with stone seating throughout the *theatron* (much of which still survives), divided by radial staircases into thirteen wedge-shaped sectors (**kerkis**, plural **kerkides**), with the rows of seats divided into upper, middle and lower bands by two broad passageways (**diazōma**, plural **diazōmata**). The upper passageway incorporated a pre-existing footpath around the foot of the Acropolis known as the Peripatos. In the front row, the priest of Dionysus and other dignitaries sat on ornate stone thrones (see p. 140, marked 3 on the plan on p. 48). Although the surviving thrones date from the Roman period (first century BC), it is likely the Lycurgan seats were similar. The *skene* was also rebuilt under Lycurgus as a permanent stone structure some 20 metres in length. It now certainly included **paraskēnia** (singular **paraskēnion**), side wings that protruded forwards (marked 4 on the plan; see also reconstruction below), first mentioned by Demosthenes (*Against Meidias* 17), as well as side doors flanking the main central doorway and used to full dramatic effect in Menander's comedies. It may possibly also have had a second storey. If the fifth-century theatre did not include a raised stage, the Lycurgan version likely did.

Reconstruction of the Lycurgan phase of the Theatre of Dionysus at Athens.

Phase 4: the late Hellenistic theatre and beyond

At some point in the Hellenistic period (probably late third or early second century BC), the Lycurgan *skene* was again remodelled: the new *paraskenia* projected less (marked 5 on the plan) and a **proskēnion** or low colonnaded portico was added to the front of the *skene* (6 on the plan), as occurred at other theatres at this time. These porticoes may represent the architectural realization, in three dimensions, of columns that had previously been represented in two dimensions in scene-painting on the facade of the *skene*. Actors now acted from the roof of this *proskenion*, called the **logeion** (or 'speaking place'), with the second storey of the *skene* now functioning as the backdrop and known as the **episkēnion** (see p. 53). By this period, plays no longer included any interaction between actors and chorus. A further set of changes was made in the Roman period under Nero (AD 54–68), including the addition of marble paving-stones in the *orchestra* and the erection of a projecting stage or *pulpitum* (7 on the plan) that gave the *orchestra* the horseshoe shape that it still has today.

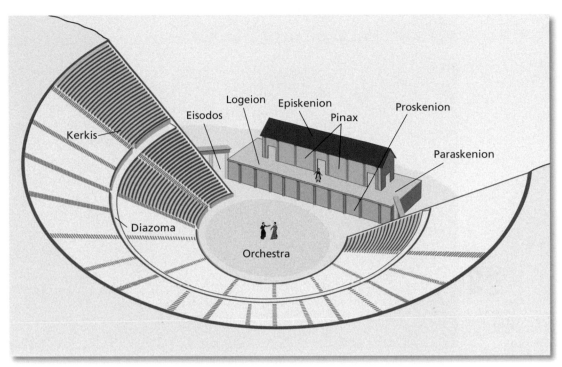

Elevation of a typical Hellenistic theatre, after Malyon (in Csapo and Slater 1994).

Other theatres

Thorikos

The theatre that served the coastal deme of Thorikos has been quite well preserved. It dates back to the early fifth century and so gives us a good idea of what one early theatre looked like (see p. 54). It has a roughly rectangular *orchestra* lined by a stretch of straight stone seating that curves around at both ends. Its shape is irregular and asymmetrical, the altar is off to one side of the *orchestra* instead of at its centre, and the small temple bounding the west end of the *orchestra* is not particularly aligned with the theatre proper. Its orientation and shape respond to the physical terrain and are partly a result of the expansion of its seating area over time (the original central stretch of seats was first expanded laterally, then later the upper rows were added, reaching a final capacity of *c.* 6,000 spectators); it is therefore dangerous to make the unwarranted assumption that other early theatres which did not face the same topographical constraints would have looked similar. Holes bored into the rock-face have been interpreted as sockets for the supporting framework of a wooden stage. The theatre was probably also used for holding public assemblies and may have originally been built for this purpose. In fact, many ancient theatres served multiple functions in this way. When the apostle Paul visited Ephesus, a mob was roused to oppose his teachings; they seized two of his companions and held an impromptu town meeting in the theatre (Acts 19).

The theatre at Thorikos.

Many towns in the ancient world had their own theatre, and sites such as the sanctuary of Apollo at Delphi and of Asclepius at Epidaurus also offered theatrical performances and other forms of entertainment for visitors in large theatres built within the sanctuary complex. Unfortunately, many theatres had their stone plundered for reuse as building material in later centuries; other theatres were modified and reused for new purposes, were buried by the accumulation of deposits, or were built over. Nevertheless, a sizeable number of theatres survive and new discoveries continue to be made. In 2007, for example, substantial remains of what appears to be the theatre of Acharnae (a deme important to the cult of Dionysus and celebrated in Aristophanes' *Acharnians*) were unearthed during construction of an apartment complex in Menidi, a northern suburb of Athens.

Epidaurus

The theatre at Epidaurus (built in the late fourth or early third century BC) is rightly famous. It is a marvel of architectural perfection, incorporating architectural refinements that rival the Parthenon. It is also one of the largest theatres in Greece (it seated around 14,000 spectators) and the best preserved. The theatre was designed as a perfect study in mathematical proportions based on the cubit, a unit of measurement taken from the human lower arm. To the Greeks, the human body, whose various parts relate to the whole according to precise mathematical proportions, exemplified the order of the cosmos and therefore carried religious significance. Thus the refinements of the theatre of Epidaurus may have been a specific tribute to Asclepius, god of healing, beside whose sanctuary it was located, and were not typical of theatres in general.

The photograph offers an oblique view of the theatre: the original lower section of the *theatron* is divided into twelve wedges (*kerkides*) by radial staircases; to this was added an upper tier of seating in the second century BC, separated from the lower by a broad passageway known as the *diazoma* ('girdle') and in turn divided into twenty-two wedges (since the wedges got increasingly wide as they radiated from the *orchestra*, having more staircases in the upper section helped avoid congestion). The *orchestra* is perfectly round and has its circumference marked out in stone. Its centre point where the altar (the **thymelē**) would have stood is also marked, allowing modern visitors to conduct an experiment testing the theatre's remarkable acoustics. If you drop a coin onto the ground at the centre of the *orchestra*, the clink will be heard perfectly from the very back row! A study by acousticians from Georgia Institute of Technology published in 2007 determined that the limestone seating functions as a filter for low-frequency background noises. The two *eisodoi* are framed by monumental gateways.

Unlike the Theatre of Dionysus at Athens, which developed piecemeal from rather primitive beginnings, the theatre at Epidaurus was built out of stone from the start. In its final phase, the *skene* building was two storeys high, and actors would have stood on the projecting roof of the ground-floor *proskenion*, as is typical in theatres of the late Hellenistic period (see drawing on p. 53).

The theatre at Epidaurus, where performances of ancient plays are still put on every summer.

Syracuse

In its heyday, the city of Syracuse on the south-east coast of Sicily rivalled Athens in power and wealth. It was also a hotbed of creative talent, home to Simonides, Pindar, Theocritus and the scientist Archimedes, and host to the theatrical talents of Aeschylus, Epicharmus (comic playwright) and Sophron (writer of mimes).

One of the ways in which it displayed its influence was by building a large theatre. This new theatre, constructed *c.* 230 BC under Hieron II, replaced the earlier theatre in which Aeschylus performed his plays when he lived at the court of Hieron I. Much of the seating of the new theatre, which could hold around 15,000 theatre-goers, was quarried out of the live rock that is a natural feature of the area, in itself a massive feat of construction. Carved into the wall of the *diazoma* or walkway half-way up can still be seen inscriptions dedicating the theatre to Olympian Zeus and to members of the royal family; above the *theatron* was a covered portico offering shelter from the elements. Like many Greek theatres, this one faces south: if, as in Athens, plays were put on in the late winter and early spring, this orientation would have allowed the audience to enjoy the warming rays of the sun.

The evidence of the original stage-building and stage that survived the inevitable Roman alterations suggests that in Hellenistic times it consisted of a *skene* at least two storeys high, fronted by a *proskenion* with projecting *paraskenia*. In the area in front of this, a trench and some cuttings in the rock have been interpreted as evidence of a wooden stage.

Greek theatre and the proscenium theatre

Modern theatres offer increasingly varied and flexible performance spaces. In fact, large theatres may have a large proscenium stage, a smaller thrust stage, and a flexible studio space, allowing them to put on any given piece in the space that most suits its artistic needs. It is rare, however, that we experience theatre as the Greeks did, performed in a huge, open-air theatre. Most of the great works of modern drama were written for the proscenium stage, and generations of actors have been trained for performing on this stage. Even today, budding actors are often taught the first principles of blocking (movement on stage) on it and learn to head downstage for the moments of greatest intensity. The characteristics of the Greek playing space are very different, and these differences have an important effect not only on the kind of plays that were produced but also on the relationship between actors and audience.

The proscenium stage is, in essence, an enclosed space. The proscenium arch, from which the curtain is dropped, frames the acting space and marks a clear line of separation between actors and audience. For the audience looking through the arch at the stage behind it, the acting space is a rectangular box closed in on three sides, and the strong lines of the arch accentuate the sense that the audience

A modern proscenium stage.

is looking in at an interior scene through a transparent fourth wall. It is hardly surprising that in modern drama many scenes are set indoors, in the intimate setting of a kitchen or living room, and that a door at the back of the set will often open out onto an imagined street.

The Greek theatre was fundamentally different. Performances took place *al fresco*. Even when a permanent stage-building was built, spectators in many of the seats would enjoy clear sight lines beyond it into the surrounding landscape. Plays were generally set in the open, and characters usually emerged from the stage-building to report interior scenes. There was no pronounced separation between the acting space of the *orchestra* and the *theatron* that encircled it. Those sitting in the front rows could at any time find themselves targets of direct address in comedy (see **6.9**). Those looking down at the scene from the back or occupying seats in the side wedges would have seen the chorus and actors enfolded by the mass of audience members. Unlike the proscenium theatre, which is primarily frontal, the Greek *theatron* wrapped around more than half of the *orchestra* or performance space, so that audience members could see each other and each other's reactions. David Wiles, in his book *Greek Theatre Performance* (2000: 112), cogently expresses the effect this would have had:

> Many modern performers feel that performance in a huge space is a constraint upon subtle delivery and the development of an actor–audience relationship … This is to miss what lent Greek theatre its power. The spectator 100 metres away was part of a single crowd, bonded by a space that created no vertical or horizontal boundaries, and concealed no group from all the rest. If all 15,000-plus tightly packed people were listening to the same words at the same time, and shared the same broad response, the power of emotion generated would have been quite unlike that created today in a studio theatre.

A reconstruction of the Theatre of Dionysus at Athens in the late fifth century BC.

There is no modern theatrical equivalent – even performances on thrust stages or in theatres in the round usually perform to much smaller audiences (3,000 is a large audience nowadays) and take the audience out of the equation through the use of stage lighting that focuses attention solely on the stage. Watching a Shakespeare play in the reconstructed Globe theatre on the South Bank in London may allow a modern audience to experience a comparable immediacy. But even here, those standing in the Pit and nearest the action are looking up at actors performing on a raised stage, while those in the galleries are separated from the stage by the expanse of the Pit. The ideological implications of layout are perhaps best seen in the many church congregations that have moved away from front-facing pews in favour of seating arrangements that eliminate the architectural division between clergy and laity and characterize worship as a collective experience.

1   Does your school or university theatre have a proscenium stage or an open stage?

2   What type of dramatic action might be best suited to performance in a Greek theatre? You might approach this question by thinking about what would *not* work in such a setting.

3   On a proscenium stage, the dominant position is downstage at centre, where the apron projects out beyond the proscenium arch. If an Athenian actor occupied a similar downstage position right at the front of the *orchestra*, his voice would be muffled by the heads of those sitting in the front rows. Where in the *orchestra* of a Greek theatre do you think the dominant position might be, both visually and acoustically?

4   In a Greek theatre, most of the audience-members look down on the action instead of up. What effect does this bird's-eye view have on the general use of space? For example, what kinds of choreography would be most effective for the chorus?

5   Given the scale of the Theatre of Dionysus at Athens, with a seating capacity of *c.* 15,000 by its Lycurgan phase, what forms of modern entertainment are most comparable? Can you think of large-scale events nowadays in which audience-members being able to see each other has an effect on the atmosphere?

6   Have you ever attended an open-air performance? If so, did you find it gripping or distracting to be outdoors?

7   Think back to theatrical performances that you have attended: what different kinds of venues and acting spaces have you seen? Has any stage design struck you as particularly innovative?

Elements of the theatre

The wooden stands

> Photius was a scholar living in Constantinople during the ninth century AD who compiled a mammoth lexicon drawing on earlier works. The following is his entry on the word 'stands' or 'benches' (***ikria***).

3.1   the stands in the Agora from which they watched the Dionysiac contests before they built the theatre of Dionysus.

> The following note on Pratinas is found in the tenth-century AD lexicon known as the *Suda*.

3.2   [Pratinas] of Phlius, a tragic poet. He competed with Aeschylus and Choerilus during the 70th Olympiad [i.e. 499–496 BC], and was the first to write satyr-plays. While he was putting on a play, the stands on which the spectators were placed collapsed, and as a result of this the Athenians built a theatre. He put on 50 plays, of which 32 were satyr-plays, and won once.

> If this account is at all true, then the stands set up in the Agora must have been a temporary structure of wooden planks bound or nailed together to form a scaffolding of tiered planks, which then collapsed under the weight of the spectators. The verb here translated 'placed' can also mean 'were raised' or 'stood'. References to the *ikria* in the theatre of Dionysus indicate that spectators sat on them (and they are therefore translated 'benches' in this context) – the natural incline of the slope would have eliminated the need for raised stands.

The stage

Sicily and southern Italy (especially the region of Apulia in the heel of Italy) have yielded a large number of vases, most dating to the fourth century, that either show dramatic performances themselves or scenes inspired by the theatre. A few of these depict a wooden stage, raised on wooden supports, and sometimes a wooden ladder or short flight of steps leading up onto the stage is also shown.

A bell-krater dating to *c.* 380 BC is an example of one such vase-painting that comes from Apulia in southern Italy. An old man labelled Chiron is being helped up a set of steps onto a low stage by two men; one, labelled Xanthias (a slave name), grabs him by the hair while the other pushes him from behind. He is probably a comic parody of the centaur Chiron, a mythological character who was half-man, half-horse. The ludicrous posture assumed by his smaller assistant as he latches onto his rear end in an attempt to propel him up the staircase creates a visual reflection of just such a hybrid creature. In the top right-hand corner, two grotesque crones converse behind what may be the outline of a rock. They are labelled *Mousai* (Muses) in what must be another humorous parody of the supposedly beautiful goddesses of artistic inspiration. A young boy, who shows no indications of being a character in the play, watches on at bottom right.

What most interests us at this point, however, are the features of the stage that have been depicted: a low and shallow platform raised on wooden supports, led up to by a narrow flight of steps. Judging from the scale of the figures, the stage is only one metre or so high. At the back of the stage is a flat backdrop, the *skene* facade, with an overhanging roof.

3.3

For many years scenes such as this were thought to be depictions of a local Italian genre of farcical drama called the **phlyax** (plural **phlyakes**), but with the discovery of some that can be clearly identified as scenes from Athenian Old Comedy, this theory has now fallen out of favour.

Athenian drama (tragedy and, as Oliver Taplin has convincingly argued, also comedy) was by this time being exported overseas. It could very well be that the simple stages shown in these vase-paintings are temporary contraptions used by travelling actors for re-performances of Athenian plays in southern Italy.

The issue is complicated, however, by the fact that similar scenes are found on vases from Athens, and that Attic vases, along with Attic terracotta figurines of actors, were being produced for export. So does a vase such as this one (or the Choregos Vase, **1.7**) commemorate a performance of Old Comedy in southern Italy by a travelling cast of actors (most scholars think so), or is it simply a souvenir of an Athenian performance, with no connection to southern Italy?

Another complicating factor is that vase-painters are not often interested in verisimilitude (the realism offered by a photograph) but tend to paint a more schematic representation of what most interests them, often simplifying a scene because of space constraints. Thus what appears to be a small, temporary stage may in fact be standing in for the full-size stage of the Athenian theatre (see also **3.4**).

3.4 is a drawing that recontructs a badly damaged vase dating to *c.* 420–410 BC. This vase was found at Anavyssos (ancient Anaphlystus) in southern Attica and shows another comic performance. A single actor is on stage. He is probably playing the part of the hero Perseus after slaying the Gorgon Medusa with the sickle that he holds in his left hand – another comic depiction of this scene on a vase-painting actually shows Medusa's head poking out of the bag. The man's contorted pose and grotesque features and his body-suit (a costume worn to represent naked flesh), whose hem is visible at his ankles and wrists, make it clear that we have an actor of comedy (though whether this is Old Comedy or some other comedic genre such as mime or farce is debated). He performs a vigorous scene on a low stage. There is no indication of a *skene* facade, but what appears to be a curtain drapes across part of the stage and a flight of four steps leads up to it.

What is most unusual is the depiction of two seated audience members at the foot of the stage, the only one of its kind that survives. One is a bearded man,

3.4

the other probably a youth. They are seated on individual wooden chairs, not the benches of the theatre.

What exactly are we seeing? Some have argued that this is a schematic representation of a comic performance in the theatre of Dionysus: the older and the younger man then stand in for the audience as a whole (and, indeed, authors frequently mention the different generations when describing the theatre audience). The artist communicates the direct connection between actor and audience typical of comedy by eliminating the dead space of the *orchestra* that would normally separate them and by showing the actor looking out at his audience. Perhaps they should be seen as sitting in the special seats in the front row (these were, in real life, stone thrones that imitated the shape of the particular type of chair shown). Alan Hughes (2006) has recently proposed that the bearded man is a judge accompanied by a younger colleague.

Others read this as a rehearsal scene taking place in a private setting, and suggest that those watching the actor may be the *choregos* and the poet. Alternatively, it may depict a performance in a setting other than the large open-air theatre of Dionysus. If actors were taking comedy on tour in southern Italy and Sicily (for which there is good literary evidence, albeit for the third century rather than the fifth), then it is not unreasonable to suppose that smaller-scale performances also occurred in or around Athens in more informal settings. It is interesting that in Plato's *Laws*, in which three fictional speakers discuss the ideal city-state, the Athenian suggests (817b–c) that he would not allow foreigners to show up and put on a performance in this imagined ideal city-state, since such performances could not be vetted by the city's magistrates to ensure that they did not undermine the values of his *polis*. 'So,' he would respond to an enquiry by a foreign tragedian, 'do not think that we will ever allow you to simply set up your stage-building (*skene*) in our market-place and bring on your mellifluous actors, whose voices are louder than ours, and let them hold forth in front of women and children and the whole populace.'

When we examine the evidence of this Attic vase-painting, then, we face the same conundrum that presents itself in the southern Italian vase-paintings. Where a stage is depicted, it is always low and narrow; the actors are shown performing from the stage, but are also sometimes acting from ground level. Is it possible to conclude from this that Athenian drama in the late fifth and fourth centuries used a low and shallow wooden stage that the actors mounted in certain scenes? That there is no archaeological evidence for such a stage is not surprising given that it would have been a wooden and makeshift structure.

- Try to track down some production photos of a modern play. How clearly do they indicate the details of the staging?

The stage-building

Fragments of another vase from Apulia (this one an example of Gnathian ware, in which the pot received a black glaze and then decoration was added in multiple colours), dating to *c.* 350 BC, offer intriguing evidence of what may well be the backdrop for a theatrical performance.

The surface of the painting is badly worn in the right-hand fragments, and parts of it are missing; however, we can see four figures framed by an elaborate columned building. At far left, a woman stands in an open doorway. Her body is turned sideways and her head cocked and partially hidden, so that she appears to be eavesdropping on the men from her concealed vantage point. At the far right, another female figure, damaged beyond clear recognition, appears to be adopting a similar pose in another open doorway. In the centre of the field, a young man approaches an older, bearded man to his right, who holds out a shallow bowl from which he will pour a libation. The young man wears a traveller's hat (the *pilos*) and carries a walking stick, while the older man is dressed in long, flowing robes and is perhaps a king standing in front of his palace.

3.5

Various attempts have been made to identify the scene in question, of which Eric Csapo and William Slater's reading of it (1994: 62–3) as a scene from Euripides' *Peleus* seems the most convincing. However, attention has chiefly focused on the architectural features that the artist has included. The open doorway on the left, with its double leaves and meticulously drawn jambs and lintel, stands within a projecting side-porch drawn in three-quarter perspective. The decoration of its coffers is painted in loving detail, and its shape and dimensions match those of the theatrical *paraskenion* (see p. 52) to a remarkable degree. Although it is true that the painter has not represented the characters with masks, this does not argue against it being a theatrical scene. When representing scenes from tragedy, vase-painters tended to show the action without any tell-tale signs that it is theatrical make-believe (e.g. masks and stage), as we can tell from test cases that are demonstrably connected to a particular tragedy.

If, then, the artist here has depicted the theatrical backdrop, he could either be representing scene-painting, painted onto the flat surface of the *skene* (perhaps through the use of painted panels – see below), or he could be representing a porch that was now actually part of the architectural structure of theatres. The first possibility is perhaps more likely than the second given the date of the vase, which predates any archaeological evidence for the *paraskenion*, while we know that wall-painting was a highly developed art-form by this time. Of course, there is always the possibility that in the fourth century such elaborate palace facades could have been constructed out of perishable wood, though in the absence of evidence this must remain purely hypothetical.

Scene-setting and scene-painting

Hellenistic and Roman theatres had all sorts of clever stage devices, listed in rapid succession by Vitruvius (first century BC) and Pollux (second century AD); these authors refer to them as features of the Greek theatre, but most of them must belong to its later phases, when the *skene* was now a solid stone structure. They mention the use of painted panels known as **pinakes** (plural of **pinax**) that could be inserted between the columns decorating the theatre facade (see illustration on p. 53), thereby allowing the scenery to be quickly and easily changed – not just between plays but perhaps even to indicate changes of setting within a play. We also hear of movable set units (called *periaktoi*), which seem to have swung into place, perhaps early forerunners of the revolving sets of the modern theatre.

But the early Greek theatre was a simple affair and did not rely on technical wizardry to impress its audience. Aristotle (*Poetics* 1449a) credits Sophocles with introducing scene-painting (**skēnographia**). His comment suggests that such scene-painting was not an original element of Greek drama, but an innovation added at a later time. This makes sense, especially if the earliest phase of the theatre of Dionysus did not even have a *skene* building, as many believe. On the other hand, it is likely that even Aeschylus' *Persians*, our earliest surviving play (472 BC), was performed against the backdrop of some kind of *skene* that represented the Persian palace at Susa, mentioned in passing by the chorus at line 141, even if it was only a rudimentary hut or the facade of a makeshift set rather than a three-dimensional building.

However, we must beware of assuming that every reference in the plays to a physical feature was represented in some way or other in the set. The very impulse to look for such special effects is a fundamentally anachronistic one, a product of modern realism. Ancient theatre, in contrast, was a theatre of the imagination (or 'theatre of the mind', as Oliver Taplin (1978: 3) has termed it). Even the few physical props that were used were emblems given their significance through the words and stage-action of the characters. If Athenians had entered the theatre of Dionysus with a realistic mindset, they would have been sadly disappointed by what they saw. Euripides' *Helen* is set in exotic Egypt and, in the opening line of the play, Helen points to the fair-flowing waters of the mighty Nile. Some modern set designers might have water coursing across a stage covered in sand; but in the original production of 412 BC, there would not have been a drop of water or grain of sand anywhere in sight! In the original, non-realistic conception of the play, the Nile only exists in the mind's eye, and Helen can refer to – and even point to – 'these waters of the Nile, with its beautiful nymphs' (line 1) without describing anything that is visible on stage.

Anything is possible in the world of theatre: the tragedy *Rhesus* (attributed to Euripides, probably spuriously) is set at night-time and has Odysseus and Diomedes give the slip to a chorus of Trojan night-watchmen even though its performance took place in broad daylight, while characters in Aristophanes' *Frogs* can row across the river Styx and enter the Underworld without ever leaving *terra firma*. The Greek 'stage' was an 'unlocated scene', a *tabula rasa*, whose features and boundaries were set by the words and movements of the actors. The same was true of the Elizabethan stage.

The following is an extract from Euripides' *Bacchae* (lines 576–626), a play that was produced posthumously, perhaps in 405 BC. Pentheus, king of Thebes, tries to suppress the worship of Dionysus; he has captured and imprisoned the god, who appears in this play disguised as a human leader of the Dionysiac cult.

3.6 DIONYSUS	Io! Hear, hear my call!	
	Io bacchants! Io bacchants!	
CHORUS	What is this cry? Where is it from,	
	The cry of Bacchus that calls me?	
DIONYSUS	Io! Io! Again I cry!	580
	I, the son of Semele, son of Zeus!	
CHORUS	Io! Io! Lord, lord,	
	Come now to our band of worshippers,	
	Bromios! Bromios!	
DIONYSUS	Shake the floor of the world, spirit of earthquake!	585
CHORUS	Ah, soon the palace of Pentheus	
	Will be shaken apart and collapse!	
	Dionysus is in the palace!	
	Worship him!	
	– Ah, we worship him!	590
	Can you see the stone lintels	
	Above the pillar flying apart?	
	Bromios is raising his cry inside the house!	
DIONYSUS	Set light to the bright blaze of lightning!	
	Burn, burn the house of Pentheus!	595
CHORUS	Ah! Ah!	
	Do you not see the blaze of fire	
	Around the sacred tomb of Semele?	
	The flame she left when she was struck by lightning,	600
	The thunderbolt of Zeus?	
	Throw your trembling bodies to the ground!	
	Maenads, to the ground!	
	For our lord, the son of Zeus, is attacking the palace,	
	And has turned it upside-down!	
DIONYSUS	Women of Asia, are you stricken with terror that you have fallen to	605
	the ground? You can feel **the Bacchic god**, it seems, shaking the house	
	of Pentheus apart. Stand up! Take courage and stop trembling!	

Io bacchants!   Dionysus calls out from within the palace to the chorus of bacchants (i.e. worshippers of Bacchus, another name for Dionysus). The chorus-women have just prayed to Dionysus to punish Pentheus for his impiety; the god answers their prayer immediately, and in this scene we get an interpretation, in dramatic form, of a divine epiphany, which the Greeks imagined to be a truly terrifying event. Dionysus' epiphany manifests itself in the form of an earthquake accompanied by lightning-bolts that strike the palace, leaving his worshippers trembling with fear as well as exhilarated.

Bromios   a cult name for Dionysus, meaning 'thunderer'.

the Bacchic god   Dionysus reappears on stage; he is at once the god and also the leader of his worshippers who refers to Dionysus in third person. As the god of theatre, it is not surprising that he appears in other guises and is hard to pin down.

CHORUS	Supreme light of our ecstatic Bacchic worship! How happy I am to see you after feeling so abandoned!
DIONYSUS	Did you fall into despair when I was taken away? Did you think that I would be thrown into Pentheus' dark dungeons?
CHORUS	How could I not? Who would look after me, if you were to come to harm? But how were you freed, after falling into the hands of that unholy man?
DIONYSUS	I freed myself, easily, without effort.
CHORUS	Did he not tie your hands in binding knots?
DIONYSUS	That is exactly how I humiliated him: when he thought he was binding me, he did not touch or hold me, but was living on empty hopes. He found a bull in the stables, the prison he took me to, and he tied knots around its knees and hooves, panting his rage, his body dripping with sweat, and biting his lips. I was close by, sitting peacefully and watching. It was at this time that Bacchus came, and shook up the palace, and made the fire blaze up on his mother's tomb. But when Pentheus saw it, thinking the palace was on fire, he dashed this way and that, ordering his servants to bring him the river Acheloüs. Every slave was put to work, but toiled for nothing. *At the end of the scene, Pentheus emerges from the palace, furious and baffled by Dionysus' escape.*

Line references in right margin: 610, 615, 620, 625

1 How might this scene have been staged in a time before *Jurassic Park* and the era of computer-generated special effects? The scene refers to many spectacular sights and sounds: was everything to be imagined, or do you think there was some kind of enactment of the god's epiphany through stagecraft (e.g. a drum roll for the earthquake, smoke ascending from backstage for the fire, the collapse of some stage scenery)?

2 In this scene Dionysus makes repeated mention of appearances and illusions. Look back closely over his words. Might he be describing an essential quality of theatre: its ability to create (through make-believe or through stage-effects) an illusion of reality? Or is he describing a psychological phenomenon, a delusion with which he has struck Pentheus that makes him imagine things? Or is he saying something else?

Mechanical devices

Although most of the technical inventions mentioned by Vitruvius and Pollux belonged to later centuries, there is clear evidence that two contraptions were already in use in the fifth century: the ***ekkyklēma*** and the ***mēchanē***.

The ekkyklema

The *ekkyklema* literally means 'the wheeled-out thing'. It was a wooden wheeled platform, rolled on at key moments. Its chief function in tragedy was to display to the audience indoor tableaux such as the bodies of those murdered off stage. Comedy may have used it for similar purposes: Aristophanes' *Clouds* opens with Strepsiades and Phidippides in bed: Strepsiades lies awake, tossing and turning, while his son Phidippides lies sound asleep and dreaming of horse-racing, despite his father's best efforts to rouse him. The use of the *ekkyklema* in staging this bedroom scene would seem likely. There are two comic scenes, however, in which the *ekkyklema* is explicitly referred to (**3.8**; also *Acharnians* 402–17), both of which use the device as a source of humour.

> The following is an extract (lines 1028–52) from Euripides' tragedy, *Heracles*, performed *c.* 417–416. Heracles has gone mad and killed his wife and three sons, as we learn in a messenger speech. Here the chorus describe the tableau they see on the *ekkyklema*.

3.7	CHORUS	Alas, alas! Look, the tall bolted doors of the palace are swinging apart! Ah me! Look at the poor children, how they lie in front of their wretched father, who sleeps a terrible sleep after killing his sons. He is bound up with ropes tied with many knots, which prop up the body of Heracles, fastening him to the stone **pillars** of his house.	1030
			1035

Amphitryon (Heracles' mortal father) emerges from the skene (which represents the palace at Thebes).

	CHORUS-LEADER	Here comes the old man, like a bird mourning the fledglings it has borne, wending his sad way with slow steps.	1040
	AMPHITRYON	Elders of Thebes, won't you keep quiet and allow him to rest in sleep and forget his woes?	
	CHORUS	I weep tears for you, old man, and the children, and the man who won **great victories**.	1045
	AMPHITRYON	Come forward, further away from him. Don't make a sound, don't shout, don't awaken him from the **tranquillity of sleep**.	1050
	CHORUS	Alas! What bloody gore ...	
	AMPHITRYON	Ah, ahh! You are destroying me!	
	CHORUS	... was shed and now comes into view.	

pillars   his father Amphitryon has tied him in this way to prevent further destruction.

great victories   Heracles, who successfully completed his Labours before being struck with madness by Hera.

tranquillity of sleep   later in the scene, Heracles wakes up, now restored to his senses, and discovers the terrible truth of his crazed killings when Amphitryon explains to him why his wife and children lie dead next to him, with his bow and arrows close by.

> 1 What does this scene tell us about the *ekkyklema*? Try and envisage how the bodies and other elements on it might have been set up and where the *ekkyklema* may have been positioned in relation to the actors.
>
> 2 Why do you think Greek theatre developed this technique of bringing interior scenes out onto the stage? What is gained by viewing these scenes that could not be communicated through words alone?

The following is an extract from Aristophanes' comedy, *Women at the Thesmophoria* (lines 95–9). Euripides is in big trouble with the women of Athens, who don't like the way in which he portrays women in his plays and have decided to hold a political assembly that could result in his death sentence. In desperation he comes up with a crazy plan: he will send the tragic poet Agathon to the women's assembly, disguised as a woman! In this extract, Euripides is talking to a relative as Agathon is wheeled out of the *skene*.

3.8

EURIPIDES	Shh! Be quiet!
RELATIVE	What is it?
EURIPIDES	Agathon's coming out!
RELATIVE	Where is he?
EURIPIDES	You don't see him? He's the chap over there being **wheeled out**!
RELATIVE	Then I'm going blind – 'cos I don't see any *man* there, only a **Cyrene**!
EURIPIDES	Be quiet! He's getting ready to sing.

Agathon then sings a choral ode from one of his tragedies. At the end of the scene, he asks to be rolled back into the house as quickly as possible.

In this scene, the *ekkyklema* is used to great comic effect. It allows the audience to spy on Agathon as he sings to himself in the 'privacy' of his house, quite unaware that he is performing in front of an audience of thousands! The domestic setting adds to the feminization of Agathon, since in Athens women spent most of their time within the confines of the women's quarters in their house.

---

wheeled out although Euripides doesn't actually mention the *ekkyklema* by name, it is clear from his use of the verb 'wheel out' (from which the word *ekkyklema* is derived), that it is being used in this scene.

Cyrene a prostitute – Euripides' relative is suggesting that Agathon is so effeminate that he looks like a woman (which makes him an excellent candidate for his secret mission!). From the relative's later disparaging remarks, it seems that Agathon is wearing women's clothing, is surrounded on the *ekkyklema* by feminine items such as a perfume bottle, mirror, hairnet and bra, and is missing the phallus that male actors normally wear in comedy. Agathon explains that he is trying to get into the right mindset to write the women's parts for his play.

- Aristophanes likes to poke fun at Euripides in his plays, and portrays him as an innovator. This leads some scholars to suppose that the *ekkyklema* was a recent invention when this play was performed in 425 BC. If true, this means that earlier tragedies (e.g. Aeschylus' *Oresteia* trilogy, performed in 458 BC) must have used another way to bring out bodies for display. Can you think how such scenes could have been staged *without* the use of the *ekkyklema*?

The mechane

Another stage device that was already in use in Athens during the fifth century was a contraption called the *mechane* (this gives us our English word 'machine'). It was some type of crane that was used to make actors fly through the air; the actor was attached by a harness to the crane's arm, which would swing into position from behind the *skene*. Its use in comedy is confirmed by explicit references to it in the plays, while in tragedy its use is attested by ancient authors.

In a number of tragedies, seemingly impossible situations are resolved through divine intervention. A god suddenly appears from on high at the end of the play, and gives instructions to the human characters. The frequent use of this as a closing device for plays resulted in the coining of the phrase **deus ex machina** (Latin for 'god from the machine') to describe the kind of unexpected divine intervention that Aristotle criticized (see **3.10**). Other ancient authors make similar objections. In Plato's *Cratylus* (425d), we find the following remark: 'When they reach an impasse, the tragic poets resort to their machines and raise the gods aloft.' And we start seeing the term being used proverbially when in Demosthenes (*Against Boeotus* 2.59) a witness who materializes out of the blue to give testimony at a trial is described as appearing 'as if from the *mechane*'.

One play that makes use of the *mechane* and is actually mentioned explicitly by Aristotle is Euripides' tragedy, *Medea*. In it the protagonist Medea kills her children to punish her estranged husband Jason, who left her for a younger woman. In the final scene of the play, Jason rushes out to try and save the boys only to discover that he has arrived too late; then Medea makes a dramatic appearance from the *mechane* (1311–22).

3.9	CHORUS	The children are no more. You must accept it.	
	JASON	Where did she kill them? Indoors or out here?	
	CHORUS	Open the door, and you will see the murder.	
	JASON	Undo the bolts there, servants! Quickly!	
		Open up! Let me see the double horror –	1315
		The children's bodies and ... take my vengeance on her.	

MEDEA   Why do you rattle and batter the doors here?
Are you looking for the corpses and me, who did it?
Stop it. If you want me, say what you wish.
You will never lay hands on me again.   1320
This chariot the Sun has given to me,
My father's father, to save me from the hands of enemies.

This scene makes use of the element of surprise. We are led to believe that the bodies of Medea's children lie inside the palace, and that they will soon be revealed, in the normal fashion, through the use of the *ekkyklema*. Instead, Medea makes a striking entry on the *mechane*, riding in the chariot of her grandfather, the sun-god Helios. She has with her the corpses of her children and refuses to let Jason hold them; they are hers, and she will bury them elsewhere. While Jason laments in the *orchestra* below, Medea enjoys her moment of triumph high above. The play comes to an abrupt end, with Medea poised to fly off and seek sanctuary at Athens and Jason unable to stop her.

It is hard to know exactly how the *mechane* would have been used in this scene. Perhaps Medea was swung into view by the *mechane*, which then hoisted her onto the flat roof of the *skene* to mount her chariot and deliver her lines.

Aristotle in his *Poetics* (1454a–b) makes the following criticism of the play.

3.10   It is clear that the resolution of a plot should come out of the plot itself, and not from the *mechane* as in the *Medea* and **the home-sailing scene** in the *Iliad*. But the *mechane* should be used for events outside the drama: for events that happened beforehand, which mere humans could not know about, or events that will happen afterwards and that need to be foretold or announced (for we grant the gods the capacity to see everything).

> 1   Why does Aristotle object to the use of the *mechane* in Euripides' *Medea*?
>
> 2   Why do you think that Aristotle approves its use in the particular circumstances that he lays out?

---

the home-sailing scene   the episode in Book 2 of Homer's *Iliad* when Athena intervenes to prevent the Greeks from sailing home after Agamemnon has given orders to depart and when the sailors were already dragging their beached ships down into the sea. This is a metaphorical use of the *mechane*, not a literal one.

In tragedy, the *mechane* elevated gods above their mortal counterparts; but comedy, which loves to turn things on their head, pokes fun at the practice of dangling actors from a crane. The *mechane* is used to comic effect in Aristophanes' *Women at the Thesmophoria*. This time he has Euripides fly through the air to rescue his male relative, whom he has sent on a mission, disguised as a woman, to speak to the women on his behalf after Agathon refused to do so (see **3.8**). When the women discover that he is a male infiltrator and tie him up, Euripides dresses up as the hero Perseus (whose winged sandals allow him to fly through the air) and comes flying in on the *mechane* in a failed attempt to carry out just the kind of *deus ex machina* intervention that Aristotle disliked in tragedy.

> In the following extract from Aristophanes' *Peace* (154–79), the protagonist Trygaeus flies up to heaven on the back of a dung-beetle in an attempt to bring the goddess Peace back to earth.

3.11   Giddyup, **Pegasus**, be on your merry way! Prick up your ears with gusto and rattle those golden chains on your bridle. No! What are you doing? Don't! Where 155 are you pointing your nostrils? Are you heading for the back-alleys? Launch yourself boldly away from the ground! Spread your swift wings and head straight 160 for the palace of Zeus! Keep your nose away from **crap** and away from the food of mortals. Hey, mate – yes, you down there in the Piraeus taking a crap in the 165 **red-light district** – what are you doing? You'll get me killed! Please dig a hole and cover it up with soil – lots of it! And grow some thyme over it, and pour on perfume! Because if I fall from this height and get hurt, the city of Chios will have to pay a **fine of five talents** for wrongful death – and all because of your butt! 170

Oh boy, I'm so scared – and I'm not joking any more! Hey, *mechane*-operator,

---

Pegasus   the winged horse ridden by Bellerophon. Trygaeus addresses the dung-beetle in mock heroic language, imagining himself as a hero mounted on an immortal steed.

crap   a dung-beetle instinctively gravitates towards faeces or left-over food. Trygaeus is terrified that it will catch a whiff and nose-dive to the ground.

red-light district   the Piraeus was the harbour for Athens and, like many ports, was an area frequented by prostitutes. In an age before indoor plumbing, back-alleys must have been a regular place for bodily excretions.

fine of five talents   if an Athenian citizen was killed in an allied state, the state was required to pay a fine (five talents was a huge sum). The reference to the Chians is probably an allusion to an incident that had just happened.

mechane-operator   the actor breaks the dramatic illusion, addressing the stage-hand operating the *mechane*, who might have been working a pulley to hoist him aloft. This is an instance of what is known as **metatheatre**: when drama calls attention to the act of performance. Such metatheatrical moments are more common and far more explicit in Greek comedy than they are in tragedy.

take care, because I'm feeling **a wind whirling around my navel**, and if you don't 175
watch out, I'll feed the beetle. But I think that I am near the gods – yes, I spot the
house of Zeus. **Who guards the door of Zeus?** Open up, if you please!

> 1 Comment on the accumulation of comic effects in this scene. What are the
>   different kinds of humour that are being employed, and how successful are
>   they?
>
> 2 Aristophanes' plays (and Old Comedy in general) are full of explicit
>   references to bodily functions, sex etc. Do you find his language and subject-
>   matter excessively vulgar? How should his obscenities be handled – should
>   his plays be banned, should portions be expurgated or altered, or should
>   they be presented as he wrote them?
>
> 3 Do you feel that there is something lazy about dramatists' use of this device,
>   or is there a valid rationale in its use in the scenes presented here?
>
> 4 Which seems more important to Greek drama: the words spoken by the
>   characters, or what is seen occurring in the playing space?

a wind whirling around my navel Trygaeus' bumpy flight has made him feel queasy,
and he warns that he may soon feed the beetle – out of one end or the other!

Who guards the door of Zeus? the call to the doorkeeper indicates that Trygaeus has
landed. With a few descriptive words, he indicates that the setting is now the palace of
Zeus.

4 The chorus

A person who cannot dance and sing is a person with no education, says Plato (*Laws* 654b). Choral dance was for the Greeks the ultimate expression of community; it was not restricted to theatrical contexts, but was a key element of many occasions – from the joyful dance accompanying the wedding hymn or *hymenaios* to the dances put on in honour of the dead Patroclus at his funeral (Homer, *Iliad* 23). When the Athenians finally surrendered to the Spartans and their allies to bring an end to the Peloponnesian War, the victors demolished the Long Walls that protected Athens 'with great enthusiasm and to the music of female pipers' (Xenophon, *Hellenica* 2.2.23). Whether in moments of great joy or great sadness, music was the natural way to express solidarity.

Choral dance and music were at the core of several genres of ancient poetry. The lyric poetry of sixth-century poets such as Sappho and Archilochus was composed for performance by a chorus of dancers led by a chorus-leader. Dithyramb, tragedy, satyr-play and comedy also featured a chorus and chorus-leader. The chorus dominated early drama and it is likely that actors were a natural development out of the role of chorus-leader. Archaeological evidence suggests that the *orchestra* or 'dancing place' was the original element of the theatre, and it seems that in the fifth century actors were performing predominantly in the *orchestra* alongside the chorus. Just as the chorus-members were not separated from the actors, so too nothing separated them from the audience, of which they were a natural extension. When in comedy (both Old and New) characters address their supposed audience using the plural form of 'you', it is often hard to tell whether they are talking to their internal audience (the chorus in the play), their external audience (the spectators) or both audiences without differentiation.

Of the various elements that went into putting on a play, the training of the chorus was the one that must have required the most attention. The recruitment and funding of the chorus were entrusted to the *choregos*, while the task of training the chorus-members was originally handled by the playwright himself and then by a professional chorus-trainer (the *chorodidaskalos*). Participation in such a chorus was a major investment of time, lasting some eight months from selection to performance. During this time, participants were excused military service so that they could concentrate on rehearsing. Like army training, it taught discipline and teamwork and required a great degree of precision, since it called for a chorus of up to 24 participants (in the case of comedy) to dance in formation and sing in unison in a wide range of lyric metres. In the case of tragedy/satyr-play, chorus-members would have to learn the words, melodies, rhythms and movements for three tragedies and a satyr-play.

Dance is at the heart of the function of the chorus; in fact, the Greek word *choros* is related to the verb *choreuein* ('to dance'). We know little about the dance movements, though they seem to have differed by genre (e.g. the *sikinnis* of satyr-play, the **kordax** of comedy) and included set pieces or figures with given names (e.g. the 'owl', the 'sword-dance'). In tragedy, the chorus usually entered the *orchestra* by one of the side entrances (*eisodoi*) early on in the play and remained on stage until the end of the performance. Their first piece sung as they entered was called the *parodos*. Over the course of a play, they performed a series of set pieces known as **stasima** (singular **stasimon**) or choral odes that also combined singing and dancing. Some of these respond to what has just occurred on stage, others foreshadow what is about to occur, while others transport us into the distant past or into the mythological realm. The chorus sing these odes using lyric metres and an artificial quasi-Doric dialect that marks them as more self-consciously poetic and further removed from ordinary speech than the everyday iambic metres and regular Attic dialect of the lines spoken by the actors or by the chorus-leader. Characters also occasionally sing in lyric metres or engage in lyric exchanges with the chorus at moments of heightened emotion (e.g. laments or outbursts of joy).

Choral song and other sung portions of plays were accompanied by music, usually provided by a piper. Over time, the piper became an increasingly prominent member of the cast and the music played became more innovative and complex. While professionalism led to increased fame for musicians and actors, the role of the (still volunteer) chorus declined – in quantitative terms (the proportion of lines that they were given declines) and in qualitative terms (they lose their centrality to the plot).

> • The existence of all these technical terms may give the impression that Greek tragedy was more strait-jacketed than it actually was. Dramatists show such freedom and variety in the way they handle these formal elements that they cannot in any meaningful way be described as constrictive. What comparable structural elements can be found in modern plays?

The chorus in tragedy

Athenaeus, in his *Learned Banqueters* 21d–22a (written *c.* AD 200), describes the early development of the tragic chorus.

4.1   Aeschylus not only invented the beauty and dignity of the costume that is imitated by the **priests and torchbearers** when they robe themselves, but he also invented

---

priests and torchbearers they officiated in the Eleusinian Mysteries, an important Athenian cult that took place annually at the sanctuary of Demeter and Persephone at Eleusis. The priests and torchbearers will have been dressed in ornate costumes, and it is no doubt this that led Athenaeus to believe that they imitated the lavish costumes worn by participants in Greek tragedies.

many dance steps and passed them down to his **choreuts**. For **Chamaeleon** says that he [Aeschylus] was the first to choreograph his own choruses and did not use dance-trainers, instead creating the dance steps for his choruses himself, and in general taking on the entire management of the tragedy himself. So in all likelihood he acted in his own plays. For Aristophanes – and reliable evidence about the tragic poets *can* be found in the comic poets – has Aeschylus himself say: 'I myself created the dance steps for my choruses.' Aristphanes also says 'I know from watching his *Phrygians*, when they came with Priam to help ransom his dead son, they danced many steps like this and like that and in this way.'

The dance-trainer Telesis (or Telestes) also invented many dance steps, **closely illustrating the lyrics with his hands.** The musician Phillis of Delos says that the **citharodes** of old made minimal facial movements, but moved their feet a lot in marching steps and dance steps. For Aristocles says that Aeschylus' dancer Telestes was so accomplished that when he danced *Seven against Thebes* he made the action clear through his dancing. They also say that the poets of old – **Thespis, Pratinas, Cratinus, Phrynichus** – were called 'dancers' because they not only arranged the dances for their own plays but also – quite apart from their own works – taught dance to anyone who wanted to learn.

---

choreuts   participants who sang and danced in the chorus.

Chamaeleon   a Greek philosopher (*c.* 350–280 BC) whose writings included works on satyr-play and comedy as well as on Aeschylus, preserved only in snippets through quotation, as here. Most of Athenaeus' claims are based on inferences that he makes from the passages he quotes.

Phrygians   a lost play by Aeschylus. Aristophanes' play was probably parodying the dance steps of the tragic chorus.

closely illustrating the lyrics with his hands   such hand-gestures are frequently mentioned as a staple element of choral dancing. They are also described as being *mimetic* – that is, they convey in dance the meaning of the accompanying words. Similar claims are made about the musicians who accompanied them. For example, Aristotle (*Poetics* 1461b) criticizes performers who use a lot of movement 'supposing that the audience won't notice anything unless they themselves convey it' and illustrates his point by citing second-rate pipers who twirl around if they are representing the throwing of a discus or who attack the chorus-leader if they are piping about the monster Scylla. Quite how the dancing imitated the words is not clear. We should not assume direct miming of actions just as we cannot rule it out.

citharodes   those who sang to the accompaniment of the cithara, a type of lyre.

Thespis, Pratinas, Cratinus, Phrynichus   Thespis, Pratinas and Phrynichus were early figures in the history of Athenian drama: Thespis (late sixth century BC) was credited with inventing tragedy, Pratinas (early fifth century) with inventing the satyr-play, while Phrynichus (early fifth century) was said to have first introduced female characters into tragedy. Cratinus (late fifth century) was a famous comic poet and rival to Aristophanes. We also hear of Sophocles dancing in his own choruses.

In the following extract (*Poetics* 1456a), Aristotle discusses the integral role that he believes the chorus should play in tragedy.

4.2   The chorus should be considered as one of the actors, as a part of the whole and as a contributor to the performance – not as in Euripides, but as in Sophocles. In the works of later poets, the songs are no more closely connected with the plot than with any other tragedy. And so they now sing interludes, a practice first started by **Agathon**. And yet how is singing interludes different from inserting a speech or whole episode from a completely different work?

The Greek word for 'interludes' (embolima) that Aristotle uses here literally means 'throw-ins' or 'inserts' and is used to describe choral songs that have no direct connection to the plot; these appear to be the norm by the second half of the fourth century when Aristotle is writing (see p. 16).

Aristotle insists that the chorus should be involved in furthering the plot of the play – and indeed they frequently do perform this function. For example, the chorus of sailors in Sophocles' *Philoctetes* are active and savvy conspirators in the plot to deceive Philoctetes, and it is they who urge Neoptolemus to take advantage of Philoctetes' incapacitating attack of pain and make off with the bow. So too it is they who first pity Philoctetes; their sympathy for the helpless outcast could well have been an important factor in Neoptolemus' change of heart and would probably also have evoked a sense of pity in the audience. Thus the chorus also functions as the emotional barometer for a play – at once a participant in the action and a witness to it. The influential German writers Friedrich von Schiller and August von Schlegel both characterized the chorus of Greek tragedy as the 'idealized spectator'; but their role as representatives of the community at large need not imply passivity or distance from the action any more than their involvement in it prevents them from serving as mediators when characters come into conflict.

Aristotle's claim that the chorus loses its centrality over time is, in broad outline, borne out by the evidence of surviving plays. In the early plays of Aeschylus, the chorus has the bulk of the lines and is the main interlocutor. Even when two or more speaking characters are on stage together, they often direct their comments to the chorus. In some of Euripides' plays, in contrast, they do play a relatively minor and passive role. However, Aristotle generalizes about Euripides' practice somewhat unfairly. In some plays by Euripides, the chorus does play an integral role. For example, in his *Trojan Women*, performed in 415 BC, the chorus of captive Trojan

---

Agathon   a tragedian writing at the end of the fifth century (see **3.8**). Purists (e.g. Plutarch, *Moralia* 645e) accused him of other musical innovations that they saw as corrupting the simple vigour of earlier tragedy.

women accompany their queen, Hecuba, in her grief throughout the play, and their danced odes are a poignant testimony to the therapeutic effect of communal song in situations of great anguish. Even in his *Bacchae* (*c.* 405 BC), put on after his death and probably one of his two last plays, the maenad chorus, dancing with raw energy in honour of Dionysus, carries many of the central themes of the play. It may be that Aristophanes' characterization of Euripides as the incorrigible innovator resulted in all blame for change being laid at his doorstep. In fact, it is in Aristophanes' later comedies (*Assembly-Women*, *Wealth*) where we see clearest evidence of the choral interludes described by Aristotle.

A number of sources indicate that the chorus entered the theatre in set formation by row and file. Pollux (second century AD), for example, describes the arrangement as follows in his *Onomasticon* (4.109), a thesaurus of terms arranged by subject-matter.

4.3   And in the tragic chorus there were five files of three, and three rows of five, since there were fifteen in a chorus. **They entered** in threes if the *parodos* was by file; if it was by row, they entered in fives.

Further clues are found in Aristides' *In Defence of the Four* (3.154). In this work, also written in the second century AD, the sophist Publius Aelius Aristides makes the following remark.

4.4   Well then! Where in the chorus or in which row shall we place Miltiades of Marathon? Isn't it clear that he belongs in front of the audience and in a position where everyone can get a good view of him? Though in fact he is not really a **stander-on-the-left** but is rather on the right wing of the Greek battle-line.

They entered   this set formation is described specifically for the *parodos*, the initial procession of the chorus into the theatre; it is not safe to imply that chorus-members kept this formation by row and file throughout the performance. Like the *pompe*, the *parodos* was probably a piece of great pageantry. In Aeschylus' *Persians*, the chorus come on at the beginning of the play and sing for 150 lines; their description of Xerxes' glittering army must have been matched by their own stately entry wearing the elaborate costumes of Persian elders. More commonly, the chorus' *parodos* occurred after a prologue delivered by one of the actors.

stander-on-the-left   an expression also used by the comic poet Cratinus to describe a chorus-member who was placed in the left row (i.e. the one closest to the audience). Those who occupied the middle row were known as 'alley-standers' – they were the weakest members of the chorus, and so were tucked away from view. Here Aristides is cracking a joke: although Miltiades, the famous Athenian general, deserves to occupy the place of honour and thus should be the 'left-stander' in theatrical terms, on the battlefield the bravest soldier occupied the position on the right end of the battle-line, since he would not have another soldier's shield protecting his right flank.

The scholiast (ancient commentator) on Aristides added the following explanation.

4.5 This is a metaphor taken from the choruses at the Dionysia. When they entered, the choruses sang their songs while moving obliquely and kept the spectators on their left, and the first-rate choreuts held the left-hand side. So when he says 'where in the chorus', he is referring to what was performed in front of the theatre audience: for in choruses, the left side is the position of greater honour, while in battle it is the right … When the chorus entered the *orchestra* (where the altar is), they entered it from the left, and so were located on the right-hand side of the archon; therefore the good choreuts were drawn up on their left side, so they were located facing the people.

- The sources suggest that choreuts were strategically arranged according to ability. Do similar practices occur in modern performance genres (e.g. ballet, musicals, marching bands)?

In the following passage, Athenaeus (*Learned Banqueters* 628c–f) distinguishes between good and bad types of dancing.

4.6 Quite rightly **those around Damon of Athens** say that songs and dances must be produced by the soul being moved in some way; noble and beautiful dances produce noble and beautiful souls, while the opposite produce the opposite. This is the origin of the clever comment of **Cleisthenes, ruler of Sicyon,** that gave proof of his educated mind. For, as they say, upon seeing one of his daughter's suitors (it was Hippocleides of Athens) dancing in bad taste, he declared that he had danced away his marriage – believing, it would seem, that the man's soul was also base.

---

those around Damon of Athens   Damon was said to have been a tutor and adviser to Pericles, and also to have taught Socrates (*Diogenes Laertius* 2.19); the term 'those around Damon' refers to his circle of pupils – one of whom, Dracon, was said to have given musical instruction to Plato. Damon argued that music had an inherent moral quality, and therefore that certain forms of dancing/song improved the soul while others corrupted it. But other ancient authors (e.g. Philodemus, *On Music* 4.122 Delattre) challenged the notion that music can affect character.

Cleisthenes, ruler of Sicyon   he ruled Sicyon, a city west of Corinth, *c.* 600–570 BC. The story is told by the fifth-century historian Herodotus (6.126–31), who adds that Hippocleides had already excelled in singing and public speaking and had a clear lead over the other suitors until he ruined his chances by indulging his love of dancing: he danced on a table to the music of the piper, finishing off his routine by standing on his head and waving his feet in the air!

For in dancing as in walking, grace and orderliness are beautiful, while bad taste and disorder are ugly. For this reason from the beginning the poets arranged their dances for free citizens, and only used dance movements that **illustrated what they were singing**, making sure that nobility and manliness were always maintained in them … For the kind of dancing of the choruses back then was graceful and of great dignity, as if representing the movements of those fighting. This is why Socrates in his poems says that those who dance the best are also best in warfare, expressing it thus:

> Those who honour the gods best in dances are best in battle.

For dancing was almost like military training, and was a display not only of discipline in general, but also of care for the body.

---

1 Who dances nowadays, and in what contexts? What functions does dance fulfil in modern society? Does dance still teach discipline? And are there dances that teach combat readiness?

2 Nowadays, are certain types of dancing seen as good and others as immoral? If so, what is it that distinguishes them?

The following is the first *stasimon* (472–515) from Sophocles' *Electra*. The word *stasimon* literally means 'standing song', but what this means is far from certain, since it is clear that the chorus danced as they sang the *stasima* (plural of *stasimon*). This particular ode is composed of the three basic units of choral song: the **strophe**, **antistrophe** and **epode**. The strophe and antistrophe are metrically identical to each other, while the epode has an independent metrical pattern and often also differs in subject-matter and tone. The Greek words *strophē* and *antistrophē* respectively mean 'turn' and 'counter-turn', while *epōdos* means 'additional song'. Atilius Fortunatianus, a Latin grammarian writing in the fourth century AD, claims that choruses circled the altar from the right for the strophe, circled it in the opposite direction for the antistrophe, and then stood still for the epode. However, his comment may be little more than guesswork based on the meanings of these Greek words.

In this ode the chorus of older townswomen of Argos react optimistically to the news that the hated Clytemnestra has had a frightening dream. Their loyalties lie with Electra, who mourns her father Agamemnon's murder and longs for her brother Orestes to return to avenge their father's death.

---

illustrated what they were singing Athenaeus means that the dancing fitted the heroic themes of the songs, which were noble and dignified, and wasn't exaggerated or inappropriate. Hamlet's advice to the players bears comparison: 'Suit the action to the word, the word to the action, with this special observance, that you o'erstep not the modesty of nature' (3.2.15–16).

4.7   **Strophe**   **Unless I am a prophet without sense,**
                                          Lacking in wise judgement,
                                     Justice will come, as she has prophesied,   475
                                       Winning just victories with her hands;
                                  She will come after them, child, before long.
                                         I am bolstered by confidence,
                                           Now that I have heard
                                      This dream with its sweet breath.   480
                                          For your father, the lord
                                         Of the Greeks, will never forget,
                                           Nor will the ancient axe,
                                      Bronze-striking, double-edged,   485
                                  Which killed him in a shameful act of violence.

       Antistrophe   **She shall come with many feet and many hands**
                                        Concealed in fearful ambush,   490
                                          The brazen-footed Fury.
                                  A murderous lust to marry, unsanctioned
                                           And unholy, seized those
                                        For whom it was forbidden. And so,
                                   I am confident that never could this omen   495
                                         Draw near and not bring harm
                                       To the doers and their accomplices.
                              For surely there is no power of prophecy for mortals
                                        In fearful dreams or oracles,   500
                                          If this vision of the night
                                         Does not come safely to land.

Unless I am a prophet without sense   here the chorus, though singing in unison, refer to themselves with a collective 'I'. Often they respond to plot developments or build anticipation for what is about to happen. They also serve as a sounding-board for the issues of the play. In this play, they often sympathize with the tragic heroine and join her in her mourning, but also call into question her behaviour as being excessive. The chorus, however, should not be seen as the 'voice of the playwright' steering the audience towards a particular point of view. Their predictions can sometimes be misguided – for example, in Sophocles' *Oedipus the King* (1086–1109), their optimism that the problem of Oedipus' mistaken identity will turn out well could not be further from the truth.

Bronze-striking   the language of choral odes is both rich and vivid. Often the poet uses unusual or even invented words, as here; they set a poetic tone through bright flashes of imagery. Choral odes include some of the most beautiful passages of Greek literature.

She shall come with many feet and many hands   the chorus describe the approach of the Fury, the Underworld deity who hunts down those guilty of bloodshed; they portray her as a terrifying monster whose many feet make escape impossible and whose many hands make her invincible. Their words may also have been reflected in their own movements on stage, though quite how dance would have related to words is not known.

Epode

Your coming long ago,
Chariot-race of Pelops,   505
Brought us only trouble,
Blighting this land
Forever.
For since Myrtilus
Plunged to his death in the sea,   510
Uprooted and
Hurled from his
Chariot of gold
With monstrous cruelty,
Never yet has violence full of troubles   515
Left this house.

---

1   What parallelism can you see in structure and subject-matter between the strophe and antistrophe?

2   What is different about the epode (structure, subject-matter, mood)?

3   Can you think how the words of the chorus might be reflected in simple choreography?

The following scene is taken from Aeschylus' *Agamemnon* (1331–71). Agamemnon has entered the palace in triumph, but the chorus of old men of Argos sense that his joy will be short-lived. Their stasimon or choral ode is cut short by cries from within the *skene*. These are followed by an urgent exchange among members of the chorus; many scholars believe that the twelve outbursts are each delivered by a different choreut, and that this confirms that early tragic choruses consisted of twelve members. At the end of this exchange, Clytemnestra emerges from the palace with the bodies of Agamemnon and Cassandra.

Your coming long ago   choral odes frequently interrupt the plot and take us back in time to the mythological past. Here the origin of the violence plaguing the royal family of Argos is traced back to Myrtilus' curse on Pelops for deceiving him.

4.8	CHORUS	Success is by nature something no man	
		Has enough of; no one rejects it and keeps it	
		Out from a home that men point at,	
		Saying 'Enter here no more.'	
		The blessed gods even granted this man	1335
		To capture the city of Priam.	
		Honoured by the gods he arrives at his home,	
		But if he now is to pay for the bloodshed of times gone by	
		And by dying for those who have died	
		Cause others to die in revenge,	1340
		Who then of mortals would boast he was born	
		With a *daimōn* that protects him, when he heard about this?	

AGAMEMNON	Aagh – in here – I have been stabbed – a fatal blow!	
CHORUS	Quiet! Who screams that he is wounded by a fatal blow?	
AGAMEMNON	Aaagh, another – I have been stabbed again!	1345
CHORUS	From the screams of the king, I think the deed is done.	
	Still, together let us think of a safe course of action.	
	– I will tell you my suggestion:	
	Summon the citizens to bring help here to the house.	
	– I think we should rush in as quickly as possible	1350
	And seize the freshly dripping sword to prove the deed.	
	– I too share your thoughts:	
	I vote we do something: the main thing is that there be no delay.	
	– It is clear to see: this is the prelude,	
	A sign that they plan tyranny for the city.	1355
	– While we waste time, their hands do not sleep;	
	They trample the very name of hesitation to the ground.	
	– I know of no plan that I might sensibly suggest.	
	Even the man prepared to act must first think what to do.	
	– That is my opinion too, since I know no way	1360
	To raise the dead man up again with words.	

daimōn   a spirit that accompanied a person through life and was credited with bringing good or bad fortune.

Summon the citizens   the chorus consider taking action, but do not do so (in tragedy killings happen behind closed doors, and choruses almost always remain on stage for the duration of the play). Often the chorus represent weak groups such as old men or war-captives dependent on others for aid (the chorus of Euripides' *Phoenician Women* is triply marginalized in that they are not only women but slaves and barbarians at that!).

– **Shall we drag out our lives** by letting those
Who defile the house rule over us?
– **That I could not bear** – death is better:
It is a milder fate than tyranny. 1365
– Are we to divine that our master has been killed
With these screams as our proof?
– We must have certain knowledge when we speak about this,
For having certain knowledge is different from guessing.
– I feel, then, that we all agree to this, 1370
To find out for sure what has happened to Atreus' son.

1 What is the purpose of the chorus' words in the stasimon which opens this extract? What is the effect of having these sentiments expressed *before* the killing of Agamemnon?

2 Does the chorus in this scene become a participant in the action or does it remain an observer?

3 How do you think this scene might have been choreographed? Would the abrupt shift from choral unison to agitated discussion have been reflected in a striking change in movement?

4 In the final scene of the play, the chorus of elders face off against Aegisthus, who is rejoicing at the death of Agamemnon, though their feeble old age is no match for the tyrant. How do you think the chorus' helplessness is conveyed by their words and movements?

In Aeschylus' *Eumenides*, the chorus of Furies pursue Orestes, who has killed his mother Clytemnestra to avenge his father Agamemnon's death. Tracking the scent of shed blood, they follow him to Athens; they proceed to perform a 'binding dance' on him, of which this extract (303–33) includes the first part.

4.9 CHORUS So you won't answer me, but scorn my words, you who have been
fattened and set apart for me as a victim? You won't be slain at an 305
altar; I will eat you alive. So listen to this song that will bind you.
Come now, let us link the dance, since we are intent on performing
our grim art and declaring the right by which our company oversees 310
the affairs of men. We deem that we deliver just verdicts: the man
who holds out hands that are pure is safe from the violence of our

Shall we drag out our lives ... That I could not bear the chorus convey important lessons about the relationship between individual and community. Through them we see how the actions of individuals can have a terrible impact on the community at large; they also teach us, through their words and movements, how individuals can cooperate harmoniously. Even when individual voices can be discerned, as in this passage, the chorus still comprises individuals who have chosen to cooperate and communicate as a collective body of citizens. Thus choruses are, in a fundamental sense, civic performances.

anger, and lives out his life unharmed; but whenever someone 315
transgresses, as this man has, and tries to conceal hands that are
bloody, we present ourselves as just witnesses for the slain, and appear
against him as avengers of bloodshed right through to the end. 320

Strophe 1 O mother Night, mother who bore me to punish the dead and the
living, hear me! **Leto's son** deprives me of my honour, taking away
from me that miserable wretch who must offer fitting atonement for 325
his mother's blood.

Refrain Over our sacrificial victim we sing this song – crazed, frenzied,
maddening the mind, the chant of the Furies, **accompanied by no** 330
lyre, which binds the wits and shrivels up a man.

Antistrophe 1 is then followed by a repetition of the Refrain.

The binding dance of the Furies illustrates a number of elements of ancient
magic such as the use of chant and of repetition (in the recurring refrain). The
ancients believed that such spells had to be performed aloud to be effective.
Although rituals in plays are often dramatic interpretations rather than exact
re-enactments of such rituals as performed in real life, they are nevertheless
frequently represented as achieving their goal. In this instance, Orestes is
protected from the savage power of the Furies by Athena, to whose statue he
is clinging, and the primary purpose of the song is to heighten the potential
threat posed by the terrifying Furies.

This choral ode is particularly suggestive in its recurring references to the acts
of singing and dancing. In lines 370–1, for example, the chorus sing of the
effect on their victims 'of our black-clad attacks and the vindictive dances of
our feet'. They then intone the following refrain (372–6): 'Leaping up high I
bear down from above with the heavy force of my foot, limbs that trip even
those in full flight, a dire fate.'

- The Furies' words are frightening, and their appearance, according to the
  colourful if fanciful anecdote in the *Life of Aeschylus* (9), preserved by
  an anonymous ancient biographer, was so fearsome that women in the
  audience miscarried! What might their movements have looked like, and
  how might their grim dance have been choreographed in relation to their
  intended victim?

Leto's son Apollo, who has instructed Orestes to kill his mother and has promised to
protect him.

accompanied by no lyre the lyre, whose strings are tuned to each other according to
precise musical ratios, was seen as a symbol of harmony and grace, and its music was
considered to be noble (in contrast to other instruments, such as the cymbal and double-
pipe). The wild dance of the Furies aims to disorder its victim's wits and drive him to
distraction.

This scene on an Attic red-figure krater dating to *c.* 500–490 BC is unusual in that it shows a tragic chorus in action. The identical open-mouthed expressions of the faces suggest that these are masked actors, and the coordinated steps and gestures portray a choreographed dance. They are wearing military costume, so this may be the *pyrrichē*, an energetic war-dance often mentioned by ancient sources.

The six choreuts approach what appears to be a stepped altar, on which ribbons and garlands have been placed as offerings. This could be a representation of the *thymele* or altar in the middle of the *orchestra* and, given the size and placement of the shrouded figure behind the altar, it may be doubling as a tomb, from which the spirit of a dead hero is rising out of the earth (as in Aeschylus' *Persians*). In a similar scene in Aeschylus' *Libation Bearers*, the chorus join with Electra in a rite of libation at the tomb of her father Agamemnon. Electra appeals to her father to bring Orestes home, and the chorus join in with their own invocation. At the beginning of the scene, the chorus-leader sets the sacral tone when she says to Electra: 'I revere the tomb of your father like an altar' (106). It may well be that the altar, prominently positioned in the centre of the *orchestra*, doubled as the tomb of Agamemnon in this play. Certainly this would facilitate the staging of the subsequent scene, in which Electra, reunited with her brother Orestes and his companion Pylades, joins with the chorus to rouse her dead father to action, a scene that would seem to call for all to congregate around the tomb.

4.10

The chorus in satyr-play

The satyrs that formed the chorus of every satyr-play seem from the surviving evidence to have been central to the plot. In fact, satyr-plays are sometimes referred to as simply 'the satyrs'. The late Hellenistic author Demetrius (*On Style* 169) described satyr-play as 'tragedy at play', and the many titles and fragments of satyr-plays that survive do suggest that the genre treated many of the same mythological figures as did tragedy (e.g. Odysseus, Heracles, Theseus), but that the myths were treated in a playful manner and the heroes, who acted in tragic costume and spoke using a similarly elevated diction, were surrounded by a riotous and raunchy chorus of satyrs.

This raunchiness is reflected in the satyrs' comments, which often voice their appetites for food, wine and sex, the basic instincts of these half-animals/half-men. However, it must have been most apparent in their physicalities (i.e. their postures, gestures and movements).

An Attic vase dating to *c.* 480–470 BC shows a satyr chorus in action. Although there are many vase-paintings of satyrs behaving outrageously (e.g. performing sexual acrobatics or groping maenads), many of them have no discernible connection with the theatre, depicting the satyrs not as men in satyr costume but as 'real' satyrs. In this scene, the presence of the piper, who wears an elaborate full-length robe, marks this out as a performance, as do the woolly breeches that the satyrs are wearing, complete with trademark erect leather phallus, and their identical masks. Behind the piper stands a younger man, who may be the playwright. The five satyrs are carrying pieces of what appears to be an ornate banqueting couch, which they are perhaps getting ready to assemble on a low stage at the front. They are all shown in lively postures, and it seems as if the painter was interested in showing a variety of movements. Their footwork, expressive hand gestures and entire body language contribute to their obvious excitement at the festivities that await them once they have set up the banquet. If the piece of furniture is a throne rather than a banqueting couch, then it may be that they are preparing for a joyful reunion with Dionysus, the god they worship.

4.11

1   What impressions do you get from the body language of the satyrs?
2   Do you think that Athenaeus (see **4.6**) would have approved of this form of dancing? Why, or why not?

In the following extracts from Sophocles' *Trackers* (Greek *Ichneutai*) (124–60, 176–212), the chorus of satyrs are searching for Apollo's stolen cattle, enticed by the promise of a finder's bounty. They have split into three search-parties, and are tracking the scent of the cows with their noses. They must have presented a comical sight, scurrying about the *orchestra* with their noses to the ground and jumping at the slightest sound. Silenus, father to the satyrs (who functioned as chorus-leader in early satyr-plays, but has by now been given a separate role, played by an actor), pokes fun at them and gives us clues as to what their antics might have looked like.

<table>
<tr><td>4.12</td><td>SILENUS</td><td>What is this technique then that you've invented for yourselves, what novelty is this: the way you hunt, lying flat on the ground? What kind of behaviour is that? *I* certainly don't know! You lie face down like hedgehogs in a thicket, or like a monkey bending over to let off a fart. What is this? Where on earth did you pick it up? Where? Tell me! That kind of behaviour is **entirely foreign to me**.</td><td>125

130</td></tr>
<tr><td></td><td>CHORUS</td><td>Oo-oo-oo-ooh!</td><td></td></tr>
<tr><td></td><td>SILENUS</td><td>Why are you howling like that? Who is scaring you? What do you see? Who is throwing you into a tizzy? Why on earth do you keep acting crazy? Are you **trying to find millet**? Why are you now silent – till this moment you were such chatterboxes!</td><td>

135</td></tr>
<tr><td></td><td>CHORUS</td><td>Be quiet!</td><td></td></tr>
<tr><td></td><td>SILENUS</td><td>What is that over there that keeps making you jump?</td><td></td></tr>
<tr><td></td><td>CHORUS</td><td>Just listen!</td><td></td></tr>
<tr><td></td><td>SILENUS</td><td>How can I listen when I hear nothing?</td><td></td></tr>
<tr><td></td><td>CHORUS</td><td>Do as I ask!</td><td>140</td></tr>
<tr><td></td><td>SILENUS</td><td>You will be no help to me in my hunt.</td><td></td></tr>
<tr><td></td><td>CHORUS</td><td>Listen for yourself, father, just for a moment, to the noise that terrifies us and drives us mad, a **sound never before heard** by mortal man.</td><td></td></tr>
<tr><td></td><td>SILENUS</td><td>Why on earth are you so scared of a sound? You mannequins moulded from wax, you dirty pieces of animal dung! You see terror in every shadow, you are afraid of everything. You are spineless, slovenly and slavish attendants, nothing but bodies, tongues and phalluses! If you're ever needed, you sound loyal, but run away from the action. And yet, you worthless beasts, you have such a father as me – who, when young, graced the dwellings of the nymphs with **many monuments to his manliness**. He did not turn in flight, he feared nothing; he never cowered at the sound of cattle grazing in the hills; instead, he wrought with his spear glorious deeds, which you now tarnish as soon as you hear some shepherd's coaxing call...</td><td>145

150

155

160</td></tr>
</table>

In the next few lines, Silenus persuades the satyrs to regroup under his command and approach the cave. Suddenly the noise repeats.

---

entirely foreign to me   Silenus' behaviour is usually just as ludicrous and outrageous as that of his satyrs.

trying to find millet   millet was kept in underground storage pits; when satyrs are this excited, they are usually looking for food!

sound never before heard   the sound that frightens them is the infant Hermes playing the lyre that he fashioned from a tortoise shell. The primitive satyrs have no experience of such refinements as lyre-playing.

many monuments to his manliness   Silenus describes trophies normally set up to commemorate courage in battle, but here the wording suggests that he is claiming to have shown his 'manly courage' through his sexual prowess in encounters with nymphs.

CHORUS   Oo-oo-ooh, psss, aaah – tell us what is the matter? Why do you groan and gibber and glower at me for no reason? **Who is this caught at the first turn?** You're caught! He's here, he's here! You're mine, I'm taking you prisoner. Who is this at the second...   180

There is a break of twenty lines that are mostly lost...

SILENUS   Ah!   205
CHORUS   What is it?
SILENUS   I'm not staying.
CHORUS   Please stay!
SILENUS   Can't be done. If you want, *you* search for them and track them down and get rich by catching the cattle and getting the gold. I've decided not to stay here any longer and waste my time.
CHORUS   No, I won't allow you to desert me or to sneak off from the job before   210
we know for sure who is in this chamber.

The mountain-nymph Cyllene, who is rearing the infant Hermes, emerges from her cave (i.e. the skene*) and scolds the satyrs for disturbing the peace with all their stomping and twirling.*

- • Below is a list of various types of humour. Which do you see operating in this scene?

Verbal humour

- • wit: clever comments
- • verbal creativity: using words in unusual and humorous ways (e.g. puns and other word-play)
- • verbal disjuncture: when tone and subject-matter don't match (e.g. use of mock heroism, bathos)
- • use of hyperbole (exaggeration for the sake of effect) and other rhetorical devices

Visual humour

- • comic movement and gesture (the physicality of the clown or the mime)
- • comic blunders (e.g. tripping and falling – see also *Schadenfreude* on p. 91)

Who is this caught at the first turn   the satyrs, frightened by the sound coming from the cave represented by the *skene*, seem to be milling about in pandemonium, grabbing each other as they think they are catching their assailants.

The chorus in Old Comedy

> The following extract from Aristophanes' *Birds* (performed in 414 BC) forms part of the initial entry of the chorus of birds (260–96). Two Athenians, Peisetaerus and Euelpides, have arrived at the kingdom of the birds, hoping to persuade them to found a new colony with them in the sky. So the birds are summoned to council by Tereus, a human transformed into a hoopoe, who is now ruling as king of the birds. The extract begins with the last lines of his song, in which words are interspersed with sounds that imitate bird calls.

4.13

TEREUS	Come now, all of you, to our council, hither, hither, hither, hither!	
	Torotorotorotorotix,	260
	kikkabau kikkabau,	
	torotorotorolililix!	
PEISETAERUS	Do you see a bird anywhere?	
EUELPIDES	By Apollo, I sure don't, though I'm gaping up at the sky trying to spot one.	
PEISETAERUS	So the Hoopoe, it seems, did his whooping for nothing when he entered the thicket and copied the curlew.	265
TEREUS	Torotix torotix!	
EUELPIDES	Hey, mate, look over here, there's a bird coming!	
PEISETAERUS	By Zeus, it *is* a bird. What kind of bird? Surely not a peacock?	
EUELPIDES	The Hoopoe here will tell us. What bird is that?	270
TEREUS	That isn't just the common variety of bird that you humans see every day: he's a marsh bird.	

EUELPIDES	**Wow, how beautiful he is**, all flaming pink!
TEREUS	Of course – that's why he's called Flamingo!
EUELPIDES	You there – hey – yes, you!
PEISETAERUS	What is it?
EUELPIDES	Over here there's another bird!
PEISETAERUS	By Zeus, you're right, there *is* another one. He too is decked out in extraordinary colour. **Who on earth is this musical prophet**, this exotic mountain bird?	275
TEREUS	This one's called Mede.
EUELPIDES	Mede? Lord Heracles! Then if he's a **Mede**, how did he fly here without a camel?
PEISETAERUS	Here's yet another bird – he's got himself a crest.
EUELPIDES	What marvel is this? So you are not the only hoopoe, but he is one too?	280
TEREUS	This one is the son of **Philocles' hoopoe**, and I am his grandfather, just as you might say Hipponicus son of Callias, and then Callias son of Hipponicus.
PEISETAERUS	So this bird is Callias. He's losing a lot of feathers!
TEREUS	That's because he's a pure-bred, so he gets plucked by money-grabbers, and the females also pull out his plumage.	285
EUELPIDES	By Poseidon, here's yet another brightly coloured bird. What is his name, I wonder?

Wow, how beautiful he is   the spectacle offered by the chorus – its costumes and masks, dancing, song and musical accompaniment – must have had a strong visual as well as auditory impact on the audience members. Aristotle identifies spectacle (*opsis*) as an element of tragedy that is missing in epic (*Poetics* 1462a), and Plutarch states (*Moralia* 1095c) that even the philosopher Epicurus acknowledged that the wise person is a 'lover of sights' and enjoys hearing and seeing Dionysiac performances as much as anyone else.

Who on earth is this musical prophet   a quotation from Aeschylus' *Edonians*. Aristophanes liked to transplant lines from tragedy, often into contexts where they seem humorously out of place.

Mede   Greeks often referred to Medes and Persians interchangeably. The Persian expedition against Greece in 480 BC had used camels. The bird in question is probably a cock, referred to as the 'Persian bird'.

Philocles' hoopoe   Aristophanes seems to be making a joke about the many plays that feature Tereus as a character. The Tereus in this play may identify himself with the protagonist of Sophocles' *Tereus*; 'Philocles' hoopoe' refers to a play about Tereus written by Philocles, a nephew of Aeschylus. Perhaps Aristophanes is suggesting that Philocles plagiarized from Sophocles by including a Tereus (and so Philocles' hoopoe is the next generation). The young hoopoe that Aristophanes has just brought on stage would then be the third generation of hoopoes. He is also poking fun at a rich aristocratic family who for several generations had kept calling their sons either Callias or Hipponicus.

TEREUS	That one's Gobbler!
PEISETAERUS	You mean Cleonymus is not the only gobbler?
EUELPIDES	This one can't be Cleonymus – **Cleonymus** would have thrown 290 away his crest.
PEISETAERUS	Actually, what is the reason for the crests on these birds? Have they come to race in full armour?
TEREUS	No, my dear fellow, they're like the Carians: **they live on crests**, for security.
PEISETAERUS	By Poseidon, just look at the number of damn birds that have congregated!
EUELPIDES	Lord Apollo, what a cloud! Whoa, whoa! You can't see the *eisodos* 295 any more for all the birds flitting around.

By now the remainder of the twenty-four chorus-members have hopped in,
and in the following lines Peisetaerus and Euelpides start calling out bird
names in rapid succession. The birds quickly realize that two humans have
invaded their territory. They line up in battle-formation and start 'nose-
diving' their enemies, who try to shield themselves from attack with the pots
they are carrying.

1   What is the term used to describe comments such as Euelpides' remark
about the chorus blocking the *eisodos* that deliberately call attention to the
fact that this is all a performance?

2   What types of humour does this scene use that were not present in the
earlier scene from satyr-play?

3   How might you choreograph the scene? Think about the placement of
Euelpides, Peisetaerus and Tereus, where the birds enter from, what they
might do on stage, and how these birds may behave as chorus-members (are
they coordinating their movements or not?).

4   What elements of this scene might have surprised its original audience?

Cleonymus   an Athenian politician accused of greed (hence 'the gobbler') who fled after
the battle of Delion (424 BC). Since helmets were often crowned by a crest, Aristophanes is
saying that this crested bird cannot be Cleonymus, who threw away his helmet in flight.

they live on crests   Carians lived in a mountainous region of Turkey; they built their
settlements on the crests of hills, which allows Aristophanes to get in yet another pun on
the word 'crest'.

A number of early Attic vase-paintings show scenes of animal choruses in performance. This black-figure oinochoe (wine-jug) dates to *c.* 480 BC, around the time that comedy was first introduced into the City Dionysia; but others date back half a century earlier, suggesting that comedy was already a thriving art-form at Athens before it was incorporated into this festival.

In this painting, two chorus-members dressed in identical bird costumes dance to the accompaniment of the *aulos* or double-pipe. With the left figure, the underside of the wings is shown, so that we can see the performer's arms strapped to the wings, while with the other the arms are visible in silhouette through the wings. On their heads, both choreuts wear a crest or cock's comb; their beards have been painted a fiery red to match, and they have pointed noses suggesting a beak. The body-tights they wear carry a pattern that represents feathers. Attached to their knees are bright red extensions. Richard Green (2007: 168) offers an attractive interpretation of their function. They represent the birds' feet, he argues. While dancing, these feet would have been raised high off the ground, indicating that the birds were flying; when the birds came to rest, the performers would have knelt down, allowing the feet to perch on the ground. Certainly on this vase, the painter shows the performers in mid-flight, with wings outstretched and legs leaping into the air. Both turn their heads back towards the music of the piper (just visible on the far left).

4.14

1. Why might the vase-painter have chosen to show the underside of one of the chorus-members' wings and thereby represent him as a human actor with strapped-on wings instead of sustaining the illusion that these are real birds?
2. In this vase-painting, as in most depictions of choral performance, the chorus-members wear identical costumes, thereby emphasizing their collective identity. Why do you think that Aristophanes in his *Birds* chose to have each choreut represent a different species of bird?

The chorus in New Comedy

In the following extract from Menander's *Girl with the Cropped Hair* (*Perikeiromenē*), lines 261–6, the arrival of the chorus is announced by the character Daos, who then leaves the playing space for the chorus to perform their interlude. The lyrics of the chorus are not given in the text. Similar descriptions of the chorus as young revellers bursting in on the scene are found in several other plays of New Comedy.

4.15 There's a crowd of drunken young men approaching. I give high praise to **my mistress**: she has taken the young girl into our household. She's a true mother. I have to go look for her foster-son. It would be **the perfect moment** for him to show up here without delay, in my opinion.

Music

Sophocles wrote a lost work titled *On the Chorus*. It would have been interesting to have the insights of a practising playwright; most of our information on music and dancing was written by scholars interested in music theory rather than by practitioners. Their writings are usually dry and often baffling. They use a wide variety of technical terms to describe music; many are hard to pin down, and some have no exact modern equivalent. Even the word 'music' is a much broader term in Greek. It encompasses the words, the dance or movement, as well as

---

my mistress Myrrhine, the mistress of the household. The play has the classic plot of twins separated at birth. One of them, Moschion (i.e. the foster-son), was adopted by Myrrhine; the other, Glycera, happens to live next door! Having been kicked out of the house by her lover Polemon, she is taken in by Myrrhine. Daos is the family slave, and departs to look for Moschion.

the perfect moment New Comedy is full of references to the coincidences that drive its plots. Here Daos may be speaking ironically, implying that wherever a gang of young hooligans is forming, his wayward young master is sure to join them.

what we would call the music – to the Greeks, the whole poetic composition was inspired by the Muses and therefore constituted *mousikē*. Ancient music theorists attributed different emotional effects to different metres (rhythmic patterns) – but their pronouncements are often contradictory, and the surviving plays don't entirely support their cut-and-dried conclusions, since many metres show an incredible range.

Similarly, ancient authors discuss a number of modes – different modes seem to have used different scales of notes and these were said to have had different characters (the Dorian was seen as strong, the Ionian as soft). Nowadays minor keys are often seen as mournful, while major keys are upbeat. However, in the ancient world these distinctions were complicated by the fact that these modes were associated with different ethnic groups: the Dorians, Ionians, Aeolians, Lydians, Phrygians were all peoples with their own dialects of Greek (or, in the cases of the Lydians and Phrygians, their own languages), so the descriptions of different modes carry ethnic prejudices and are further complicated by the characterization of certain modes (e.g. the Dorian) as manly and others (e.g. the Lydian) as effeminate.

What ancient writers object to most forcefully is the increasing mixing of modes characteristic of what modern scholars have termed the 'New Music'; instead of choosing a mode appropriate for the genre, poets start to range freely between modes, blending them and even breaking out of them altogether. To use a modern example, similar objections might be lodged if in a Christian wedding the organist played a rock-and-roll number for the bridal processional instead of Wagner's wedding march. This 'slide' towards more freeform music seems to have begun relatively early – a fragment of a comedy by the poet Pherecrates (active in the 430s and 420s) preserved in Pseudo-Plutarch (*On Music* 1141c) has Music (a character in the play) blame a contemporary dithyrambic poet called Melanippides for ruining her.

The melody or pattern of notes must have added yet greater variety to the pieces, though it is impossible to determine how melody related to mode, how the melody of the accompanying instrument related to the singing, and whether the antistrophe used the same pattern (or what we might call 'tune') as the strophe. Hardly any ancient musical notation has survived, so it is hard to determine what the music would have sounded like.

The *aulos* in performance

The **aulētēs** or piper played a wind instrument known as the *aulos* (sometimes referred to in the plural *auloi* since they were usually played as a pair of pipes, one with each hand). The player wore a head-strap (**phorbeia**) while playing and, as with the modern oboe, blew into the instrument through a reed. Its sound must have been quite high pitched given its narrow bore.

The piper provided musical accompaniment for dithyramb, tragedy, satyr-play and comedy alike. He played a leading role during training as well as during the performance. The scholion on Aeschines' *Against Timarchus* 10 mentions that the piper stood in the centre of the dithyrambic chorus; numerous sources suggest that he led the choral procession into the theatre. We see him occupying a similarly prominent position on vase-paintings showing rehearsals and performances (see **1.3**, **1.6**) and on inscriptions commemorating victorious casts. In fact, the selection of pipers was decided by lot so that no *choregos* would have an unfair advantage. Demosthenes recounts how his piper Telephanes took over the training of the chorus when the chorus-director proved disloyal (see **2.7**). Top pipers gained celebrity status and started commanding hefty fees for solo performances at festivals. The polymath Athenaeus (*c.* AD 200) records the annoyance of the fifth-century playwright Pratinas of Phlius at the increased prominence of pipers: they no longer played to accompany the chorus, he complained, but instead the choruses now sang to accompany the pipers (*Learned Banqueters* 617b–c)! Clearly the piper was an integral element of the drama, even though his presence is rarely discernible from the bare scripts of the plays.

A piper performing on a double-pipe. The musician seems to be moving to his music. Clearly visible is the phorbeia *or head-strap.*

The Attic red-figure vase in **4.16** dates to *c.* 470 BC and shows a scene from tragedy. An actor playing the part of a maenad, a female worshipper of Dionysus in a divinely induced frenzy, holds in her left hand the hind-quarters of an animal that she has torn apart, while in her right she brandishes a sword. She is depicted mid-step, with her costume swinging out in front of her; her gestures are vigorous and her face looks out at the viewer askance.

The presence of the piper, which indicates that this is a live performance, also suggests that the maenad is a member of the chorus. Peter Wilson, in a stimulating study of the *auletes* or *aulos*-player (1999), points out that the *aulos* held a problematic position in Athenian society – its music was a vital part of dramatic performances, yet at the same time was seen as a corrupting influence, driving people to lose their self-control and act in an irrational manner. In this vase-painting the 'dangerous' *aulos* and the frenzied maenad are presented in close juxtaposition so that it seems as if the former is stirring up the latter.

4.16

Ecstatic music

The following extract is from a fragment of Aeschylus' *Edonians*, a play in which Dionysus and his religion are rejected by the Edonian king Lycurgus, who is then punished by the god. Here in the *parodos* the chorus describe the instruments used in ecstatic rites.

4.17 One holds in his hands a pipe worked on the lathe, and fills the air with its fingered melody, the call that sets off frenzy. Another with cymbals sounds a clash … while the rumble of the kettledrum, like the roll of subterranean thunder [i.e. an earthquake], spreads great terror.

> 1 Are there certain musical instruments nowadays that are seen by some as dangerous in some way? What are they, and why do they carry these negative associations?
>
> 2 How does modern interpretative dance communicate meaning? Do its dance movements use a vocabulary that communicates discernible plot elements to the viewer?

In the following extract from Aristophanes' *Birds* (658–84), an *aulos*-player, dressed up as a nightingale, actually seems to be playing a part in the play. The plot of the play revolves around the idea of humans trying to turn into birds: the two main characters, Euelpides and Peisetaerus, want to grow a pair of wings; the king of the birds, Tereus, used to be human but was turned into a bird. The appearance of the piper (whose name was apparently Chaeris, 858) as the mute character of the nightingale, a bird known for its beautiful song, is just one more instance of Aristophanes' inventiveness.

4.18

CHORUS-LEADER	(*to Tereus*) Take these men with you and dine them well. But that sweet-singing nightingale who performs with the Muses – bring her out here and leave her with us, so we can **play with her**.	660
PEISETAERUS	Yes, by Zeus, grant their request! Bring the chick out from among the reeds.	
EUELPIDES	Do bring the nightingale here, by the gods, so we too can take a look at her.	
TEREUS	If that's what you want, we'll do it. **Procne**! Come out and show yourself to the guests!	665
PEISETAERUS	Zeus in high heaven! What a pretty chick! So delicate and fair!	
EUELPIDES	You know, I'd really like to spread her legs!	
PEISETAERUS	And what a lot of gold she's wearing – quite the diva!	670
EUELPIDES	Me, I fancy giving her a kiss.	
PEISETAERUS	You idiot, her beak's like a **pair of skewers**.	
EUELPIDES	So I'll have to peel the shell off her head, like an egg, before I kiss her.	
TEREUS	Let's go!	
PEISETAERUS	You lead the way, and may fortune accompany us!	675

Tereus, Euelpides, Peisetaerus and their two slaves leave through the skene *door.*

---

play with her   their words carry a double-entendre. Female pipers played at male banquets such as the one to which Tereus is inviting his two guests; they were expected to perform sexual favours as well as provide the musical entertainment.

Procne   in myth, Procne punished her husband Tereus for raping her sister by killing their son Itys; she was then transformed into a nightingale, forever singing her mournful song. But comedy can wipe the slate clean, and here there is no evidence of this terrible family history.

pair of skewers   pointed spits used to grill meat. Since Procne is a piper, this is probably a reference to the double-pipe, which protrudes from the mouth like a beak.

CHORUS

Beloved triller,
Dearest of birds,
Who accompanies all my songs,
My companion the nightingale,
You have come, you have come into view,   680
Bringing me your sweet melody.
So now, you who weave springtime tunes
On your fair-voiced pipe,
Lead us in our anapaests!

---

1   What types of modern theatrical performance make greatest use of dancing
    and of music?

2   The soundtrack is a key artistic component of many films. What different
    functions does music fulfil in film? (You might think about how it
    communicates tone, genre, emotion, suspense.) Does film suggest useful
    ways of thinking about the role of music in Greek theatre?

3   In modern performances of Greek drama, directors often reduce the chorus
    to a handful of members or eliminate it completely. What, if anything, is lost
    by doing this? And what reasons might they have for doing so?

4   From the extracts presented in this chapter, what has changed about how
    we think of music compared with ancient Greeks?

Lead us in our anapaests   a rhythm in which the chorus often chants or sings when it is
marching in. The beginning of the choral ode marks a shift in perception: the nightingale/
piper is no longer the sexualized female piper but is now the acknowledged leader of the
choral performance, lending it beauty and direction.

5 The actors

The masterpieces of modern western drama certainly have their origins in ancient Greek theatre. But theatrical practices have changed considerably over time, and we should not make the mistake of imagining that watching a play in ancient Athens was anything like our own experiences at the theatre when we take in a play by Ibsen, Chekhov, Miller or Stoppard. We will be much better off if we recognize that there is a lot about ancient plays that is different from their modern counterparts, including when, where, how and by whom they were performed. Over centuries of experimentation, modern theatre has developed a huge repertoire of possibilities. If we say that we're taking in a theatrical show, we might be in Central Park watching an open-air performance of Italian opera, in a smoky bar watching a one-man comedy routine, or in prison watching a travelling cast perform with Javanese shadow-puppets. Modern directors have great freedom to put their own interpretative stamp on their production, and the audience almost expects to encounter the unexpected.

Athenian theatre, in contrast, offered a narrower palette. All the actors were male; they wore masks, performed in the open air in a large, outdoor theatre, and shared the playing space with a large chorus. In short, the possibilities were restricted by a set of conventions that accompanied this developing art-form. To us as we look back, these conventions may seem overly limiting. However, the surviving evidence suggests that there was wide variety within these parameters. Take, for example, the convention in tragedy that no more than three actors played the speaking characters. This convention certainly did not limit the number of speaking characters to three, since masked actors could easily change mask and costume and play multiple parts in succession: at least four surviving Euripidean tragedies have ten or more speaking characters!

Much modern theatre, like modern cinema, aims at *naturalism*. The set, costumes, script and acting all imitate real life, and the audience could be forgiven for believing that it was looking through a window into the neighbours' house and observing a family dispute. Greek theatre never aimed at naturalism; rather, it developed its own repertoire of theatrical props, costumes, language, gestures and movements that were recognizably theatrical. In fact, characters in comedy would often break out of the dramatic moment to poke fun at an individual in the audience. Tragedy especially used elevated words that marked its verses as poetic rather than 'realistic'. Characters often spoke in extended speeches; even when they engaged in dialogue, it was an artistic form of dialogue that did not reproduce a real-life exchange. Characters in tragedy could interrupt each other, rush onto the scene or dissolve into fits of raving, but these happenings were staged in what we might describe as a *formal* rather than a *naturalistic* manner.

Perhaps a modern counterpart might be opera; its Romeos and Juliets exchange declarations of undying love in melancholy arias and with graceful gestures that move the audience with their lyricism but don't usually resemble the steamy love-affairs that are a staple of many TV soaps.

Dramatic action

Posture

The intense emotions of the characters in tragedy are conveyed in their words, outbursts and songs; but they must have also been communicated through movement and stance. In a huge outdoor theatre without the advantage of spotlights, small motions would have been lost on the audience.

Greek tragedy has far less movement than most modern drama, and so many modern productions of Greek tragedy seem static and perhaps even visually drab to modern audiences used to the rapid action of television and film. And yet precisely because there is less 'background noise' caused by the kind of constant movements of modern naturalistic drama (in which a character might, for example, get up off the sofa and start pacing, light a cigarette and then pull up the blinds), the movements that do occur gain greater significance. They are often slower, more stately and more deliberate. Japanese Noh theatre offers a useful point of comparison to Greek tragedy; it too has a repertoire of highly stylized movements that often carry symbolic meaning to an audience familiar with the genre.

> Euripides' *Trojan Women* (performed 415 BC) is set in the immediate aftermath of the destruction of Troy. Poseidon opens the play from the *theologeion* (the roof of the *skene*) by describing the smouldering ruins and utter devastation; he then draws attention to the sole character on stage (and the only character in surviving Greek tragedy to remain on stage from beginning to end) – the figure of Hecuba, queen of Troy (36–8).

5.1   Look at this poor woman – if anyone wants to see her – it is Hecuba, lying here in front of the door, weeping many tears on many counts.

> The figure of the widow of Priam lying prostrate in the dust speaks powerfully of the sorrow that engulfs this play – even before Hecuba has uttered a single word. She remains in this position of grief and subjection for another sixty lines until she finally delivers a lament over herself and her city (98–121).

5.2 Up you get, ill-fated woman! Raise your head and neck from the ground! Troy is no more, and we are no longer Troy's rulers. Your fortune has turned, so bear it! Sail 100 through the straits, sail with your fortune; do not set life's prow towards the wave of calamities. Ah me! Is there any lament that I cannot voice? My fatherland, my 105 children, my husband have all been destroyed. O mighty dignity of my ancestors: you are now ended; you were nothing! What should I keep quiet, and what not? 110 I am beset by a heavy fate. My limbs lie there piteously, **my back is stretched out on a hard bed**; my poor head, my temples, my ribs; how I long to roll my back 115 and spine, shifting to each side of my body in turn as I constantly sing my tears' laments! **For those in adversity this too is music: to sing their troubles that** 120 **cannot be danced.**

> 1 What do Hecuba's posture and movements communicate about her characterization?
>
> 2 Why does Hecuba describe her movements when the audience can see them?

Silences

Just as the absence of movement could convey deep meaning, so too a character's silence could be expressive. Aristophanes' *Frogs* offers tantalizing clues to the role played by silences in some plays. The play stages a contest between Aeschylus and Euripides as to who is the best playwright. With Dionysus, the god of theatre, presiding over the contest as judge, the two rivals engage in ridiculing each other's plays. Euripides begins his attack on Aeschylus with the following criticism (907–21).

5.3 EURIPIDES   Well then. With regard to myself and the kind of poet that I am, I will speak in my later comments. But first I will expose this fellow,

---

my back is stretched out on a hard bed   Hecuba is referring to the hard beaten earth of the *orchestra* floor. To an Athenian audience, for whom a woman's place was within the protective walls of her house, Hecuba would have seemed particularly exposed and helpless lying on the ground in front of what are described as the smouldering ruins of Troy.

For those in adversity this too is music: to sing their troubles that cannot be danced   Hecuba poignantly expresses a seeming paradox: laments over the dead are in many senses a cacophony, a discordant song; and yet the very act of self-expression, and the gift of music in particular, have a therapeutic effect and are music to the soul. She then expresses another striking truth: the acts of violence that she has witnessed have no rhyme or rhythm to them, they are too horrible to be put to dance; and yet tragedy does just that: it stages choral dances that are an attempt to act out a response to the terrible misfortunes that beset the characters.

showing you what a con artist and sham **he was**, and by what tricks
he deceived his audience-members. For he inherited them from
Phrynichus and they were dim-witted by having been raised on his   910
plays. Right at the start he would have a single character sit there
– an Achilles or a Niobe – all wrapped up, not showing their face,
emitting not even a mutter.

DIONYSUS   By Zeus, you're right!

EURIPIDES   They would keep up their silence while the chorus rattled off four
salvos of choral songs in a row without stopping!   915

DIONYSUS   I enjoyed the silence; I liked it just as much as the chatterboxes we
get nowadays.

EURIPIDES   Then you sure were silly.

DIONYSUS   I guess I was. But why did he do this?

EURIPIDES   Because he was a con artist. He did it so that the spectator would
sit waiting for when Niobe would finally say something; and   920
meanwhile the play just kept going.

DIONYSUS   What a rascal! He sure tricked me!

> Euripides singles out Aeschylus' silent characters as the first trait to parody.
> Euripides himself will later be lampooned for putting characters on stage
> who think themselves too clever by half and cannot stop talking. It is to be
> expected that Euripides will cast Aeschylus' silent characters in the worst
> possible light and suggest that they are part of Aeschylus' attempt to bluff his
> audience; but it is worth noting that Dionysus, the god of theatre, says that he
> enjoyed these scenes.

The plays that Euripides mentions have not survived; however, we can imagine
that Achilles and Niobe each played the tragic protagonist. Vase-paintings show
Achilles with his head wrapped in grief as he broods over the loss of Briseis,
taken away from him by Agamemnon. Such a gesture of grief is more frequently
associated with women, and Agamemnon's act of aggression in a sense has
emasculated Achilles, who has lost status in the eyes of his peers. Niobe mourned
her seven sons and seven daughters, killed by Apollo and Artemis; she became a
byword for a figure caught in perpetual grief. Both are individuals isolated and
afflicted by loss; an opening scene in which the character sat silently shrouded
in grief could have been very effective in drawing in the audience; Euripides'
description of the playwright as con man is a satirical way of describing the effect

he was   the playwrights are now dead and in the Underworld and are trading insults
about the plays they put on while alive.

Phrynichus   a tragedian who was a slightly older contemporary of Aeschylus; he is
credited with several theatrical innovations, including introducing female characters to
the stage.

that a play (which is, after all, fiction!) has on its audience when it moves it to tears. Thus a well-crafted silence might have been as powerful an element of the tragic repertoire as an impassioned speech.

Entrances and exits

Arrivals and departures are often among the most significant actions of Greek tragedy and reward close analysis, as Oliver Taplin showed in his influential book *Greek Tragedy in Action*. In this extract from Aeschylus' *Agamemnon* (performed in 458 BC), Agamemnon departs into the palace at the invitation of his wife Clytemnestra, treading on expensive purple tapestries (944–57).

5.4   **If you think it right**, then **let someone quickly undo**
    My boots, foot-servants on my travels.   945
    May no evil eye of resentment strike me from afar
    As I tread on this **ocean-purple fit for the gods**.
    There is great shame in damaging one's own property,
    In destroying expensive cloth paid for in silver.
    Well, so be it. Now, welcome in   950
    This foreign girl graciously; god smiles from afar
    On the master who is gentle;
    No one willingly submits to the yoke of slavery.
    This girl, a flower picked out from our hoard of booty and
    Given to me by the army, comes with me.   955
    Now, since I am forced to heed you in this matter,
    I will enter the halls of my house, trampling on this purple.

If you think it right   in the lines leading up to this, Clytemnestra persuades Agamemnon, against his better judgement, to trample on the precious tapestries that she has strewn in his path. Agamemnon is duped by Clytemnestra into believing that she wants to give him a royal welcome after his long absence. In fact, she seeks revenge for the death of their daughter Iphigenia, who was sacrificed by Agamemnon to secure fair winds for the Greek fleet as it sailed for Troy. His earlier decision to sacrifice his daughter to advance his public cause is mirrored by his action on stage: he tramples on the tapestries, the laborious handiwork of women, to make his triumphal entry into the palace.

let someone quickly undo My boots   comments such as these are our only indication of the presence of mute characters such as the slave who here unties Agamemnon's boots, or the brooding war-captive Cassandra ('This foreign girl') who accompanies him as war-booty and remains silent in this scene.

ocean-purple fit for the gods   purple cloth was produced by extracting the dye from thousands of tiny murex shellfish, and was therefore very expensive. Agamemnon's act of trampling on these precious tapestries is represented as a religious violation.

Well, so be it   characters in tragedy frequently face a choice that carries grave consequences; here Agamemnon's decision leads to his murder inside the palace.

This scene is one of the climaxes of the play and offers a striking example of the rich symbolism at the heart of Greek tragedy. Here, the symbolism is conveyed by the dramatic action as much as the words. Over the course of this speech and Clytemnestra's subsequent response, Agamemnon walks along the purple tapestries. The two speeches span thirty lines, so that his progress into the palace, where death awaits him at the hands of Clytemnestra and her lover Aegisthus, is a movement that unfolds at a measured and solemn pace, thus heightening its significance. What should have been the triumphant homecoming of the victor at Troy is turning into his death-march into the den of his treacherous wife. The attention of the audience is focused on the figure of Agamemnon, his symbolic action and the vivid stage prop of the purple tapestries which, from the elevated vantage point of most of the audience, would have been visible stretching across the floor of the *orchestra* and up to the double door of the *skene*.

Relatively little movement occurs in most Greek tragedies, but what action takes place is imbued with great significance. Scenes of rapid movement, such as Chrysothemis' breathless entry in Sophocles' *Electra* to announce the return of Orestes or the agonizing writhing of the hero in his *Philoctetes*, are generally reserved for moments of extreme pathos and would have been all the more startling. Such movements were commonplace in comedy, where characters rushed around all over the place, thereby adding to the humour.

Other significant dramatic acts

Tragedy, according to Aristotle, is chiefly about plot: 'plot is the first principle and, so to speak, the soul of tragedy' (*Poetics* 1450a); the plot, as he goes on to discuss, is communicated through words and through gestures (1455a). It is this marriage of verbal and non-verbal communication that is a hallmark of Greek drama. The direction that a play is taking, and the choices that its characters are facing, are discernible through their words *and* through their movements. We have already seen a significant act played out on stage in the scene from Aeschylus' *Agamemnon*; in it, Agamemnon's fateful entrance into the palace is accompanied by his description of the act. Although modern theatre might let the stage action do the talking, in Greek drama, words and stage-action usually go hand in hand.

Although Greek tragedy usually spared the audience the horror of seeing acts of death performed before their eyes, many other significant acts were enacted before the audience's eyes. Supplication and prayer are among the most common.

Supplication

In the following extract from Sophocles' *Philoctetes* (performed in 409 BC), the abandoned Philoctetes supplicates Neoptolemus in the hope that he will save him from his miserable life as an outcast by taking him with him (468–87).

5.5　By your father, child. By your mother – by anyone you love back home, **I beg you as your suppliant**. Don't leave me here on my own like this. You have seen 470 how lonely I am, how I live, you have heard how great my troubles are. Let me come along. I know it's no easy matter to have something like me on board, but do it. A good man hates to do wrong. Noble deeds bring glory. Your failure to act 475 would bring dishonour, but if you do this, child, you will earn yourself **a glorious reputation** if I get to the land of Oeta alive.

Come, your suffering will hardly last a day. Be brave. Put me where you like, but 480 take me: the hold, the bows, the stern – wherever I am going to cause **least trouble to the others**. Say 'yes', child, **I beg you, by Zeus, the suppliant's god**. Do what I ask. I am on my knees to you, though I am a poor, helpless cripple. Just don't leave 485 me here, alone, far from any trace of man.

- Aristotle defined tragedy as 'a *mimesis* (imitation) of an action which is serious, complete and great … in dramatic, not narrative form' (*Poetics* 1449b). He went on to argue that the particular actions that make up the play's plot are the most important and only indispensable elements of tragedy. In what ways is *seeing* actions such as supplication actually performed on stage different from *hearing* about such actions, as we do in other genres such as epic poetry?

I beg you as your suppliant　supplication was a formal act in which one person put himself at the mercy of another. He indicated this by kneeling before the supplicated, clasping his knees with the left hand and his chin or beard with the right. This gesture indicated that the suppliant was weaponless and appealing for pity to the supplicated, who was constrained by the act of supplication to consider the request.

a glorious reputation　Philoctetes and Neoptolemus belong to an 'honour' culture in which a glorious reputation was all-important. Neoptolemus is the son of Achilles, the great Greek hero of the Trojan War who exemplified the heroic ideal when he chose a short and glorious life over a long life of anonymity.

least trouble to the others　Philoctetes had been abandoned on the deserted island of Lemnos by the Greeks en route to Troy because he had been bitten by a snake, and his cries of anguish and the smell of his gangrenous wound had become more than they could bear.

I beg you, by Zeus, the suppliant's god　Zeus is the god who oversees justice; the vulnerable of society such as beggars and suppliants particularly enjoy his protection. In the lengthy appeal of which this passage is an extract, Philoctetes adds many reasons why Neoptolemus should take him along. His words themselves invite pity, but the sight of the once great hero now crippled and reduced to a bestial existence, kneeling before the young Neoptolemus, reinforces the empathy felt towards Philoctetes by the chorus, Neoptolemus, and no doubt the audience watching the play.

Sophocles' *Oedipus the King* was a play particularly admired by Aristotle for its tightly constructed plot; he specifically singled out for praise (*Poetics* 1452a) the following scene, which sets in motion Oedipus' tragic reversal from revered king of Thebes to disgraced exile. Earlier in the play, the prophet Tiresias identifies Oedipus as the murderer of King Laius; Jocasta, however, recalls an oracle that declared that her first husband Laius would be killed by his own son; since her only son by Laius was exposed to die as an infant, she concludes that Oedipus, her new husband, cannot be the murderer of Laius. In this passage (911–34), Jocasta comes out of the palace and prays to Apollo.

5.6	JOCASTA	Lords of our land, the thought has come to me
		To visit the shrines of the gods, taking in my hands
		These wreathed branches and offerings of incense.
		Oedipus is overwrought; his mind is prey
		To every kind of anguish. He does not judge
		Fresh events by past ones, like a man of sense,
		But listens to anyone who talks of terrors.
		So, since my own advice is achieving nothing,
		I turn to you, Lycean Apollo – you are nearest –
		In supplication with these tokens of prayer:
		Give us deliverance from this plague and cleanse us.
		For now we are all afraid when we look at him
		And see his terror – the helmsman of our ship.
	MESSENGER	Could you tell me, friends, where I will find
		The palace of your ruler, Oedipus?
		Best of all, tell me his whereabouts, if you know.
	CHORUS	This is his house, friend, and the master is at home.
		Here is his wife, the mother of his children.
	MESSENGER	May she always be happy, and surrounded by
		Happiness, as the wedded wife of a man like him.
	JOCASTA	The same to you, my friend, for you deserve it
		For these kind words. But tell me why you are here:
		What do you want from us? What do you wish to tell us?
	MESSENGER	Good news for this house, and for your husband, lady.

Line numbers: 915, 920, 925, 930

This is one of many moments in Greek drama in which a character prays to the gods. In Greek religion, prayer followed a defined pattern. It was accompanied by offerings, as here, intended to make the deity receptive to the prayer. Prayers to the Olympian gods were uttered aloud while the speaker stood with hands raised aloft. Often such prayers were addressed to a statue of the divinity in question, present in the acting space, as was likely for this scene. Her offerings placed on the altar in the *orchestra*, as well as her posture and gestures to the statue of the god, would have been a visual accompaniment to the words of her prayer.

Jocasta asks Apollo to deliver Thebes from the plague that is ravaging it and to set Oedipus' mind at ease. Her prayer is immediately followed by the arrival of a messenger from Corinth, who announces that he brings good news for the king and his family. It seems from the way the scene is structured that he arrives as a direct answer to Jocasta's prayer. The messenger's announcement that King Polybus is dead and that Oedipus is set to become the next king of Corinth seems to Jocasta to confirm that Oedipus' fear of killing his father is misplaced. However, the messenger then reveals that Oedipus is actually the adopted son of Polybus and the plot continues to unfold until Oedipus finally comes to know the terrible truth: he *is* the son of Laius and Jocasta, and has in fact killed his father and married his mother.

The audience is aware that Jocasta's confidence is horribly misguided and that the very evidence in which she places her optimism actually points to a dark truth. The tight plot of this play is full of structural **ironies** such as the messenger's arrival 'in answer' to Jocasta's prayer.

Stage props

Greek plays have come down to us without the stage directions that accompany most modern scripts. Since in Greek drama the playwright himself was usually involved in putting on his play, such written directions were not necessary. Although we shall probably never know what else might have been visible on stage in a given play that *isn't* explicitly mentioned by the characters, their words indicate that Greek drama used a wide range of stage properties (or 'props'). The scholar and writer Iulius Pollux, writing in the second century AD, includes daggers, sceptres, spears, bows, quivers, messenger staffs, clubs, lion skins and suits of armour among the objects worn by male characters in tragedy (*Onomasticon* 4.117) – and he is focusing more narrowly on costuming, so omits objects that are carried. Even animals made the occasional appearance: a number of tragedies (e.g. Aeschylus' *Persians* and *Agamemnon*, Euripides' *Trojan Women*, *Electra* and *Iphigenia at Aulis*) bring characters into the *orchestra* on horse-drawn carriages, while in the opening scene of Aristophanes' *Frogs* Xanthias enters riding a donkey.

Some props, such as Heracles' club and lion-skin, are a standard element of a character's wardrobe. Others are incidental to a scene, just as in the boat scene in *Frogs* Charon hands Dionysus an oar and tells him to row. But sometimes props receive sustained attention in a play and acquire symbolic meaning. We have already seen the purple tapestries put to such use in Aeschylus' *Agamemnon*. The bow in Sophocles' *Philoctetes* is another physical object that becomes laden with a rich web of meanings, as Oliver Taplin (1978: 89–93) has argued. It is a magical talisman without which the Greeks are unable to take Troy. It is also a symbol of friendship, a guest-gift given to Philoctetes by Heracles in gratitude for his loyalty. And yet it is also a deadly weapon. The whole plot of the play revolves around Neoptolemus' mission to acquire the bow. When Philoctetes entrusts it to Neoptolemus for safe keeping while he himself is incapacitated by the pain of his leg wound, Neoptolemus is at a crossroads: should he abscond with the bow now in his possession, or should he honour the bond of friendship that led Philoctetes to give it to him? At first he refuses to give it back, and we witness Philoctetes' maelstrom of rage and helplessness. But then he has a change of heart, and he returns the bow to its now angry and dangerous owner. The restoration of the bow softens Philoctetes' attitude towards Neoptolemus somewhat, and he promises to protect him against the Greeks if they come to punish him; but he is still not willing to come to Troy. The impasse is resolved when Heracles makes a *deus ex machina* intervention and gets Philoctetes to accompany Neoptolemus: the two of them, Heracles adds, are to fight side-by-side like a pair of lions, each protecting the other, and Troy will fall a second time to Heracles' bow (he himself had taken Troy in an earlier expedition). Throughout the play, the bow has been a visual symbol of the choices that both Neoptolemus and Philoctetes face and a token of the ties of friendship between them.

Another play of Sophocles that uses a stage prop to powerful effect is his *Electra*. In this play, all Electra's hopes are pinned on the return of her brother Orestes to avenge their father's death. Orestes does return home at the start of the play, but he does so in secret, and devises an elaborate scheme that will put his enemies off guard and allow him access to the palace. First his Tutor arrives with news that Orestes has been killed in a chariot race. Then Orestes himself appears, carrying an urn that supposedly contains the ashes of his own body (1113–42).

5.7	ORESTES	He is dead, and we come carrying	
		His meagre remains in a little urn, as you see.	
	ELECTRA	O misery! Then this is it, **clear before my eyes!**	1115
		I see **a burden of grief within my reach.**	
	ORESTES	If you grieve for Orestes' misfortunes,	
		Know that this vessel contains his body.	
	ELECTRA	Stranger, give it to me, by the gods!	
		If this urn conceals him, let me take it in my hands,	1120
		So that I may weep for myself and for my whole family	
		As I mourn these ashes.	
	ORESTES	Bring it here and give it to her, **whoever she is**;	
		This is not an unfriendly request;	
		She must be close or related by blood.	1125
	ELECTRA	O last testament to the life of Orestes,	
		The one I loved most dearly! I sent you away with such hopes,	
		And this is how I receive you!	
		Now I hold you in my hands, as nothing,	
		But you shone brightly, child, when I sent you away.	1130
		How I wish I had left this life	
		Before I stole you away with these hands,	
		Rescued you from murder,	
		And sent you off to a foreign land.	
		You could have died here on that day	
		And taken your allotted place in the tomb of our ancestors.	1135
		But instead, you have perished miserably,	
		Far from home, an exile in a foreign land,	
		Separated from your sister.	
		I never washed and dressed your body – ah me! –	
		With loving hands, nor gathered up	
		Your pitiful remains from the blazing fire, as is right;	1140
		They were strangers' hands that tended you.	
		And now you arrive, a tiny weight in a tiny urn.	

clear before my eyes   the whole scene is loaded with dramatic irony. Electra focuses on the urn and fails to recognize her brother who is carrying it. In an earlier scene, her sister Chrysothemis rushed on with the joyful news that Orestes had returned, which she had deduced from the clear evidence of his footprints and a lock of his hair left at the tomb of their father, but Electra refused to believe her, having already heard from the Tutor that Orestes was dead.

a burden of grief within my reach   Electra's description of the lightness of the ashes not only contrasts with the weight of grief that they cause but also reminds us of the transience of human life, so easily passing from dust to dust.

whoever she is   Orestes does not yet recognize his sister.

Electra's lament over the urn continues until Orestes, overcome by pity, can no longer contain himself and feels compelled to reveal his identity. However, Electra, disappointed so often in the past, is slow to believe him (1202–24).

5.8

ELECTRA	You're not some relative of ours, are you?	
ORESTES	I would tell you, but are these women our friends?	
ELECTRA	Yes, they are. You can trust them.	
ORESTES	Then let go of this vessel so that you can learn everything.	1205
ELECTRA	No, by the gods, don't do this to me, stranger!	
ORESTES	Do as I say – you will never regret it.	
ELECTRA	**By your beard, I beg you**, don't take away my dearest treasure!	
ORESTES	I tell you, I won't let you keep it.	
ELECTRA	Ah! I am lost, Orestes, if I may not bury you.	1210
ORESTES	Be careful what you say! You have no reason to mourn.	
ELECTRA	How can I have no reason to mourn my dead brother?	
ORESTES	You are wrong to address him like that.	
ELECTRA	Am I even deprived of my right to mourn the dead?	
ORESTES	You are deprived of nothing; but this is not for you.	1215
ELECTRA	Of course it is, if this is Orestes' body that I hold.	
ORESTES	But it is not Orestes' – except in fiction.	
ELECTRA	Then where is the poor man's tomb?	
ORESTES	There isn't one – the living do not have tombs.	
ELECTRA	What are you saying, young man?	1220
ORESTES	All that I say is true.	
ELECTRA	Then is he alive?	
ORESTES	If I am alive, then yes.	
ELECTRA	So are you he?	
ORESTES	Look at this signet ring –	
	My father's – and see if I speak the truth!	
ELECTRA	O dearest light of day!	
ORESTES	Dearest indeed, I bear witness!	

> **1** Why is Electra so reluctant to hand over the urn, and why is it psychologically important that she do so?
>
> **2** This scene features two significant props that carry symbolic import – the urn that Electra holds and Agamemnon's signet ring that Orestes wears. What meanings are inherent to each and how does each contribute to the development of the plot?

By your beard, I beg you the sight of Electra clinging to the empty urn as she clasps her brother in supplication but fails to recognize him is a memorable moment of theatre.

Aristophanes' plays feature a still wider array of props; indeed, their crazy multiplication is a characteristic feature of his comedies. Often these are everyday items put to at times bizarre new uses, as in the following extract from Aristophanes' *Lysistrata* (742–57). Produced during the Peloponnesian War (411 BC), it offers a novel plan for bringing about peace: the women of Greece sign on to a sex strike and refuse to sleep with their men until a peace treaty is signed. This extreme measure, however, takes its toll on the women too. Here Lysistrata (the leader of the women) catches yet another woman trying to sneak out of their stronghold on the Acropolis to get together with her husband.

5.9	THIRD WIFE	O **goddess Eileithyia**, delay my delivery until I get off **holy ground**.
LYSISTRATA	What is this nonsense?
THIRD WIFE	I'm just about to give birth.
LYSISTRATA	But you weren't pregnant yesterday!	745
THIRD WIFE	Well I am today! Please, Lysistrata! Send me home to the midwife at once!
LYSISTRATA	What are you talking about? What's in here? It's hard.
THIRD WIFE	It's a boy.
LYSISTRATA	By Aphrodite, it's more like something metallic and hollow. Let me take a look. You silly girl, you mean you're pregnant with the **sacred helmet**?	750
THIRD WIFE	But I *am* with child, I swear!
LYSISTRATA	Then what is this for?
THIRD WIFE	In case I went into labour while I was still on the Acropolis. I'd climb into the helmet and give birth – like a pigeon!	755
LYSISTRATA	Nice try! But it's obvious what's going on.
	You'll just have to stay here until your helmet's **naming day**!

---

1 How would you characterize the type of acting that this scene calls for?

2 How might an actor communicate the wife's sexual frustration?

---

goddess Eileithyia   Eileithyia was the goddess of childbirth.

holy ground   the Acropolis was sacred to the gods, so the woman pretends to want to avoid giving birth there.

sacred helmet   she has taken the helmet from the statue of Athena in the Parthenon!

naming day   a festival at which the newborn baby was welcomed into the home and carried around the hearth.

Masks

To act in a Greek play was to wear a mask. Every actor and chorus-member in every play – tragedy, satyr-play and comedy – wore one. Judging from the many vase-paintings in which actors stand with mask in hand as they prepare for a performance, the act of wearing a mask was synonymous with the experience of acting; and dramatists, both tragic and comic poets, creatively exploit the dramatic possibilities that the mask offers.

For a modern thespian to understand the place of masks in Greek theatre requires a good deal of effort since masks have largely been marginalized in the modern theatre. We might expect a clown to wear a mask, or a harlequin figure perhaps. Sometimes a villain will appear in a mask, or a monster will take to the stage as a giant puppet. But we expect to be able to see the faces of the main characters; the face gives them their distinct identities and helps us to relate to them. We associate masks with contexts other than the theatre. The masks that tourists bring back from vacations in far-off countries may titillate them with visions of grisly human sacrifice, make them feel more connected to their Earth Mother through an artefact associated with a more 'primitive' and 'unspoilt' culture, or suggest the spontaneous exuberance of a tribal festival.

The evidence for the use of masks in ancient Greece does, on the face of it, invite similar responses. We hear of masks used in religious contexts such as the festival of Artemis Orthia in Sparta. A number of vases represent Dionysus in the form of a mask erected on a pole in scenes that are non-theatrical (perhaps part of the spring-time Anthesteria festival). And there is evidence that masks were dedicated to Dionysus after theatrical performances. However, we must be careful not to exaggerate the religious significance of their use in drama because of their use in other, overtly religious contexts. Our ancient sources and the evidence of the plays themselves suggest that other, more practical concerns were at least as important in explaining their use in the Greek theatre.

Masks in tragedy

The fragment of a vase from Taras dating to *c.* 340 BC, which also appears on the cover of this book, shows an actor holding his mask in his right hand, while in his left hand he holds a sword that serves as a prop. Sometimes such props help identify a character and are simply an extension of his costume (e.g. as a warrior or a king); at other times they play a crucial role in the plot itself (e.g. the sword with which Ajax commits suicide in Sophocles' *Ajax*).

This vase-painting offers an excellent close-up view of a tragic actor. That he is a tragic actor is clear from the *kothornoi* or tragic boots that he is wearing (not visible in the close-up on the cover). As well as the knee-length sleeved undergarment or *chiton*, tragic actors also wore an outer garment or cloak (either a *himation* or *chlamys*). Here the actor wears his *himation* draped around his left arm and partly concealing the sword.

The masks worn in Athenian theatre were full-head masks. In this case the mask has been given a thick shock of white hair with a receding hairline and a full white beard. Each mask projects a certain persona, in this case conferring age and dignity on the character, perhaps here a king or wise old messenger (the tasselled fringe on the *chiton* may suggest that his character is a non-Greek). Such masks were constructed of stiffened linen, cork or wood. Although Greek men were normally bearded, this actor has shaved his beard in order to wear the mask.

- What practical advantages might the wearing of a mask offer, judging from this vase-painting and the facial features of the actor and the mask he is holding?

In the following extract from Aeschylus' *Agamemnon* (1384–94), Clytemnestra is providing an account of her killing of Agamemnon.

5.11   Twice I strike and in the space of two screams
His body collapsed on the spot, and as he lay fallen   1385
I add a third, a thank-you prayer
To Zeus of the Underworld, guardian of the dead.
So he falls, driving the spirit out of him,
And as he gasps out his gushing death-blood,
He sprays me with a dark shower of gory dew,   1390
And I revel no less than the crops in the ecstasy
Zeus grants them when they give birth from their husks.
In this situation, you elders of Argos,
Rejoice, if you would rejoice; I glory in it.

In this scene, performed over the bodies of Agamemnon and Cassandra probably on the *ekkyklema*, Clytemnestra revels in her success. Her confidence is suggested by her use of the number three, which functions as an important *leitmotif* throughout this set of three plays. Just as Zeus is the third and final king of the gods, so Clytemnestra utters the third and final cry, a prayer of thanksgiving to Zeus that her hold on the throne of Argos is now secure. In a vivid if macabre figure of speech that is a horrific perversion of the imagery of fertility, she compares the spray of blood from her dying husband which spattered her to the life-giving rain that falls on crops.

How might her joy be conveyed in masked acting? In naturalistic acting without a mask, the actor could break into a fiendish grin, but this is not possible when the actor is wearing a mask whose expression is fixed. Greek drama does not seem embarrassed by this restriction; in fact, we get many explicit references to facial expression. In Sophocles' *Electra*, for example, Orestes warns his sister Electra after their joyful reunion (1296–9).

> And see that when we enter the house
> Our mother does not find you out
> By your radiant expression; rather, act as if
> You are grieving at the false news of my death.

Electra has been mourning the reported death of Orestes; now her radiant face could tip off Clytemnestra. Electra reassures him that she won't give the game away (1309–13).

> Have no fear
> That she will ever see my face radiant with smiles.
> Prolonged hatred is deep-set in me.
> And besides, now that I have seen you,
> I shall never stop weeping for joy.

First, it is important to realize that the tragic mask is a relatively neutral mask. Unlike the masks of comedy, whose facial features are distorted for comic effect, masks in tragedy have natural facial features. The one prominent feature is the mouth, which is permanently agape to allow the actor's voice to project. This open mouth is ideally suited to communicate strong emotion of any kind. Wild anger, wild grief or wild joy are equally expressed by an open mouth; the particular emotion in a given scene is communicated by the words that are emitted, the tone in which they are spoken, and the body language that accompanies them. This body language was likely to have been more schematized than we are used to in modern naturalistic drama.

So in the scene from Aeschylus' *Agamemnon*, Clytemnestra's jubilation is communicated through her words: 'I revel' and 'I glory' mark her emotion as pure joy, despite the grisly scene at her feet. But her impassioned words would have been accompanied and reinforced by gesture and stance. In this case, her prayer to Zeus invites an upturned face and arms raised in prayer, a posture that would also communicate the pleasurable sensation of feeling raindrops falling on one's face that Clytemnestra evokes in her description of the shower of blood.

In fact, masked acting accentuates the use of gesture and stance: since the viewer cannot use facial expression to read emotion, even slight shifts in posture can signal a change of emotion. And the mask itself can also communicate emotion. An upturned head will suggest confidence, as in this scene, while a drop of the head will communicate dejection. Thus the mask offers a remarkable degree of versatility. The tragic mask in **5.10** allowed a scruffy, balding, ordinary-looking actor to take on the noble bearing of a tragic character. Moments later, the same actor could, if the script required, transform into a female character through a simple mask and costume change. The distinct identities of characters in a play were, to some extent, defined by their masks, which would have been immediately recognizable to an audience familiar with the specific attributes of each mask type. Characters in tragedy were not individuals as we might think of them; their actions were as much defined by their social position and their ancestry as they were by their own personalities. Thus Oedipus was first and foremost a king and member of the royal house of Thebes. And this identity would have been communicated through his mask and regal robes.

Masks in satyr-play

The red-figure bell-krater in **5.12** dates to the early fourth century and comes from Apulia, southern Italy. It shows three choreuts in a satyr-play with their masks, and offers a good close-up view of their costume. They all wear short breeches to which is attached an erect phallus; also visible on the right-hand figure is the horse-tail that hangs from his breeches at the back.

In this scene, we again see the part that the mask played in conveying an identity. However, for chorus-members, it is a shared identity, and the identical appearance of the masks accentuates this. Satyr masks – with their characteristic high forehead, snub noses with flared nostrils, pointed animal ears and long shaggy beard – help transform a cast of ordinary-looking Athenians into the half-animal retinue that dance in honour of Dionysus.

We witness this transformation in progress on this vase. The central and left figures are still out of character and standing at ease. The right figure, however, has donned his mask and begun to dance. And everything about him – from his arched back and tense musculature to his thrust-out pelvis – indicates that he is now impersonating a satyr, a creature that has some human traits about him but whose nature is also fundamentally animalistic. The transformation effected when an actor becomes a character (i.e. someone other than himself) has been seen as a form of *ekstasis* or 'standing outside oneself', a divine inspiration that is a feature of Dionysiac religion. This divine possession has a terrible outcome in Euripides' *Bacchae* because of Pentheus' resistance to Dionysus; but for true worshippers, it is a state that offers temporary release. In other cultures, the wearing of masks plays a key role in festivals in which participants dance and impersonate a character and enter an ecstatic trance. However, in the absence of any direct link between the worship of Dionysus in ecstatic rites and masked acting, readings of theatrical performance in honour of Dionysus as a form of *ekstasis* must be seen as an attractive hypothesis rather than as fact.

5.12

Masks in comedy

In Aristophanes' plays, masks and costumes are an aid to staging the bizarre. Choruses of wasps, frogs, birds and clouds give their name to surviving plays by Aristophanes; and a number of vase-paintings show other animal choruses. And yet these animals talk like humans and contribute to the plot as a human chorus would. Their masks function as a visual reminder of this hybrid identity: they expose them as human actors masquerading as animals rather than concealing their human traits under a full disguise.

The chorus of clouds in Aristophanes' *Clouds* is a good example of this tendency. In a parody of his highfalutin ideas about the cosmos, Aristophanes' Socrates prays to the clouds as deities, asking them to come and receive his sacrifice. From his description of them as 'awesome goddesses of thunder and lightning' (265) we might expect something otherworldly and frightening. But when the chorus of clouds first enter the *orchestra*, the main character Strepsiades seems disappointed by their appearance (340–50).

5.13   STREPSIADES   Tell me, then, what this is: if they really *are* clouds, why do they look   340
like women? For those clouds (*pointing up to heaven*) don't look like these.

SOCRATES   Then what *do* they look like?

STREPSIADES   I don't know for sure; they look rather like unfurled fleeces, certainly not at all like women. But these ones have noses!

SOCRATES   Now, then, will you answer some questions that I have for you?   345

STREPSIADES   Go right ahead – ask me whatever you want.

SOCRATES   Haven't you ever looked up and spotted a cloud that looks like a centaur, or a leopard, or a wolf, or a bull?

STREPSIADES   Sure thing. But so what?

SOCRATES   Clouds can turn into whatever they choose. So if they see a long-haired hillbilly, one of those shaggy types – the son of Xenophantes, for instance – they make fun of his fixations by making themselves   350
look like centaurs.

> • What do you think the point is that Aristophanes' Socrates is making in his response to Strepsiades' concerns?

Most of the characters in Aristophanes' plays, however, are humans; his characters include real-life people (such as Socrates) or thinly disguised alter egos (the Paphlagonian tanner in Aristophanes' *Knights*, for example, represents the powerful Athenian demagogue Cleon, who came from a family of tanners). It is quite likely that some of these characters wore masks that were caricatures of the people that they represented, with features exaggerated for comic effect. An off-hand remark in Aristophanes' *Knights* seems to be the exception that proves the rule: a slave remarks that the Paphlagonian is not wearing a lifelike mask (of Cleon), since 'none of the mask-makers was willing to make a mask of his likeness, out of fear' (230–2). Even if it is in fact true that Aristophanes did not put the Paphlagonian on stage in a mask resembling Cleon, this seems to be an anomaly that the dramatist uses against Cleon as part of his characterization of him as a vindictive strong-man terrorizing the population. He certainly did not do this to protect Cleon's identity, since the target of his criticism is patently clear. In fact, the slave himself goes on to make this point (233): 'in any case he will be recognized, since the audience is clever'.

The writer Platonius (date unknown) remarks in his *On Differences between the Comedies* that masks in Old Comedy resembled the individuals they were parodying; in Middle and New Comedy, he says, masks were given distorted features so that the Macedonian rulers would not mistake them as representations of themselves. In fact, Platonius oversimplifies the issue. For a start, not all masks in New Comedy have noticeably distorted features: the young girl mask, for example, tends to have attractive if well-defined features, with no obvious distortion. Furthermore, the distorted features that he cites for Middle and New Comedy (the sweeping eyebrows, and the enlarged mouth) are already present in masks of Old Comedy.

Vase-paintings of scenes from Old Comedy such as the Choregos Vase (**1.7**; see also **3.3** and **3.4**) show actors wearing masks that are somewhat larger than life size. Facial features such as protruding chins and hooked noses are exaggerated for comic effect. But other features too are made more prominent: the furrows on a balding forehead are heavily delineated, while the large open mouth is framed by the goatee that encircles it. These features make the mask more readable from a distance (in a similar way, the strong facial features of certain Hollywood actors – Angelina Jolie's prominent lips, Arnold Schwarzenegger's chiselled jaw – are ideally suited for the screen, communication experts tell us). When you consider that, seen from the top row of the theatre, actors would have been thumb-size, the advantages of wearing masks over attempting to communicate through facial expression are readily apparent.

In New Comedy, the exaggerated facial features of comic masks have become an important element of characterization. However, instead of individualized characters such as Socrates or Aeschylus, we now find characters who are recognizable as types. The stern father, the young lover and the crafty slave become staple figures, and each is immediately recognizable through his mask.

The following extract (143–78) is from Menander's *Old Cantankerous* (Greek *Dyskolos*). In this scene, Knemon makes his first entry. He is the father of the girl whom the protagonist Sostratos has fallen for. Unfortunately for Sostratos, Knemon dislikes all contact with people and lives the life of a hermit on his farm, along with his daughter and an old female slave. In fact, Sostratos' slave Pyrrhias has just rushed breathlessly onto stage. When he went to talk to Knemon on Sostratos' behalf, the old man chased him off his property and pelted him with pears!

5.14	PYRRHIAS	Oh! Here he is here himself! I'm off, sir! *You* talk to him.
	SOSTRATOS	I couldn't possibly! I'm always so bad at persuading people when I talk. What should I say to the man? By Zeus, the way he's looking at me doesn't seem friendly at all! How serious he is! I'll step back from the door a bit. That's better! He's walking on his own and shouting! He doesn't seem to be in his right mind. By Apollo and the gods, I'm afraid of him – I might as well admit it!
	KNEMON	That fellow **Perseus** was fortunate in two respects: he had wings and so never had to meet any travellers on the ground; he also had a device with which he turned into stone anyone who bothered him. I wish I could do that now! Nothing would be more common than stone statues all over the place. But as matters stand, life is intolerable, by Asclepius! People are now traipsing all over my property, chattering away! Am I in the habit of wasting time by the side of the road, by Zeus? I don't even work that part of the farm – I steer clear of it because of the passers-by. But now they chase me up onto the hilltops! Oh the thronging masses! Woe is me! Here is another one standing at our door!
	SOSTRATOS	(*aside*) Is he going to hit me?
	KNEMON	A man can't find solitude anywhere – not even if he wanted to hang himself!
	SOSTRATOS	Is he mad at me? Sir, I'm waiting for someone here – we arranged a rendezvous.
	KNEMON	See – just as I said! Do you people think that this is a **stoa**, or the shrine of Leos? If you want to see someone, just arrange to meet him at my door! Sure! And why not build a bench, if you like – or better yet, a council-chamber! Oh poor me! It's abuse of the worst kind, if you ask me.

Line numbers: 145, 150, 155, 160, 165, 170, 175

Knemon disappears into his house.

Perseus the hero Perseus was given winged sandals by Hermes that allowed him to fly through the air. He killed the gorgon Medusa by cutting off her head; it turned anyone who looked at it to stone.

stoa stoas were roofed colonnades, often built in public spaces such as the *agora* or market-place. They were popular meeting-places, offering a shady spot for people to conduct business or even hold philosophical discussions (the Stoics were named after the stoa in which they regularly met). The shrine of the Athenian hero Leos was located in the busy Athenian Agora.

1   How would you describe Knemon's character? If you had to design a mask
    to fit his temperament, what features would you give it?

2   How does Sostratos come across in this scene? What features might his mask
    emphasize?

Masks from New Comedy were popular decorative items, as were terracotta figurines such as the ones shown on p. 17. A small terracotta plaque found in northern Greece and dating to the Early Hellenistic period features six masks; they still show the bright colours with which they were painted. The masks in the top row represent (left to right): the father, the young girl and the slave; in the bottom row are shown (left to right) the young man, the wife and the old crone. These are the main characters of many plays of New Comedy. The young man falls in love with the young girl – the father of one or other of them objects to their liaison, while the slave usually plays the part of facilitator. The old crone is frequently a procuress or madam who serves as pimp to young girls. If this is the case in this cast, then the young girl is likely to be a courtesan (a type of prostitute) – which, in New Comedy, often leads to a recognition scene: the girl was abandoned as an infant and sold as a courtesan, but is then reunited with her family during the course of the play. Thus the mask of the wife may in fact be that of the mother of the young girl.

5.15

Iulius Pollux, writing in the second century AD but drawing on earlier sources, provides an extensive list of different masks, arranged by dramatic genre, as part of his treatment of the terminology of the theatre in book 4 of his thesaurus known as the *Onomasticon*. Although his lists may be overschematized, they give a good indication of the variety of masks and the small differences that distinguished them. The following (4.151–4) is the section that describes the different masks for young women in New Comedy, which follows descriptions of the various masks representing different types of old men, young men, slaves and old women.

5.16   The masks of young women are: the chatterbox, the curly-haired girl, the maiden, the **false maiden**, the second false maiden, the chatterbox with a sprinkling of grey hair, the concubine, the mature courtesan, the little courtesan, the courtesan decked out in gold, the courtesan wearing a bonnet, the girl with a top-knot, the pretty girl with all her hair shorn, the little slave-girl with smoothed-down hair. The chatterbox has long hair, carefully brushed to the side; her eyebrows are straight, her skin is pale. The curly-haired girl differs from the chatterbox in her hairstyle. The maiden has a centre parting to her hair, which she brushes to the side; she has straight black eyebrows and a yellowish pallor to her complexion. The false maiden has a whiter complexion, and has her hair tied at the front. The second false maiden is distinguishable only in that her hair doesn't have a parting. The appearance of the chatterbox with a sprinkling of grey hair is obvious from her name, identifying a courtesan who has retired from her profession. The concubine looks like her, but has long hair. The mature courtesan is of a ruddier complexion than the false maiden, and has curls around the ears. The little courtesan is without adornments and wears a small ribbon around her head. The courtesan decked out in gold has a lot of gold in her hair. The courtesan wearing a bonnet has her head wrapped in a bonnet of many colours. The **top-knot** gets its form through the braided hair, which tapers to a point, from which the girl gets her name. The pretty girl with all her hair shorn is a little slave-girl with her hair cut short, wearing only a white tunic (*chiton*) with a belt. The slave-girl with smoothed-down hair has a parting in her hair; she is flat-nosed and serves as slave to the courtesans; she wears a scarlet tunic (*chiton*) with a belt.

false maiden   this refers to an unmarried girl who has become pregnant, usually as a result of a one-night stand at a festival. Since the Greek word for 'maiden' (*korē*) means both 'unmarried girl' and 'virgin', the term 'false maiden' (*pseudokorē* in Greek) points to the troubled status of being unmarried yet with child.

top-knot   the term literally means 'torch' and is used to describe both the hairstyle created by binding the hair into a top-knot and the girl who wears her hair in this way.

Costume

We have already described the forms of costumes worn in the various genres as we encountered them on vase-paintings (see **1.3** for the costumes of dithyramb; **1.7**, **4.10** and **5.10** for tragedy; **1.6**, **4.11** and **5.12** for satyr-play; and **1.7**, **3.3**, **3.4**, **4.14**, **4.16**, **5.20** and **6.16** for comedy). The costume, along with the mask, gave the audience instant visual clues to a character's identity. When a character first enters, his appearance frequently receives comment as another character makes deductions from his clothing and general appearance. In Sophocles' *Philoctetes*, for example, the outcast Philoctetes immediately recognizes the chorus as fellow-Greeks from their clothing, before they have said a word to him. He urges them not to shrink back, frightened by his wild appearance. His rags and weather-beaten mask communicate the dreadful suffering he has endured more powerfully than anything he could say and might have evoked a gut reaction from the audience too. In Aeschylus' *Persians*, a similarly pitiable scene occurs towards the end of the play. Throughout the play, the fabulous wealth of Xerxes, the great Persian king, has been emphasized, often with reference to the luxurious trappings that he and his army wear. But when he finally makes his appearance, he enters in tatters, having torn his embroidered clothing into shreds out of grief. The enormity of the reversal that he has suffered through the annihilation of his navy at Salamis is visually communicated as the chorus rends their clothing too in anguish for their king.

In comedy, references to clothing are even more frequent and are often made in ways that self-consciously draw attention to the act of dressing-up that is central to theatre. In Aristophanes' plays, in which characters come on in rapid succession, the costumes they wear and the props that they carry give the audience immediate clues to their identity. However, these identities are often fluid: characters often disguise themselves through the use of costume.

Just as props frequently function as components of costuming, so too costumes frequently function as props in both tragedy and comedy, handed from one character to another. In comedy, this often is used to humorous effect, as in Aristophanes' *Frogs* when Xanthias and Dionysus trade off the lion-skin that is part of their disguise as Heracles. But in tragedy, items of clothing are sometimes used in much more deadly ways. In Sophocles' *Women of Trachis*, for example, Deianeira gives Heracles a beautiful robe (a *chiton*) which has been smeared with the blood of the centaur Nessus. She thinks that it will function as an aphrodisiac to rekindle his love for her; but it is in fact a poison that burns through his skin and causes him an agonizing fate. When she finds out what she has done, she commits suicide.

In Euripides' *Medea*, a robe has a similarly devastating effect, this time through a deliberate ruse. Medea is driven to fury by having been abandoned by Jason in favour of a young princess (who remains the anonymous 'other woman' in the play). She summons Jason, pretending to have had a change of heart, and gives her rival gifts as a token of good will (947–58).

5.17   I'll send her gifts, the finest in the world:
A finely woven dress and crown of beaten gold.
The boys will take them. Quickly,   950
Tell a maid to fetch the adornments.
Not once, but countless ways she will be blest:
Winning so fine a man as you to share her bed,
And gaining the adornments which the Sun God,
My father's father, bequeathed to his descendants.   955
Take these bridal gifts, boys, in your hands.
Carry them and give them to the happy royal bride.
It is no contemptible gift she will receive.

The princess accepts the presents, puts them on, and dies a gruesome death, as does her father when he tries to embrace his dying daughter and his flesh also gets eaten away by the poison.

- Why might Euripides have chosen a gown and a crown as the murder weapons in this particular play?

Cross-dressing

The phalluses worn by male characters in Old Comedy not only give playwrights ample opportunity to improvise scenes of sexual humour, they also serve as a reminder of the exuberance and vitality of comedy and were likely part of the carnivalesque temporary suspension of societal constraints that distinguishes festivals from the everyday. Festivals could offer an outlet for women as well as men: in the festival of Haloa at Eleusis, celebrated in honour of Demeter and Dionysus, *women* engaged in feasting and drinking, exchanged sexual vulgarities and even held up sexual symbols. So too in Aristophanes' plays, male characters dress up as women, but female characters also dress up as men.

Male actors getting dressed for female parts in a tragedy.

Aristophanes' *Women at the Thesmophoria* offers an extended sequence of cross-dressing. After Euripides fails to persuade Agathon to disguise himself as a woman and infiltrate the women celebrating the Thesmophoria festival in order to speak in his defence and save him from their wrath (see **3.8**), Euripides' relative comes to the rescue and volunteers for the job. Euripides gets him to take off his cloak (*himation*), shaves off his beard, then asks him to bend over and proceeds to singe his buttocks and crotch. Women normally removed unwanted hair by plucking, but this method gives Aristophanes the excuse for some slapstick visual humour as the relative hops around with his buttocks apparently aflame. Euripides then sets about dressing him for his female role (249–69).

5.18	EURIPIDES	Agathon, since you're not willing to offer your services, at least lend us a dress for this chap here, and a bra – and don't say that you haven't got any!	250
	AGATHON	Here, take! Use them, by all means.	
	RELATIVE	Which should I take?	
	EURIPIDES	Take the **saffron-yellow dress** – but try it on first.	
	RELATIVE	By Aphrodite, I smell a fresh whiff of prick. Fasten it on quickly!	255
	EURIPIDES	Now hand me the bra.	
	AGATHON	Here you go.	
	RELATIVE	Now even out the dress around my legs.	
	EURIPIDES	We need a hairnet and a bonnet.	
	AGATHON	Look here is a **wig that I wear by night**.	
	EURIPIDES	My god, that is just perfect!	
	RELATIVE	But does it fit me?	260
	EURIPIDES	By Zeus, it's just great! Now give me a wrap.	
	AGATHON	Take one from the couch.	
	EURIPIDES	And we need shoes.	
	AGATHON	Here – take mine.	
	RELATIVE	Do they fit me? One likes to have them loose.	

saffron-yellow dress saffron-yellow garments were worn by women at festivals. In Aristophanes' *Frogs*, Dionysus wears a saffron-coloured costume and the soft boots (*kothornoi*) typical of tragic actors along with the lion-skin and club with which he attempts to pass as the macho Heracles. Heracles teases him for looking ludicrous.

wig that I wear by night Agathon probably means that he wears it to go out in at night, perhaps hinting at night-time antics. The Greek word used, which refers to an artificial accessory (it gives us our word 'prosthetic'), can also refer to a mask. It is possible that the actor playing Euripides' relative exchanges his mask for one with feminine features and a woman's hairdo.

AGATHON	You'd know best! Well then, since you have what you need, will someone **roll me** into the house, quick as you can!	265
EURIPIDES	Our man here is a real lady now – at least in appearance! But when you talk, make sure that you use a woman's voice, nice and convincing!	
RELATIVE	I'll try.	
EURIPIDES	Then off you go!	

---

1 How is costume being used in this scene? Would you describe the tone as playfully tongue-in-cheek, or obscene and degrading?

2 As well as their comically distorted masks, male characters in Old Comedy wore body padding to enlarge the belly and the buttocks; on their arms and legs they wore a body-stocking simulating bare skin; and a phallus dangled below the hem of their short *chiton*. How do you think a character like Euripides' relative would have looked once he dressed up as a woman?

3 Agathon has such a full wardrobe in part because he is a playwright. Euripides, another playwright, also clearly enjoys dressing up his relative. There may be a theatrical dimension too to the relative's eagerness to dress up – he may feel that he has some of Euripides' theatrical talent. What other implications does the act of dressing up carry in this scene?

Later in the play, Euripides' relative, disguised as a woman, joins the council of women and speaks up on Euripides' behalf. But when the women hear that a man has infiltrated their ranks, their suspicion falls on him, and he is exposed as an impostor. Apparently cornered, he comes up with a desperate plan: he takes as hostage the baby of Mica, one of the women, and holds a knife to it as he dangles it over the altar and threatens to slit its veins. Mica in turn threatens to burn him alive, and departs to fetch firewood. While she's away, the relative unwraps the swaddling clothes from the 'baby' only to discover that it is not a baby at all and Mica is outed as a fake mother (733–64).

| 5.19 | RELATIVE | What is this? The baby girl turns out to be a filled wineskin – wearing little Persian boots! You hot-headed women, incorrigible drinkers, always finagling a drink, a huge windfall to innkeepers but to us a curse, and the same for **our dinnerware and clothing**! | 735 |

---

roll me   on the *ekkyklema* (see **3.7** and **3.8**).

our dinnerware and clothing   Euripides' relative spouts the kind of misogyny Euripides was accused of by the women in the play: here he brands them as drunkards and claims that their habit prevents them from taking care of domestic duties such as cooking and weaving. These are comic stereotypes of women that Aristophanes recycles for comic effect.

MICA	Throw on lots of firewood, Mania.	
RELATIVE	Sure, throw it on! But tell me something: you say that you gave birth to this?	740
MICA	Yes, I carried it for ten months.	
RELATIVE	You really did?	
MICA	Yes, **by Artemis.**	
RELATIVE	I wonder, was it **a three-cup baby**?	
MICA	What have you done? You shameless man, you've stripped my little babykins!	
RELATIVE	Little babykins? It's not exactly tiny, by Zeus! How many years old – three **Choes** or four?	745
MICA	Round about that, plus a Dionysia. But give it back!	
RELATIVE	No, **by Apollo over there**.	
MICA	Then we'll burn you to a cinder.	
RELATIVE	Go on then, burn away! But the girl will be sacrificed immediately.	750
MICA	NO! I beg you! Do what you want to me – just not her!	
RELATIVE	You have quite the mother's love for your child – but she will be sacrificed all the same.	
MICA	My poor baby! Give me the sacrificial bowl, Mania, so that at least I can catch my baby's blood.	755
RELATIVE	Hold it under it, then: I'll grant you this one favour. (*The relative sacrifices the wineskin.*)	
MICA	Damn you, you're so mean-spirited and hateful!	
RELATIVE	The priestess gets **the skin**.	
CRITYLLA	The priestess gets what?	
RELATIVE	This: catch!	

by Artemis Artemis was a goddess who presided over childbirth as well as other important life stages such as the passage from childhood into womanhood. In Attica there was an important cult sanctuary of Artemis at Brauron.

a three-cup baby the relative is referring to the size of the 'baby' by liquid measurement rather than by weight because he knows that it is actually a wine-skin. The Greek measure translated as 'cup' (*kotulē*) is actually roughly equivalent to half a pint or 250 ml.

Choes the second day of the Anthesteria festival celebrating the new wine. The day was named after the *chous*, another liquid measure (one *chous* equals twelve *kotulai*); festival participants competed in a drinking competition.

by Apollo over there a statue of Apollo was often placed at the entrance of a house to protect it; from this remark, it seems that there is a statue of Apollo in front of the *skene* door.

the skin part of a sacrifice is usually reserved for the priest or priestess (in fact, inscriptions survive that stipulate exactly what portions are to be dedicated to the god and handed over to his priest). Here the hide in question is a wine-skin. The old woman Critylla, who is officiating at the Thesmophoria rituals, hears the mention of a bequest and shows up in an instant to claim her share!

CRITYLLA   My poor Mica! Who robbed you of your daughter? Who poured out   760
            your dearly beloved daughter?

MICA   This scoundrel here. But now that you're here, guard him so that I
            can go and get **Cleisthenes** and denounce this man's crimes to the
            board of officials.

> 1   How are the women characterized in this scene? Do you think they receive a
>   sympathetic treatment?
>
> 2   In what ways does this scene mirror the earlier one from the same play?

This exact scene appears on a red-figure bell-krater from Apulia. It dates to
c. 380–370 BC, some thirty years after Aristophanes first put on the play in
411 BC. A figure straddles an altar; in his right hand he brandishes a knife,
and in the other dangles a wineskin dressed up with little boots! Another
figure approaches holding a large bowl in both hands.

The painting brings to the fore a number of key elements of Aristophanic
comedy. One is the comic appropriation of the sacred. In Greek society, the
altar is a place of refuge, and so it is natural for the relative to seek asylum

5.20

Cleisthenes   an Athenian politician whom Aristophanes ridicules for his sexual orientation
and effeminacy (unlike most men at the time, he apparently did not wear a beard).

The actors   **129**

there; however, the sacrosanctity of the altar is abused by all as first the relative takes the wineskin hostage and threatens to sacrifice 'her' on the altar and then Mica and her fellow women set about turning the relative into a burnt sacrifice.

Aristophanes adds yet another layer of intricacy by writing a scene that parodies an episode from Euripides' *Telephus*. In this tragedy, Telephus comes to Argos to seek healing for a wound; he ends up taking hostage Orestes, the young son of King Agamemnon, and threatening to kill him unless his request is heard. However, what is a scene charged with horror in Euripides' tragedy has been turned by Aristophanes into absurdity, since the seriousness of the act of sacrifice is undercut by the fact that Mica's 'baby' is a wineskin and the blood that is shed is only wine. A decade earlier Aristophanes parodied the same scene in his *Acharnians* (280–357): here Dicaeopolis, facing an angry crowd of citizens of Acharnae, threatens to kill their beloved coal-bucket (coal-mining was an important industry of the region) in order to avoid being stoned.

It is interesting to see the scene through the painter's eyes. He has dressed Euripides' relative in a woman's *chiton* (longer than a man's), but makes it short enough to reveal the male body-tights underneath; thus it becomes obvious that what we have is a man dressing up as a woman. Similarly, the beardless face shows stubble, so we have a visual reminder of the earlier scene in which the relative had his beard shaved off. And the mirror on the wall marks this out as a scene concerning itself with women (or rather, one woman and one man in drag!). What is perhaps most noticeable, however, is that the phallus that male actors usually wear is not visible. The woman approaching him (probably Mica rather than Critylla or an attendant) wears the mask of an old hag.

---

1   What plausible explanations can you think of to account for how this scene on a vase from southern Italy could be remembered so vividly more than thirty years after Aristophanes put it on at Athens?

2   Violating the sanctity of an altar was to a Greek a heinous crime – and yet in comedy such taboos are regularly broken. What might be a modern equivalent? For example, what 'sacred cows' of society do modern comedy-writers use as grist for their humour?

3   What do the facial features of the mask communicate about each of the two characters?

Actors and the rise of the acting profession

Over the course of the fifth century, the part of the actor grew in relation to that of the chorus, the number of speaking actors expanded to three, and actors enjoyed increasing prominence. The increasing importance of the actor can be discerned in a number of changes to the way the dramatic competitions were organized and documented. In the early years, it seems that playwrights often performed in their own plays and that they or the *choregoi* could pick their lead actors. We hear, for example, that the actor Tlepolemus performed exclusively for Sophocles (scholion on Aristophanes' *Clouds* 1267), and we are also told that Sophocles wrote his plays to cater to the strengths of individual actors (*Life of Sophocles* 6). But then a system was instituted in which each playwright was assigned his lead actor or 'protagonist' (the Greek word *prōtagōnistēs* means 'first actor') by lot, probably in an attempt to level the playing field. This may have occurred around 449 BC, when other changes were made and we first find evidence of a separate competition for best protagonist at the City Dionysia (the Lenaea introduced this for comedy around 442 and for tragedy in the 430s). Clearly it made a difference whom you got as your lead actor, and it is not hard to see why – the actor playing a part such as Oedipus in Sophocles' *Oedipus the King* spoke almost half of the total lines; a strong performance in a key role such as this could kindle in the audience the powerful emotional response to the play that seems to have been a key element of ancient theatre.

By the fourth century, star actors had gained celebrity status, judging from anecdotes about them and inscriptions recording the huge sums that they could command. Sometimes they gave performances of chosen sections of a play as solo acts. Some speculate that the three-actor rule, which was strictly observed in tragedy, was intended to allow talented actors to showcase their versatility in playing a range of parts, though practical considerations such as preventing one-upmanship and avoiding escalating costs by standardizing the size of the cast may have also been a factor.

As well as the first, second and third speaking actors (and often one or two more in Old Comedy), plays used mute actors to play silent characters such as attendants, children (in many tragedies a source of great pathos) and minor figures such as Orestes' travelling companion Pylades in Sophocles' *Electra*, present on stage for most of the play, yet silent throughout.

In the early third century, we start to see actors organize themselves into professional guilds referred to as unions of the **Artists of Dionysus**. These troupes of actors were contracted to perform at festivals around the Greek-speaking world and, with their collective bargaining power, gained an impressive list of rights and immunities and could at times play a political role. There were separate, regionally defined guilds (e.g. a guild of Athens, of Cyprus, of Ionia, of Egypt); by the Roman imperial period (perhaps as early as the first century AD), these had organized into a 'world guild' that engaged in correspondence with emperors and enjoyed what seems to have been a mutually advantageous relationship: emperors such as the philhellene Hadrian granted the organization royal patronage and accompanying privileges, while in turn the emperor was celebrated as a patron of the arts by an influential organization in the business of communicating to the masses by putting on spectacular shows. Thus, although we tend to think of Greek theatre's heyday as the fifth century, there is ample evidence that it continued to be a thriving art-form and an important export of Greek culture for a very long time. One reason for this success was the huge reach of the Greek language, which was spoken as the lingua franca throughout the eastern Mediterranean. Inscriptions record the inauguration of new festivals, celebrate winners in a wide range of performance genres (some dramatic, others musical) and testify to the considerable financial investments that cities made in these events, which were often accompanied by athletic competitions. Just as in modern sports such as tennis and golf the top-ranked players play in the major tournaments rather than in challenger events, so too the star professional actors tended to perform at the more prestigious events, which also offered greater prize money.

6 The audience

Athenians are tireless theatre-goers, the third-century BC geographer Heraclides of Crete remarked (*On the Greek Cities* 1.4). Their love of the theatre, he added, is a habit that distinguishes Athenians from the inhabitants of other cities. Heraclides was certainly right – Athenians flocked to the theatre in droves. But it was not only Athenians but also foreigners that attended performances, especially at the City Dionysia, which over the course of the fifth century seems to have attracted increasing international attention. This may in part have been caused by the requirement for allied states to send an embassy to Athens along with their tribute, which was put on display in the *orchestra* of the theatre (see discussion on p. 25).

There is evidence that, in the Roman period at least (second century AD), citizens sat by tribe. Foreigners, resident aliens and probably even some slaves also attended. Whether women were also present is a question that is still debated, though there is increasing consensus that they did, if in smaller numbers and perhaps at the margins. That the ancient sources' attention was focused on the dominant male part of the audience should hardly surprise us given what we know about Athenian society. Along with the priest of Dionysus, certain elected officials and other VIPs had a right to the front seats.

People had to pay to attend – the price during the fourth century seems to have been two obols (see **6.11**). At some point (maybe as early as the fifth century), a dole was instituted which distributed a fixed monetary handout (the ***theōrikon***, plural ***theōrika***, literally festival-money) to every Athenian present in Athens at the time of the festival, thus making attendance possible for the poor as well as the rich.

Characters in Athenian comedy frequently address the audience directly in a bid to keep their attention and win their favour. Interaction with the audience was a two-way affair: the audience reacted noisily to the performances and behaved in other ways that might be considered disruptive in modern times.

Audience size

In this extract from Plato's *Symposium* (175e), Socrates debates the nature of wisdom; if it can be passed from one person to the next, he muses, then he stands to gain much by sitting next to Agathon at the dinner-party (they are celebrating Agathon's victory in the tragedy competition).

6.1   I think that I would be filled with much fine wisdom from you. For **my own wisdom is meagre** and as debatable as a dream; but yours is brilliant and is making great advances; young though you are, it shone forth so brilliantly and so prominently two days ago in the presence of **more than thirty thousand Greeks**.

Audience composition

Aristophanes often has characters in his play address their audience directly (modern talk-show hosts and cabaret comedians will use the same technique to draw in their audience). His comments are our best available clues as to the composition of the theatre audience at Athens during the fifth century; however, the interpretation of his offhand remarks is hotly contested. For example, several of the following extracts have been used to argue both for and against the presence of women in the theatre.

---

my own wisdom is meagre   the Delphic oracle had declared Socrates to be the wisest of mortals; Socrates came to realize that the truth of the oracle lay in his awareness of his ignorance. Here he contrasts his own form of knowledge, the so-called 'Socratic technique' that demolishes the preconceptions of his dialogue partners by asking them a series of probing questions, with that of the tragedian Agathon, whose plays aim to showcase his talent and educate his audience.

more than thirty thousand Greeks   Athenaeus (*Learned Banqueters* 217a–b) says that Agathon won this victory at the Lenaea competition of 416 BC, but his statement has been contested by scholars, since the description of the audience as being composed of Greeks rather than Athenians suits the City Dionysia better than the Lenaea, whose audience was primarily Athenian (see **6.13**). However, we must remember that Socrates is paying Agathon a compliment rather than providing a factual account; as Simon Goldhill (1997: 57–8) points out, Athenian theatre is frequently described as playing to an audience of 'the whole city' or even 'all Greece' – in fact, 30,000 is Herodotus' figure for the total number of adult male citizens of Athens (5.97). This too is likely to be the reason for the inflated estimate of the number present in the audience. At its largest after the Lycurgan rebuilding, the theatre of Dionysus only had seating for approximately half that number and, although it is certainly possible in an outdoor theatre for an overflow audience to extend beyond the fixed seating, we need not assume that this was the case.

In the following passage from Aristophanes' *Birds* (785–97), the leader of the chorus of birds describes to the audience the advantages of having wings.

6.2   There's nothing better or more fun than sprouting wings. If, for example, **one of** 785
you spectators had wings, and grew hungry and **bored with the tragic choruses**,
he could fly out of here, go home, have lunch, then fly back here again and join us
on a full stomach. Or imagine **a certain Patrocleides** in the audience needed to 790
take a crap. He wouldn't have relieved himself into his cloak; instead, he could fly
off, fart, catch his breath, then fly back here again. And if there's anyone among
you who is having an affair, and sees the lady's husband **in the seats reserved for
the council**, he'd take to the air, fly off, screw her, then fly back here again. **So isn't** 795
getting a pair of wings invaluable?

- This passage from Aristophanes' *Birds* is often cited as evidence that women
  didn't attend theatrical performances at Athens. What other possible
  explanation(s) could account for the imaginary scenario presented in this speech?

In this extract from Aristophanes' *Women at the Thesmophoria* (389–97),
Mica delivers a tirade before her fellow assembly-women (in a mock female
version of the Athenian assembly, in which only adult male citizens could
participate), complaining about Euripides' representation of women.

---

one of you spectators   instead of insisting on the dramatic illusion that the stage action
constituted the only acknowledged reality, comedy capitalized on the possibilities that
came through the fluid interchange between characters and audience, and between the
setting of the play and the theatrical space in which it was performed.

bored with the tragic choruses   in the City Dionysia, the competition for best comedy
was followed by three days of tragedies. Comedy often poked fun at tragedy like this.

a certain Patrocleides   Old Comedy often lampooned individuals in the audience.
Sometimes famous people were satirized, but other remarks ridiculed everyday people
for very ordinary traits: being fat, thin, gluttonous or oversexed. The *Birds* was performed
at the City Dionysia (in 414 BC); five comedies were performed in one day, thus testing
the stamina of the audience.

in the seats reserved for the council   the council (or *boule*, consisting of 500 members,
fifty from each tribe) was the body responsible for the oversight of much of the day-to-
day running of the administration. For example, it was responsible for drawing up the list
of Athenian citizens eligible for selection as judges for the dramatic competitions.

So isn't getting a pair of wings invaluable?   the leader of the chorus of birds is trying
to persuade the audience of the value of wings; meanwhile, the two main characters,
Athenians who are joining the birds in founding the colony of Cloudcuckooland, are off
stage acquiring a pair.

6.3 With what wickedness has he not smeared us? **Where has he not slandered** 390
us? Wherever there are spectators, tragic actors and choruses, he calls us lover-
coddlers, man-crazies, wine-guzzlers, traitresses, gossipers, sickos, man's greatest
scourge. So as soon as **our husbands come home from the benches,** they give us 395
suspicious looks, and immediately start looking around for some hidden lover.

> In the following extract from Aristophanes' *Peace* (956–67), produced at the City
> Dionysia in 421 BC, the farmer Trygaeus, who has managed to secure peace (the
> play was performed just before the Peace of Nicias during the Peloponnesian
> War), is conducting a sacrifice to the statue of the goddess Peace.

6.4 TRYGAEUS   Now then, you take **the basket and the lustral water** and circle the
altar quickly, left to right.

SLAVE   There, I've been round! What next?

TRYGAEUS   Here! I'll take this brand and dip it in. (*To the sacrificial lamb*) **Hurry
up and nod!** And you there (*to the slave*), hand me some of the
barley-corns. Wash your own hands, then give me the basin; and 960
toss some of the barley-corns to the spectators.

Where has he not slandered us?   in this satirical treatment, Euripides is being blamed
for defaming women by putting on plays in which women behave badly. There is some
evidence to suggest that his plays were indeed seen as risqué: for example, the first version
of his *Hippolytus*, which portrayed a brazen Phaedra indecently propositioning her step-
son Hippolytus, was said to have been poorly received, leading Euripides to write a second
version in which a modest Phaedra tries to overcome her passion for her step-son.

our husbands come home from the benches   does the scenario presented by Mica imply
that the wives stay at home while their husbands attend the theatre? It certainly seems to
suggest that at least some (and probably the majority) did, although it is also true that she
seems to know a lot about Euripides' plays! That the majority of women stayed at home
does not necessarily imply that they all did; given that the theatre could hold only a small
fraction of the total population of Athens, the majority of adult male citizens would not
have been able to attend the performances either.

the basket and the lustral water   this is a comic re-enactment of a sacrifice. Participants
take a handful of barley-corn, which is then thrown over the altar, the sacrificial victim and
the earth; after this, the sacrifice is performed.

Hurry up and nod   it was hoped that the sacrificial animal would nod in assent to its
sacrifice; its head was then sprinkled with barley before it was killed.

toss some of the barley-corns   this could be a stage-direction to the character to throw
some corns into the audience (similar free give-aways of paraphernalia often occur at
modern live events); other Aristophanic plays make similar mentions of fruit and nuts (see
6.19). Or it may be a parody of the practice of throwing barley before a sacrifice. Perhaps
the women don't get any because they are sitting right at the back of the theatre, out of
reach. But the word for barley-corn is also a slang word for penis. How might this passage
be understood in the light of this double-entendre? And does it suggest that women were
present, or that they were at home, awaiting their husbands' return in the evening?

SLAVE	There you go!	
TRYGAEUS	You've already given them out?	
SLAVE	By Hermes, yes I have. There isn't a spectator who doesn't have a barley-corn.	965
TRYGAEUS	The women don't have any.	
SLAVE	Well, the men will give them some tonight.	

In another extract from Aristophanes' *Peace* (50–3), two slaves open the play by setting the scene.

6.5   SECOND SLAVE   And I will explain the plot to the children, to the young men, to the grown men, to the eldest men and especially to **these supermen**.

The slave groups his audience by age, starting with the youngest, but makes no mention of women. Is this a significant omission, indicating that women were not present at performances of comedy? Or are they not mentioned because they were considered to be marginal? It is certainly the case that boys and young men are not normally mentioned either.

Jeffrey Henderson (1991: 143) describes the 'notional identity' of the audience as male – that is, adult male citizens were the audience-members that mattered to the playwright and who were normally addressed. Athenian oratorical habits developed in the assembly (where only adult male Athenians could participate), so the equivalent of the modern 'ladies and gentlemen' in ancient Athens was 'men' (*andres*). Athenian society seems to have been particularly repressive to women when its practices are compared to those of other Greek city-states, and seems to have made invisibility into a major female virtue. Thucydides (2.46) has Pericles give the following advice to the women in the audience in his famous funeral speech delivered in honour of the Athenian war dead:

> If I am to speak of female virtue to those of you who will now be widows, it can be comprised in this brief admonition: your greatest glory is not to fall short of your nature, and to be least talked of among the men, whether for good or for bad.

- What conclusions do you think we can draw from the extracts from Aristophanes' plays included above (**6.2–6.5**) about the presence or absence of women at theatrical performances during the fifth century?

---

these supermen   the slave is probably pointing at dignitaries in the front row, who are both old and venerable.

6.6   When he (Alcibiades) was *choregos*, he would **parade in a purple robe** and amaze not only the men **but also the women** when he entered the theatre.

Seating arrangements

6.7   Here **you must sit** and watch from the **outermost block of seats**, like foreign women.

---

parade in a purple robe   one of the main events of the City Dionysia festival was a procession which passed through the Agora and ended up in the sanctuary of Dionysus below the theatre, where bulls were sacrificed at the altar, after which the dithyrambs took place in the theatre. Since the *choregos* was the main sponsor of a production, it is not surprising that he occupied pride of place. Alcibiades, brought up in the household of Pericles and taught by Socrates, was a prominent and charismatic Athenian who advocated the ambitious Athenian expedition against Sicily. His magnificent costume was not unique – the orator Demosthenes tells us (*Against Meidias* 22) that he planned to wear a golden crown and robe embroidered with gold when he paraded as *choregos*.

but also the women   here the presence of women in the theatre is explicitly mentioned, though the events being described are the preliminaries to the theatrical performances and not the plays themselves.

you must sit   since the feminine form is being used, it is clear that the women in the audience are being addressed. Given the title of the play, *Gynecocracy* ('Women Power!' or literally 'Rule by Women'), it seems likely that the character speaking is trying to point out to the women in the audience their inferior status, perhaps to sting them into action.

outermost block of seats   the term used is *kerkides*, referring to the wedges into which the seating was divided by the vertical stairways. In the theatre of Dionysus at Athens at this time (following the Lycurgan rebuilding), there were twelve sets of stairs dividing the *theatron* into thirteen *kerkides* (see pp. 51 and 53). Some believe that the thirteen blocks of seating were divided in such a way that women (or foreigners) occupied the outermost block on either wing, while citizen men (divided into ten tribes – see p. 139) occupied ten blocks, with the central block perhaps going to those with special privileges, such as foreign dignitaries and ephebes (young men in military service).

A number of tokens have come down to us that some scholars have interpreted as theatre tickets. Made of lead or bronze and shaped like coins, they often show an emblem such as the head of Athena on one side, while on the other they bear letters that may be the abbreviation of the names of tribes. Symbols connected to the theatre such as masks and tripods appear on some, and the use of such tickets in Roman times is fairly certain. The earliest such tokens date to the fourth century BC. If they in fact name the tribe to which the ticket-holder belongs, this may indicate that Athenian (male) citizens sat by tribe, with each tribe occupying a separate seating block. This would make sense for the dithyrambic performances in which each tribe enrolled its own chorus, fostering the kind of rivalry that we hear about and would expect; but it makes less sense for tragedies, satyr-plays and comedies, and it is perhaps significant that Aristophanes, who makes many impromptu remarks about the audience, doesn't make any mention of seating by tribe in his extant comedies. Another possible explanation is that marking tickets by tribe was a measure to ensure fair distribution of the limited number of available seats among the tribes rather than a system to divide seating by tribe.

6.8

> 1   When ancient sources mention the presence of women in the theatre audience, what seem to be their reasons for doing so?
>
> 2   Why were women marginalized in, or perhaps even excluded from, such an important event in the life of the Athenian *polis*?

Prohedria

Aristophanes' comedies are full of direct addresses to the audience similar to those in the previous scene – sometimes an individual like Patrocleides (**6.2**) is mentioned by name; at other times, groups such as the council (see **6.2** and **6.5**) are singled out for mention. These dignitaries were given priority seating (*prohedria* or 'the right to front row seats') at the front of the *theatron*, and so were

particularly accessible for characters to interact with. Similarly, if you go to an event nowadays at which a comedian or magician is performing a live show, you had best choose a seat in the middle of a back row if you're shy and don't want to be picked by the performer to be incorporated into the routine. Marble thrones inscribed with the titles of the priests for whom they were reserved and dating from the Roman period line the entire first row of the *theatron* and extend four rows up in the central wedge; pride of place in the centre of the front row went to the priest of Dionysus (see p. 51).

The priest of Dionysus' throne, inscribed 'of the priest of Dionysus Eleuthereus'.

In the following extract from Aristophanes' *Frogs* (296–304), Dionysus himself is travelling down to the Underworld to bring back one of the playwrights to save Athens. The god, disguised as the macho hero Heracles, is accompanied on his journey by his impudent slave Xanthias. Dionysus is full of bravado – until his slave reports seeing monsters.

6.9

DIONYSUS	Where should I run?
XANTHIAS	Where should *I* run?
DIONYSUS	**Priest, save me**, so I can drink with you later.
XANTHIAS	Lord Heracles, we're done for!
DIONYSUS	Man, don't invoke me, I beg you, **don't say my name**!
XANTHIAS	All right then, Dionysus!

300

Priest, save me Xanthias claims to have heard and then seen a huge shape-shifting monster. Dionysus takes it to be the Underworld monster Empusa. Terrified, he runs to the priest of Dionysus seated on his throne in the front row of the audience. His desperate plea to his priest for help is a comic reversal, since normally the priest would invoke the god. Prayers frequently included promises of gifts if the prayer were answered. Here Dionysus (god of theatre) promises the priest that, if he saves him from being eaten, he will join him at the party to celebrate the play's victory.

don't say my name Dionysus is wearing the lion-skin of Heracles in a bid to come across as a fearsome hero; but when danger presents itself, he doesn't want anybody to notice his presence.

DIONYSUS	That's even worse!
XANTHIAS	(*To the imaginary Empusa*) Off with you now! Come over here, boss!
DIONYSUS	What is it?
XANTHIAS	Courage, man! Everything's turned out fine, and we can say, **as Hegelochus did**, 'After the storm I see once more the weasel.' Empusa has gone!

---

1   Who are the butts of this scene's jokes? Does this surprise you? Why may Aristophanes have directed his humour at them?

2   How do you think the interaction between the actor playing Dionysus and the priest of Dionysus sitting in the front row might have been staged (try to think up a humorous dramatization)? Do you think the priest saw this coming? How might he have reacted?

Along with priests and council-members, a number of other groups seem to have enjoyed the privilege of *prohedria*, including archons, generals, ephebes (young men on military service, who seem to have occupied their own section) and honoured guests such as foreign dignitaries.

The following extracts illustrate how this privilege could become a bone of contention.

Aeschines, who held a grudge after Demosthenes put him on trial for his part in the peace negotiations with Philip of Macedon, seized the opportunity to get back at him by seeking to indict Ctesiphon in 330 BC for his motion to honour Demosthenes at the City Dionysia with a gold crown in recognition for his service to the state. Aeschines accuses Demosthenes of serving the interests of Philip of Macedon, not those of Athens. He seeks to prove his point by describing Demosthenes' extravagant treatment of the Macedonian delegation at the City Dionysia (*Against Ctesiphon* 76).

6.10   It remains for me to describe his flattery. Demosthenes, citizens of Athens, though a council-member for a year, can be shown to have never once before invited a delegation of ambassadors to the seats of honour; that was the first and only occasion. He set down cushions and spread purple rugs, and at dawn led the ambassadors into the theatre, so that he was even hissed for his disgraceful and flattering behaviour. And when they departed, he hired for them three pairs of mules and escorted the delegation as far as Thebes, making our city a laughing-stock.

---

as Hegelochus did   the actor Hegelochus made a notorious slip of pronunciation in his performance of Euripides' *Orestes*: he meant to say 'I see the calm' (for which the Greek word is *galēnē*), but it came out instead as 'I see the weasel' (*galē* in Greek)!

Demosthenes, in his defence speech, responds to Aeschines' charges and makes accusations of his own, suggesting that it was Aeschines who was in collusion with Philip (*On the Crown* 28).

6.11   He [Aeschines] attacks me because, as a member of the council, I proposed that the ambassadors should be received. What should I have done? Proposed that those who came for this very purpose – to hold negotiations with you – *not* be received? Should I have ordered the **theatre manager** not to assign them seats? If I had not moved my motion, they would have watched from **the two-obol seats**.

Aeschines denounced Ctesiphon's motion on other counts as well. It was illegal, he declared, since Athenian law expressly stipulated that such acts of recognition should take place before the assembly (*ekklesia*), except in the case of foreign crowns (that is, crowns bestowed on Athenians by foreign city-states or rulers). Clearly by this time the theatre had become an alternate venue for such acts of recognition and Aeschines is insisting on the letter of a law that has fallen into abeyance. Here he details some of the practices that, he claims, the law was designed to curb (*Against Ctesiphon* 41–3).

6.12   When tragedies were being performed in the city, certain people would make proclamations without gaining the authorization of the people: some would be crowned by their tribe, others by the men of their deme; others would have the herald announce that they were setting their household slaves free, making Greece witness to the fact. And, the most invidious practice of all: those who got a post representing a foreign city-state, had it publicly proclaimed that they were being crowned – by the people of Rhodes, or of Chios, or whatever state it happened to be – on account of their excellence and manly virtue. And they did this not

---

theatre manager   the theatre manager (Greek *architektōn*) was responsible for the running of the theatre. He received the income that was generated by the cost of admission and in turn paid operational expenses, hoping in the process to turn a profit. Those granted *prohedria* by the state did not have to pay for their seats; Demosthenes' rhetorical question implies that it was standard practice to grant *prohedria* to official foreign delegations. *Prohedria* did not grant an individual exclusive use of a particular seat, but rather gave him the right to claim a front-row seat on arrival, ousting the person occupying that seat if necessary.

the two-obol seats   i.e. the paying seats (two obols being the cost of a ticket). The *theorikon*, the dole instituted to offset the cost of admission, is listed by some sources as being two obols and by others as 1 drachma (i.e. six obols). Every citizen was entitled to claim it, and he was not obliged to spend the money on a theatre ticket. Some ancient sources attributed its introduction to Pericles, though our earliest contemporary evidence for it comes from the fourth century.

like those who were crowned by your council (*boule*) or by the people, who first sought your consent and then had their motion carried, thereby laying up for themselves a great store of gratitude. Instead, they themselves sought out the honour, **without any decree coming from you**. The effect of this practice was that the spectators, *choregoi* and performers were all inconvenienced, and those who were proclaimed in the theatre received greater honours than those who were crowned by the people.

---

1 We don't honour citizens for their public service by conferring gold crowns. What are modern ways in which citizens are publicly recognized, and where do these acts take place?

2 Why do you think that the theatre was such a popular venue for public acts of recognition?

3 What objections are raised to the use of the theatre for such acts?

4 The ceremonies that took place in front of the theatre audience included the following: the ten generals poured opening libations; the tribute of allied city-states was put on display; announcements were made by a herald publicly recognizing individuals for their service to the state; ephebes whose fathers had been killed in the line of duty and who had been raised at the city's expense were presented in full armour. What do these various events have in common?

The City Dionysia as an international event

We have already seen how the delegations of city-states were officially received at the City Dionysia. But it seems that other foreigners attended too, and that the City Dionysia was a chance for the city to display her democratic and cultural credentials by hosting – and participating in – an event put on before the eyes of all Greeks. In this respect it differed from the Lenaea, as is noted in Aristophanes' *Acharnians*.

---

without any decree coming from you Athens was a radical democracy; it was the duty of every citizen to participate in civic affairs, whether by voting in the assembly, doing jury service or even just attending the theatre! But even in democratic Athens, certain individuals such as Pericles or Alcibiades rose to prominence, often because they had superior oratorical skills or because their wealth allowed them to spend lavishly on public projects and thus become noticed. As long as they were believed to have received their status through the will of the people (Greek *dēmos*), such conspicuous privileges as *prohedria* or the conferral of crowns were seen as legitimate. But it is not hard to see how these privileges could be potentially divisive if they were perceived to have been granted by a faction or sought out by the individual.

The main character in *Acharnians*, produced in 425 BC, is Dicaeopolis (whose name means 'just city'). He gets the god Amphitheus to negotiate a private peace with Sparta after he fails to persuade the Athenian assembly to consider diplomacy over war. His scheme angers the chorus of old men of Acharnae. They pelt him with stones, until he finally persuades them to let him be heard (497–507).

6.13   Do not be angry at me, gentlemen who are watching, that, **though I am a beggar**, I am about to address the Athenians about the city **while putting on a comedy. For even comedy knows what is right.** What I will say is controversial but nevertheless 500 right. **This time at least** Cleon will not accuse me of maligning the city in the presence of foreigners: this is the Lenaea contest, and we are by ourselves. The foreigners aren't here; **the tributes and delegations** from our allied cities haven't 505 yet arrived. At the moment we are by ourselves, the wheat without the chaff – I consider the **metics** to be the bran of our population.

---

though I am a beggar   Dicaeopolis has borrowed some rags from Euripides so that his appearance will arouse their pity.

while putting on a comedy. For even comedy knows what is right.   the implication is that discussion of important matters such as what is right and wrong for the *polis* might be thought more appropriate to tragedy than comedy. The word that Dicaeopolis uses here for comedy (*trugōdia*, a word derived from 'wine-dregs') is a deliberate word-play on tragedy (*tragōdia*).

This time at least   it seems that Cleon brought Aristophanes before the council, accusing him of slandering Athens in front of her allies by putting on the *Babylonians* at the previous year's City Dionysia. Dicaeopolis is quick to point out that this play is being performed at the Lenaea festival in January, with no foreigners present. Conviction for slander could result in loss of civic rights. However, as Stephen Halliwell (1991: 70) concludes, comedy seems to have enjoyed 'a virtual, though not a legally defined, immunity to the law of slander which was probably in existence throughout the **classical** period'. This might not have stopped Cleon from taking Aristophanes to court, but it is also clear that Cleon's attempted lawsuit did not stop Aristophanes!

the tributes and delegations   allied city-states were required to send a yearly tribute to Athens as a contribution to running the navy; the tribute was put on display in the theatre and the delegations would attend the plays.

metics   metics were resident aliens; they had to perform military service and pay taxes, but couldn't vote. At Athens, they made up a sizeable portion of the population (as much as 20 per cent of the total population including slaves). In his metaphor, Aristophanes describes Athenians as the grain and foreigners as the chaff (the husks that are discarded through winnowing); the metics are the bran – though rough, it is left in with the grain. They participated in the City Dionysia, parading in the opening procession dressed in scarlet robes.

This passage is informative in a number of ways. It gives us a picture of the audience composition at the Lenaea and City Dionysia. It seems that at the Lenaea the playwright could be more politically risqué than he could at the City Dionysia, when Athens was presenting her public persona to her allies. Dicaeopolis goes on to blame the war on Athens and satirizes the trivial matters that led to its outbreak. This is perhaps all the more surprising in a time of war, when freedom of speech is often curtailed and when people are usually most staunchly patriotic. However, as Eric Csapo and William Slater (1994: 165) point out, this freedom of expression does not appear to have been a privilege enshrined in law but rather a liberty that playwrights took at their own risk.

Playing to the audience

Playwrights who were selected by the archon to perform their plays at the dramatic festivals at Athens were competing to win, so it is hardly surprising that, in comedy at least, we find undisguised attempts to play to the audience.

In this extract from Aristophanes' *Clouds* (518–27, 534–52), the leader of the chorus tries to win the favour of the audience by contrasting this sophisticated play with the low-brow entertainment offered by its rivals.

6.14 Spectators, I will speak the truth to you without reservation – I swear by Dionysus who reared me. So may I win the prize and be thought clever, since I took you for 520
a clever audience and thought this the most sophisticated of my comedies, and so thought you should get the first taste of this play, which cost me a lot of work. And yet **I was defeated** by vulgar men, though I didn't deserve to lose. I blame 525
that on you clever ones, for whom I took all the trouble. But nevertheless I will never willingly betray you the clever ones ... So now this comedy of mine, **like the fabled Electra**, has come on a quest, hoping to find somewhere a clever audience. 535

I was defeated   Aristophanes took third and final place with the *Clouds* in the City Dionysia of 423 BC; it seems that these comments of the chorus-leader in the **parabasis** (see p. 180) belong to a partially completed revision of the script for a later restaging, in which Aristophanes complains about his play's poor reception; he makes similar comments about the play in his *Wasps* (1044–7), put on the following year, in which he describes it as 'the best comedy ever' and accuses his audience of having betrayed him.

like the fabled Electra   in Aeschylus' *Libation Bearers*, Electra visits the tomb of her dead father and recognizes the lock of hair left there by her brother Orestes, a token that leads to her recognition of her long-lost brother. Here, the chorus-leader, comparing his comedy to this tragic heroine, describes her ('comedy' is a feminine noun) coming in search of her lost loyal and sophisticated audience.

For she will recognize her brother's lock of hair, if she sees it. Look how modest she is by nature; for a start, she has not come dangling any **leather appendage** stitched on, red at the tip and thick, to make the children laugh. Nor does she mock bald men, nor dance the *kordax*; nor does she have an old man bashing the other fellow with his stick while he speaks his lines in order to cover up bad jokes; nor does she charge onto the stage brandishing torches and shouting 'Iou! Iou!' Instead, she has come relying on herself and her script. And I too, being a poet of the same kind, don't give myself airs, and don't try and fool you by putting on the same material two or three times; no, I have the skills to be able to bring you fresh forms of comedy every time, each unlike the other and all of them clever! When **Cleon** was at the peak of his power, I was the one who hit him in the belly; but I didn't think it right to jump on him again when he was down. As for the others, as soon as **Hyperbolus** lost his hold on power, they have not stopped trampling on the poor fellow – and his mother too!

540

545

550

---

1 In the above passage, why does the speaker make such a point of addressing 'the clever ones' in the audience?

2 How does he characterize the plays of his rivals? Which of these same tendencies have you seen in Aristophanes' own plays?

3 What are we to make of the chorus-leader's claim that male characters in comedies wear phalluses 'to make the children laugh'? What other reasons, more fundamental to comedy, might there be why phalluses are worn?

4 What serious points underlie what you have read of Aristophanes' comedies so far?

---

leather appendage   male characters in Old Comedy (including Aristophanes' own plays) typically wore a phallus. Here the chorus-leader characterizes his comedy as wearing the modest costume of a tragic female character, probably pointing at the chorus of female clouds who (not surprisingly!) would not be wearing phalluses.

kordax   an obscene dance of Old Comedy that seems to have been associated with drunkenness and lewdness.

Iou! Iou!   an exclamation of distress. Aristophanes claims that he doesn't have to resort to any of the gimmicks that his rivals try to use to cover up their weak scripts – in fact, he himself uses many of these same tricks.

Cleon   a powerful public speaker, an influential political figure and at times a sensationally successful general, Cleon was from the same deme as Aristophanes and was frequently the butt of his jokes; he was killed in battle in 422 BC (another clue that this speech belongs to a revision after the original performance of the play in 423 BC); even his *Peace*, produced in 421 BC (after Cleon's death), continues to poke fun at him.

Hyperbolus   Hyperbolus was an Athenian demagogue who rose to power after Cleon's death. Aristophanes goes on to accuse his rival comic poet Hermippus of attacking Hyperbolus and to accuse both Hermippus and Eupolis of plagiarism.

Tragedy does not usually directly acknowledge the audience (though at Euripides, *Orestes* 128–9, it seems to do so). Sometimes the audience seems to function as an extension of the internal audience of the play, thereby drawing in the spectators.

> One such case occurs in Aeschylus' *Eumenides*. Here the scene is set at Athens; Athena has just summoned a jury of Athenians to hear the Furies' case against Orestes. As the actors playing the non-speaking parts of the Athenian jury members file into the *orchestra*, Athena delivers the following words to 'the whole city'. Many assume her words are directed at a stage crowd of citizens brought in for this scene, but the audience could just as readily fulfil this function (566–73).

6.15   Herald, give the signal and call the crowd to order; and let the shrill Etruscan trumpet, filled with human breath, send its piercing call into the gathering. For while this council-chamber is filling, it is fitting that the whole city – **and these** 570 **too** – be silent and learn of my eternal ordinances, so that the case may receive a fair trial.

> This play is the only surviving tragedy actually set in Athens, and it celebrates Athens as a city where anyone – even a killer like Orestes – can receive a fair trial. At the end of the play, the Furies are clothed in the scarlet robes of metics (symbolizing the incorporation of these alien divinities into the city) and are escorted by Athena, the jurors and a retinue of Athenian women to their new home at the foot of the Areopagus in a torch-lit procession.

Other plays also cast Athens or Athenians in favourable terms. In Euripides' *Medea*, for example, the Athenian king Aegeus offers Medea refuge when he hears that she is being banished from Corinth. In Euripides' *Trojan Women*, the Trojan refugees hope that they will be sent to Athens rather than to Sparta or elsewhere. And even plays in which Athens is not explicitly mentioned implicitly affirm Athenian values. For example, the behaviour of kings such as Creon in Sophocles' *Antigone* and Oedipus in his *Oedipus the King*, who rush to judgement and who stifle dissent, affirms values such as debate and freedom of speech that are central to Athenian democracy. It is important to note, however, that this is not invariably the case – in Euripides' *Hippolytus*, Theseus, king of Athens and Athenian hero extraordinaire, is portrayed as cruel and quick to judge his own son, though he eventually admits that this was wrong.

---

and these too   it is likely that Athena accompanied her words with a gesture that made it clear to whom she is referring, probably the parties involved in the case (Orestes, Apollo and the Furies).

Comedy often makes use of a torch-lit procession to end a play. But instead of the grand and rather solemn procession that marks the end of *Eumenides*, the characters of comedy leave the theatre in a rowdy revel, sometimes announcing their intention to throw a party to celebrate the play's anticipated victory and even inviting the audience to join them. Thus the closing scenes of many comedies remind us of the festival context in which they were performed and acknowledge the importance of the audience in any live performance.

A calyx-krater from Apulia in southern Italy dating to *c.* 400–390 BC shows such a scene; an actor wearing the padded costume and distorted mask typical of comedy carries a giant torch and gesticulates off in front of him as he turns, seemingly to invite others to follow him. The huge cloak draped over his arm may parody the ornate robes worn in festival processions, though here it trails dangerously in front of his leading foot, giving the viewer the sense that this reveller is bound to trip on it. The vessel on which the scene is painted is a mixing bowl for wine, well suited for such a party scene.

6.16

Audience response

Theatre in the modern world is often seen as a highbrow activity; even whispering in the audience is likely to draw dirty looks. The original Athenian audience was much more rambunctious – more like an audience in Shakespeare's day, who might even throw eggs at characters from the pit.

The second-century AD writer Pollux mentions in his review of theatrical terms some of the typical reactions of an ancient audience (*Onomasticon* 4.122).

6.17   The practice of hitting the benches with their heels was called 'heel-banging'; they did this whenever they wanted to get rid of someone [i.e. an actor]; they would also hoot and hiss for this purpose.

Drinking appears to have been a mainstay of the festival of Dionysus (god of wine as well as of the theatre); another ancient author, Philochorus (Athenian historian of the third century BC), writes in his *Atthis* (preserved in Athenaeus' *Learned Banqueters* 464f).

6.18   The Athenians, at the festivals of Dionysus, would go to the show after having first dined and drunk wine, and would watch it wearing wreaths on their heads; and **wine** was poured and **snacks** were served throughout the festival; as the choruses came into the theatre, people poured wine, and they poured wine again when they were marching out at the end. This is attested by the comic poet Pherecrates, who says that up to his own time the spectators were not left without food.

Comments in Aristophanes' plays suggest that the distribution of snacks might have sometimes been part of the entertainment. The following example comes from the opening scene of his *Wasps*, performed at the Lenaea in 422 BC (54–66). The slave Xanthias is speaking.

6.19   Now then, time to tell the audience the plot! But first, here are a few short words   55
        of introduction. You mustn't expect anything overly grand from us – nor, on

---

wine it is not clear from the wording whether the chorus-members were being served wine as well, but this was entirely possible. Such indulgence in wine would not have seemed irreverent, but rather another way in which participants allowed themselves to be possessed by the god, as they did when acting in his honour.

snacks foods such as nuts, raisins and figs were eaten during the show and wine was consumed. In an impromptu remark, Aristotle (*Nicomachean Ethics* 1175b) noted that 'in the theatre, those who are eating snacks do so most when the actors are bad'.

the other hand, any jokes stolen from **Megara**. We don't have a couple of slaves with baskets tossing out nuts among the spectators, or **Heracles done out of his dinner**; we don't even have **Euripides** as the target of abuse, and even when **Cleon distinguishes himself** (pure luck!), we won't make mincemeat of the same man twice. We have a little plot that has a point: **no more intellectual** than you yourselves, but more sophisticated than hackneyed comedy. (*He goes on to lay out the plot.*) 60 65

> The opening of the *Wasps* is typical of most of Aristophanes' plays. Rather than launching into the plot right away, the two slave characters Sosias and Xanthias begin by exchanging a few pleasantries – a riddle and a few tongue-in-cheek bad jokes, puns and clichés. This practice is not unlike that in television talk-shows, where the host often begins with a warm-up routine before launching into the programme proper. It would give the large and boisterous audience time to settle down without missing any important plot details.

- What do you think is Aristophanes' purpose in including these 'few short words of introduction'?

Megara the town of Megara, to the west of Athens, is often mentioned as having a tradition of comedy and even credited with having invented comedy (e.g. Aristotle, *Poetics* 1448a). Perhaps it was even an influence on Athenian comedy, as is suggested in this comment; here 'Megarian jokes' seem to imply jokes that are commonplace and low-brow.

Heracles done out of his dinner a gluttonous Heracles was a mainstay of comedy; Aristophanes uses him to comic effect in his *Birds*, where Heracles comes to Cloudcuckooland as part of the delegation of gods and is eager to come to terms with the birds so that he can enjoy the banquet that will follow.

Euripides although Euripides' plays were hugely popular later in antiquity, they met resistance during his lifetime, being viewed as new-fangled and even subversive; Aristophanes pokes fun at him in his *Acharnians*, *Women at the Thesmophoria* and *Frogs*.

Cleon distinguishes himself Xanthias' comment about sparing Cleon a second drubbing is disingenuous: the play is set in front of the house of two citizens: one, called Philocleon (literally 'Love-Cleon'), is addicted to jury duty; his son, Bdelycleon ('Hate-Cleon'), has him under house arrest to prevent him sneaking off to the lawcourts, where Cleon furthers his career by prosecuting his opponents.

no more intellectual Aristophanes satirizes intellectuals – people such as Socrates, whom the general public seem to have considered dangerously clever. In turn, intellectuals such as Plato mistrusted the theatre audience; his disdainful comments about its unruly behaviour and poor taste betray his prejudices against radical democracy.

Tragedy does not have the same sort of preamble as comedy; it usually gets straight down to setting the scene, though sometimes it does so in innovative ways that must have surprised the audience. For example, Euripides' *Iphigenia at Aulis* (if this prologue is in fact original to the play) opens with a troubled Agamemnon handing over a letter to his old servant in the dead of night. It would seem that tragedy could more easily command its audience's attention from the start.

We have already considered (pp. 57–8) how the playing space may have enhanced the audience's degree of engagement. But what exactly might an ancient audience-member have gained from watching drama? The following extracts offer a variety of answers to this question.

The pleasure of anticipation

> The most famous analysis of this topic is that of Aristotle in his *Poetics* (1448b). His account of the pleasure that humans derive from *mimesis* has already been mentioned (**1.4n**, p. 6), but deserves further discussion in this context.

6.20   This is why people enjoy seeing images, because by looking at them they are able to infer and figure out what each thing is – for example, that this person is that one. For if one doesn't happen to have seen something beforehand, the pleasure derived from it won't stem from its *mimesis*, but from its artistry, colour, or some other such factor.

> For Aristotle, the intellectual pleasure derived from looking at an artistic representation of something and recognizing in it what is being depicted is universal.

Later in his *Poetics* (1450a), Aristotle goes on to identify the reversal (***peripeteia***) and the recognition (***anagnōrisis***) as 'the components of the plot by which tragedy has the greatest effect on the soul'.

His appreciation of these two plot elements of tragedy is not hard to understand given his theory of *mimesis*. Recognition scenes, in which one character in a play will come to recognize another's true identity, offer the audience too the intellectual pleasure of watching the character correctly interpret the evidence and realize that 'this person is that one'. Often the audience has long known the truth, so that the satisfaction gained from the recognition scene that resolves the plot has been preceded by another form of intellectual pleasure: the anticipation derived from seeing the recognition coming. Thus to fault tragedy for giving away its plot is to misunderstand it; if it does not offer its audience the kind of suspense that comes from not knowing what will happen next (and tragedies *do* sometimes take unexpected turns), it offers instead the suspense that comes from knowing a truth of which the characters are still unaware and watching the plot unfold from this position of knowledge.

Emotional involvement

But Athenian drama did not just entertain and intellectually engage the spectators.
It also moved them. Ancient sources that describe the audience's reaction to the
plays that they saw (especially tragedy) emphasize the intensity of the feelings that
they evoked.

An interesting example is a remark made by the fifth-century historian
Herodotus. It forms part of his account of the capture of the town of Miletus
(a Greek town on the Ionian coast in modern Turkey) by the Persians in
494 BC. After commenting on the failure of the people of Sybaris (the state
with the closest ties to Miletus) to commiserate with the Milesians on their
misfortune, Herodotus contrasts their behaviour with that of the Athenians
(*Histories* 6.21).

6.21   The Athenians expressed their deep grief at the capture of Miletus in many ways,
but particularly in this: when Phrynichus composed and directed a play called *The
Fall of Miletus*, the audience burst into tears; he was fined a thousand drachmas for
reminding them of their own misfortunes, and they decreed that no one should
put on the play in the future.

Unlike the Sybarites, who fail to show the compassion befitting their close
connection with the Milesians, the Athenians react strongly to Phrynichus'
play. The wording suggests a surprising degree of empathy, especially since at
the time of production Athens herself had probably not yet been sacked by
the Persians, as happened in 480 BC.

Athenian tragedy generally seems to have preferred to set its plots away from
Athens and in the remote past. Nevertheless (or perhaps because of this practice),
the audience-members seem to have shown a great capacity for empathy. It is also
apparent that they didn't insist on a strict divide between 'reality' and 'fiction' and
allowed themselves to respond emotionally to what they were seeing on stage.

In the following famous sentence from his *Poetics* (1449b) Aristotle attempts a definition of tragedy and describes its emotional effect on its audience.

6.22 Tragedy, then, is the imitation of an action that is serious, complete and sizeable, expressed in mellifluous language of distinct kinds in its separate parts, in dramatic and not in narrative form, effecting through pity and fear the **katharsis** of these emotions.

> Elsewhere in his *Poetics*, Aristotle fleshes out what he means by the various elements of this definition. He believes that a tragedy should represent serious subjects – that is, characters of high moral stature (1448a), like the subjects of epic and unlike the lower sorts represented in comedy. Its plot should be complete – that is, have a clear structure with a beginning, middle and end (1450b) – and be of a suitable magnitude (1450b–1451a) – not trivial, but also not so big that it can't comprise a cohesive unit. Its diction should be graceful and suit the particular section, whether the spoken dialogue of an episode or lyrics of a choral ode (1449b). Unlike epic, tragedy acts out its plot instead of narrating it (1448a).
>
> The final clause of his definition is perhaps the most intriguing and certainly the most controversial. Aristotle later explains that it is through witnessing the reversals of fortune that characters undergo that the audience experiences the emotions of pity and fear: pity is felt for characters who undeservedly suffer a misfortune, while fear is felt when these characters remind us of ourselves (1453a). It appears that for Aristotle pity and fear are the appropriate response to the suffering of tragic characters, and in turn accomplish the *katharsis* of these emotions. What is meant by *katharsis* in this context is widely debated – some have interpreted it as meaning 'release' or 'purging', others as 'purification'; what is clearer is that, for Aristotle, these emotions are an integral and valuable part of the audience's experience and that theatre-going is a healthy activity.

> • How do Aristotle's views on theatre and its effects compare with those expressed in Plato's works (see **6.19n**)? With which viewpoint do you have greater sympathy?

Democratic debate

'We are the only people,' said Pericles to the citizens of Athens in his famous funeral oration as recorded in Thucydides (2.40), 'who consider a man who is completely uninvolved in politics to be leading not a quiet existence, but a useless one.' Athens was a participatory democracy. Among its core values was a belief in the right to speak freely and a belief in equality before the law. Policy was debated by the body of citizens in the assembly, while court cases were tried before a jury of peers. The

Athenian males who flocked to the theatre, then, were well trained in listening to competing arguments. They were called on to use the same evaluative skills as members of the theatre audience. Often in tragedy, characters face difficult choices – Neoptolemus (in Sophocles' *Philoctetes*) must decide, for example, whether to follow orders and acquire Philoctetes' bow through deception or act nobly and risk jeopardizing the mission at Troy and incurring the displeasure of the army. Often, too, characters champion competing viewpoints – in Sophocles' *Electra*, for example, Electra believes that right behaviour is a moral absolute that must be followed regardless of consequences; her sister Chrysothemis just as fervently urges that potential consequences should be taken into account, and that a moral decision is one that leads to the greatest good. Many plays include a formal debate scene (Greek *agōn*) that draws on the arguments and rhetorical techniques of the lawcourts – in Sophocles' *Electra*, for example, Clytemnestra and Electra engage in one such debate about whether Agamemnon was culpable for the sacrifice of his daughter Iphigenia.

In Sophocles' *Antigone*, Creon (king of Thebes) and his son Haemon engage in a heated argument prompted by Creon's decision to punish Antigone (who is betrothed to Haemon) for burying the body of her brother Polynices who fought against his own city. Antigone faces a slow death walled up in a cave. The issues at stake are complex: Creon insists on loyalty to the *polis*; he refuses to give special treatment to any wrongdoer, even to his son's betrothed. Antigone feels compelled to obey the unwritten laws of the gods requiring proper burial, which, she believes, carry more weight than human decrees; and she puts her obligations to her family before loyalty to the *polis*. In this scene, Creon has just urged his son to show his true colours by remaining loyal to his father and city. Haemon replies that, though the city is too frightened of Creon to say anything that he wouldn't like to hear, it mourns in secret for Antigone and considers her act to be worthy of praise (719–45).

6.23	HAEMON	Let your anger go, and allow change. If I may offer an opinion, young as I am, I say that it would be best for man to be born perfect in wisdom; otherwise – and it does not tend to turn out so – it is good to learn from those whose words are wise.	720
	CHORUS	My lord, if what he says is timely, it is right that you learn from him – and for you, Haemon, to learn from your father; for you have both spoken well.	725
	CREON	So are men of my age to be taught sense by a man of his?	
	HAEMON	In nothing that is not right. If I am young, judge not my age, but rather what I do.	
	CREON	And what you do is honour those who break the law?	730
	HAEMON	I would not tell you to honour traitors.	
	CREON	Is that not the disease that has infected her?	
	HAEMON	The united people of Thebes say not.	

CREON	Will the city tell me how I must rule?	
HAEMON	You see how you speak? As though *you* were the child!	735
CREON	Should I rule this land for others than myself?	
HAEMON	It is no city at all that belongs to one man.	
CREON	Does the city not belong to its ruler by law?	
HAEMON	You'd make a good king of an empty country.	
CREON	This man, it seems, is fighting on the woman's side.	740
HAEMON	If you are a woman! My concern is for *you*.	
CREON	You worthless boy! Will you argue with your father?	
HAEMON	Yes, because I see you mistaken about what is just.	
CREON	So I am mistaken to respect the power I wield?	
HAEMON	Yes. You do not respect it when you trample on the gods' honour.	745

In exchanges such as this one, the chorus often functions as a neutral third party, but rarely as arbiter indicating whose case is more valid. Nor does the playwright weigh in with authorial comments, though sometimes the plot will reveal the negative consequences of a choice – as in this play, where Creon's change of mind comes too late to prevent the deaths of Haemon and Antigone. Often it is left to the audience to judge between the competing claims of the characters; in tragedy as in real life it is rarely a clear-cut matter of a right viewpoint pitted against a wrong one. This scene, like many others, reaffirms the value of debate in reaching wise decisions.

1   What social and political issues might this scene have raised in the minds of members of its original audience?

2   Unlike other venues for debate such as the lawcourts and the assembly, the theatre was attended by young boys (as well as grown men) and plays were seen as an important part of their education. How might this exchange between Creon and Haemon have been perceived by (i) a teenage boy in the audience and (ii) his father?

3   Do playwrights have an obligation to their audience to teach virtue? Should the good characters in plays win out in the end? This question applies to any creative artist (novelist, artist, songwriter / pop star).

Theatre and everyday life

Much of what we learn about the theatre comes from incidental mentions in ancient sources. Theophrastus (*c.* 370–286 BC) was a philosopher who was the successor to Aristotle as the head of the Lyceum at Athens; his *Characters*, reflecting his interest in behavioural psychology, provides character sketches of thirty personality types. His teachings may well have influenced Menander, who is said to have studied under him (Diogenes Laertius 5.36–7) and whose plays are peopled with stock characters exhibiting many of the same traits. Although the behaviour of the characters is obviously exaggerated, the work nevertheless offers many valuable vignettes of everyday life and offers insights into what was seen as socially acceptable and unacceptable behaviour.

> In the following series of extracts, the character types may be drawn from everyday life, but the examples make frequent reference to the ways in which these different types behave in the theatre, clearly a venue at which the audience itself was on display.

6.24   **The Flatterer** (2)   [The flatterer] is the first of the guests at a dinner party to praise the wine, and then keeps on going: 'How luxuriously you dine!' and, picking up something from the table, says, 'Now this – this is outstanding!' And he asks his host if he is cold, and if he would like something to wear, to wrap around him. And he says this leaning over and whispering in his ear. He glances at him even when he is talking to others. At the theatre he takes away **the cushions** from the slave and spreads them down himself.

6.25   **The Obsequious Man** (5)   In the theatre, whenever there is a show, he [the obsequious man] sits near the generals ... [He has] **his own wrestling-ground** complete with sand and a ball-court; he goes around lending it out to sophists, drill sergeants and musicians to perform in; and he himself comes in rather late during their shows, when everybody is seated, so that the audience-members say to each other, 'That is the man who owns the wrestling-ground!'

6.26   **The Chatterbox** (7)   When serving on a jury, he prevents them from reaching a verdict; when at the theatre, from watching the show; when at a dinner party, from eating …

6.27   **The Shameless Man** (9)   When he buys theatre tickets **for his guests**, he watches the show also without paying his share; then the next day, he brings his sons and **their tutor** too!

---

the cushions   theatre-goers would have brought along their own cushions to pad the hard stone seating. The flatterer's prominent friend has a slave for this job, but the flatterer wants to curry favour by doing this himself.

his own wrestling-ground   Greek men would normally visit a public wrestling-ground to get some exercise, but the obsequious man has his own private facilities. The rich evidently put on their own private entertainment, which could include musical and even dramatic performances.

for his guests   it seems that he is buying tickets on behalf of foreign guests (perhaps because they themselves are not entitled to purchase the tickets) and is taking advantage of them by paying for his own tickets with their money.

their tutor   the *paidagōgos* was the slave who was responsible for supervising boys. This passage suggests that slaves too could attend the theatre.

6.28 **The Obnoxious Man (11)** The obnoxious man is the kind of man who, when he meets respectable women, pulls up his clothes and exposes his privates. In the theatre he claps when others have stopped clapping and whistles at the actors whom the rest of the audience are enjoying watching. When the whole audience is silent, he tips back his head and belches in order to make the spectators turn round.

6.29 **The Absent-minded Man (14)** When he is a defendant in a lawsuit and is about to appear in court, he forgets and heads off to the country. When he is watching a play in the theatre, he falls asleep and is left behind on his own. When he has eaten a heavy meal and gets up in the night to go to the outhouse, he is bitten by **his neighbour's dog**.

6.30 **The Avaricious Man (30)** If he sells wine, he sells it watered down to his own friend. And he goes to the theatre – with his sons in tow – only when the **show organizers** grant free admission.

---

1 What do we learn about the theatre and its audience from these extracts?
2 Why do you think that the theatre is so frequently mentioned in this work?
3 What is seen as normal behaviour at shows, and what is considered bad behaviour?

---

his neighbour's dog when he comes back from the outhouse, he enters his neighbour's house by mistake!

avaricious the Greek uses a compound word that literally means 'the man who loves base gain'.

show organizers those who leased the rights to put on theatrical shows. It is not clear how often the cost of admission was waived, and whether this happened for all seats or only for some.

7 The playwrights

Aeschylus

Aeschylus. Such busts of famous poets were not intended as actual portraits but instead were representations that conveyed certain character traits.

Aeschylus was the son of a certain Euphorion, a landowner from Eleusis, a town in western Attica where the famous Eleusinian Mysteries were held in honour of Demeter. He was born *c*. 525/24 BC; his dramatic debut came *c*. 499, but it wasn't until the City Dionysia in 484 that he won his first victory. After this, he seems to have enjoyed unparalleled success, coming first on most occasions in which he competed. The number of plays he wrote is given variously by different sources, but lies somewhere between 70 and 90. The higher number, recorded in the *Suda*, may include plays that were re-performed after his death. In fact, his unique talents seem to have been acknowledged in a special decree that allowed re-performances of his works to compete with new plays. He scored 13 victories in the 19 or 20 times he competed.

Aeschylus' early career came at a time in which Athens' very existence was threatened by two Persian invasions. He himself fought at the battle of Marathon in 490 (see **7.1**) and probably also at Salamis (480) – a battle of which he gives a memorable account in his *Persians* – and Plataea (479).

Although he spent most of his life in Athens, his career included two or more stints in Sicily; on his first trip he came to Syracuse at the invitation of its ruler Hieron I (reigned 478–67), for whom he wrote his *Women of Aetna*; he returned to Sicily at the end of his life, dying at Gela in 456/55.

The following is the epitaph said to have been inscribed on Aeschylus' tomb and attributed to the poet himself (*Life of Aeschylus* 11). Epigrams such as this were commonly composed by playwrights as well as lyric poets, and this particular one is referred to by the Roman travel-writer Pausanias (1.14.5), so that it is plausible that it was written by Aeschylus.

7.1   This grave covers Aeschylus the Athenian, son of Euphorion,
Who died in **wheat-bearing Gela**.
The plain of Marathon may tell of his famed valour
– So too may the **long-haired Mede**, who knew it well.

---

1   What does Aeschylus want to be remembered for?

2   What aspects of his life go unmentioned? Does this surprise you?

Works

Of his plays six have come down to us; a seventh (*Prometheus Bound*) was attributed to Aeschylus but may not be his. The following are the names and dates of the plays that have survived, along with their placing in the competition. Tragedies were adjudicated as a set of four plays – three tragedies and a satyr-play. The three tragedies that Aeschylus put on in 458 BC are known collectively as the *Oresteia* or 'story of Orestes'.

Title of play	Date	Placing in competition
Persians	*472 BC	1st place
Seven against Thebes	*467	1st place
Suppliants	c. 463	1st place
Agamemnon	*458	1st place
Libation Bearers	*458	1st place
Eumenides	*458	1st place
? *Prometheus Bound*	Unknown – if by Aeschylus, then probably late in his life	
* Play whose date is secure.		

Particular contributions

Aeschylus was a pioneer of theatre. We may reasonably believe ancient authors who credited him with inventions such as introducing the second speaking actor (see **7.2**), though in the absence of surviving examples of the works of his peers (playwrights such as Choerilus, Pratinas and Phrynichus whom we know only by name and through a few snippets of information) it is hard to assess what set his plays apart and what his exact role was in the development of tragedy.

---

wheat-bearing Gela   a city on the southern coast of Sicily; much of mainland Greece was too mountainous to grow wheat, but Sicily was a major producer.

long-haired Mede   i.e. the Persians that fought against him at Marathon, who learnt about his courage the hard way! According to Herodotus (6.117), 6,400 Persians were killed, while only 192 fell on the Athenian side (including Aeschylus' brother Cynegeirus); the Athenian dead were all interred in a single tumulus, visible to this day.

Aristotle in his *Poetics* (1449a) describes the contributions of Aeschylus and Sophocles.

7.2   The first to take the number of actors from one to two was Aeschylus; he also reduced the part of the chorus and made speech the first actor ['protagonist']. Sophocles introduced the third actor and scene-painting.

Language and structure

Modern audiences sometimes find Aeschylus' plays hard to digest because of their language. Aeschylus is the ultimate wordsmith: his plays use an amazing range of words and tones. Often his language is deliberately archaic, drawing especially on the vocabulary of Homeric epic. In fact he himself, we are told, referred to his tragedies as 'slices from the great banquets of Homer' (Athenaeus, *Learned Banqueters* 347e). In Aristophanes' *Frogs*, the language of Aeschylus' plays provides his rival with a ready target for parody (923–40). In the comedy, the character Euripides remarks that after subjecting his audience to his protracted silences (see pp. 103–5), Aeschylus 'would then utter a dozen words with brows and crests, terrifying monster-faced creatures unknown to his spectators'. 'Not a single plainly intelligible word does he use,' he adds; instead he talks about 'griffin-eagles', 'horse-cocks' and 'goatstags'. What he is parodying here is Aeschylus' tendency to experiment with language, often by creating new compound words or by using language in bold ways; his parody is particularly clever in that his examples describe Aeschylus' neologisms as hybrid monsters, alluding to Aeschylus' tendency to draw on animal imagery.

Aristophanes' Aeschylus, however, is quick to defend his practice. His language lends his works the dignity appropriate to its subject-matter and allows him to express great thoughts (*Frogs* 1050–2). This is indeed a virtue of the real Aeschylus' language: it is supremely versatile. The awesome beauty of a descriptive turn of phrase, distilled to its essence, can be followed by plainspoken everyday expressions. Aeschylus coins one such hybrid word to describe Clytemnestra in his first reference to her – she is a 'woman with a man-thinking heart' (*Agamemnon* 11). The compound adjective 'man-thinking' conveys the essential paradox of the characterization of this queen, at times alluring in her feigned womanliness but always strategizing in the mindset of a male potentate. Even word-play has a serious point: for example, the punning on Helen's name (the Greek verb *helein* means 'to destroy') when Helen is called by the chorus 'ship-destroyer, man-destroyer, city-destroyer' (*Agamemnon* 689) poignantly describes the far-reaching devastation caused by this one woman.

Aeschylus' language, strange enough in Greek, is almost impossible to duplicate in English (though in the above example, translators try to approximate the effect with the word 'hell' – e.g. 'hell to ships, hell to men'). The award-winning translator Tony Harrison captures the poetry of Aeschylus' bold language even though he does so by introducing imagery of his own.

I've been so long staring I know the stars backwards,
the chiefs of the star-clans, kin-stars, controllers,
those that dispense us the coldsnaps and dogdays

- What is your reaction to the use of compound words? Do they seem to stand in the way of Aeschylus' meaning or do they serve him well?

In the short extract above from the opening scene of *Agamemnon*, the Watchman describes the night sky as he looks for the fire-beacon that will announce Troy's capture. His description of the myriad stars marshalled into their allotted ranks by the dominant luminaries of the night sky develops the themes of power and control; it also focuses attention on the motifs of light and darkness, imagery that will continue to be significant throughout the trilogy and that will soon recur when the beacon bursts into light later in the Watchman's speech.

Thus it is not just individual words that distinguish Aeschylus' poetry but also the sustained and interlinking imagery that ties together a play or even a set of plays. This is enhanced by elaborate patterning of individual choral odes and speeches. A famous example is the set of seven paired speeches that dominate the central portion of *Seven against Thebes*; one by one, they describe each of the seven leaders about to attack Thebes' seven gates. Such intricate structural symmetry can be seen in the poems of contemporary lyric poets such as Pindar, with whom Aeschylus has much in common. Since Aeschylus (more than Sophocles and Euripides) often put on sets of plays related in subject-matter, this structural symmetry could span several plays. Near the end of *Agamemnon*, Clytemnestra stands over the bodies of Agamemnon and Cassandra and displays the bloodied robe in which she killed her husband and which now enshrouds his corpse – a robe that she fittingly describes as a 'net' since she used it to entrap him while he was taking a bath. In the final scene of *Libation Bearers*, Orestes, standing over the bodies of Clytemnestra and Aegisthus, holds up the same blood-stained robe in a remarkable mirror-scene. What should he call it, he wonders – a hunting-net for a wild beast, the shroud for a corpse, a wrap for a bather? It is 'a fishing net', he pronounces, 'a hunter's snare', 'a robe to entangle a man's feet' (997–1000). He points at the bloodstains on the robe, evidence of the terrible crime committed against his father.

Drama and ideas

Aeschylus' plays build slowly at first. Their extensive choral odes examine issues of culpability, often tracing the roots of present troubles to origins generations earlier. Key principles of a rational universe are invoked – the principle of poetic justice, for example, or the mantra that humans learn through suffering. A strong interest in causation does not, however, minimize the real sense of human suffering; nor does divine involvement detract from the plays' clear focus on human choice. Just as in *Eumenides* Athena assigns to an Athenian jury the task of judging Orestes' case, so too in *Seven against Thebes* the play explores the motivations behind those who defend their city and those who attack it: the civil war may be a consequence of Oedipus' curse on his sons, but this does nothing to diminish their role in the conflict. This play, like other Aeschylean works, is permeated by a strong sense of foreboding and of anticipation of its climax, which comes swiftly at the end when the messenger announces that the two brothers have killed each other in hand-to-hand combat.

Aeschylus' early works were put on when Athenian tragedy was still at a relatively early stage of development. *Persians*, *Seven against Thebes* and *Suppliants* can and may have been performed without the use of a *skene*. His plays give a greater role to the chorus than many of the later works of Sophocles and Euripides and include a greater proportion of long speeches. His simple dramaturgy is often very effective. We have already mentioned the visual impact created by the arrival of Xerxes, the great Persian king, in tattered rags in his *Persians* – not to mention the apparition of the ghost of his father Darius. In *Suppliants* the chorus of Danaus' daughters, dressed in the exotic costumes of Egyptians, cling to the statues of the gods in their desperate bid to avoid deportation – at one point, they even threaten to hang themselves from the statues if King Pelasgus rejects their plea (465). Thus the stark choice that Pelasgus, king of Argos faces – welcome the refugees and incur the enmity of King Aegyptus or reject their case and violate the sacrosanctity of suppliants protected by Zeus – is played out on stage in a visually striking and symbolically expressive way.

Even more striking is the staging of the *Oresteia* trilogy; it seems as if Aeschylus is making full use of the wider range of options now available to him. *Agamemnon* opens with the Watchman appearing on the roof of the *skene* and closes with a scene that may mark the first use of the *ekkyklema* (also probably used in *Libation Bearers*); *Eumenides* makes full use of the third speaking actor, employs a bold change of setting from Delphi to Athens, and has two choruses.

The main parts in the surviving plays of Aeschylus tend to go to powerful leaders such as Eteocles, Danaus or Xerxes. The choices they make, however, have a direct impact on the city as a whole. Thus the *polis* looms large in Aeschylus' interests, and it is not hard to see how in his *Frogs* Aristophanes identified Aeschylus as the playwright most suited to saving Athens. Loving attention is given to minor characters such as the Watchman in *Agamemnon* and the nurse Cilissa in *Libation Bearers*, who serve the royal household with utmost loyalty and who stand to gain or lose everything from the events that play out on stage. Though set in the mythic past, Aeschylus' plays deal with issues directly affecting Athens. *Eumenides*, for example, alludes repeatedly (288–91, 667–72, 762–7) to the important alliance between Argos and Athens in 461/60, two years before the performance of the play. Similarly, the play affirms the importance of the Areopagus court soon after its jurisdiction had been curtailed by legislation introduced by Ephialtes and Pericles in 462/1 and urges the Athenian citizens, through the advice of the Furies (526–31) and Athena herself (696–706), to take a middle course between tyranny and anarchy, a veiled reference perhaps to the political struggle between oligarchs and radical democrats that followed Ephialtes' reforms and which led to his assassination.

> The following is an extract from *Libation Bearers* (750–60). The Nurse, devastated by the news of Orestes' supposed death, recalls the care she lavished on Orestes as an infant (wet-nursing by a household slave was common in the ancient world).

7.3   His mother gave him to me and I nursed him. His loud cries used to get me   750
up in the night; I put up with every inconvenience – but all in vain! A baby is
like a senseless animal; it needs to be fed, does it not, at the beck of its instinct.
While it's still in diapers, a baby can't tell you if it's hungry, or thirsty, or needs   755
to relieve itself. A baby's young bowels are a law unto themselves. My attempts to
anticipate their movements often failed and I would have to wash his diapers, thus
performing my duties as both laundress and nurse.   760

- Does the register and content of the speech surprise you? Does it work?

Sophocles

Sophocles was born *c.* 496 in the small Attic deme of Colonus just north of Athens. His father Sophilus was said to have gained his wealth through a weapons-making business run by his slaves. Sophocles brought immortal fame to his home town by making it the setting for his final play, *Oedipus at Colonus*, performed posthumously in 401. In it, a wandering Oedipus, now an old man, finds refuge at Colonus and is transformed from a social outcast into a source of blessing to the population that welcomes him. The playwright's fondness for his home is evident in the loving description of the natural beauty of 'white Colonus, where the clear-voiced nightingale most likes to come to sing within the green glades' (670–3).

Sophocles. Busts such as these – here dating to the Hellenistic period – often adorned ancient libraries.

His first experience on stage reportedly came as a teenager, when he performed in the choral dances celebrating victory over the Persians at the battle of Salamis in 480 (see **7.6n**). Among his accomplishments, he was said to have been a talented lyre-player, to have acted in his own plays until his weak voice forced him to give up acting, and to have written a lost treatise entitled *On the Chorus*. He won first prize in his debut as a playwright in 468, apparently beating Aeschylus. He lived on to the ripe old age of ninety and enjoyed a productive career as a playwright that spanned sixty years! He overlapped with Aeschylus by a decade and outlived his junior Euripides by a few months.

Sophocles lived and worked during Athens' period of dominance following the Persian Wars. From the snippets of biographical information that have come down to us, it is clear that he was a sociable person (even Aristophanes described him in his comedy as 'good-natured' at *Frogs* 82) and that he rubbed shoulders with many of the leading Athenian figures of his time. He also played an active role in serving his city. He was appointed as one of the *hellēnotamiai* (literally 'treasurers of the Greeks') during 443/42 BC; the title of the office is somewhat misleading, since these financial officers of the Delian league were all Athenians, appointed by the city to levy and administer the tribute collected from the allies. He also served as general alongside Pericles, probably in 441/40 BC, and was then reappointed to the position in 428 in the early stages of the Peloponnesian War; Pericles was said to have adjudged him a good poet but a poor general. After the disastrous Sicilian expedition, Athens turned to him again, appointing him as one of ten special commissioners.

Sophocles was more pious than all others, declares the writer of the *Life of Sophocles* (12), quoting the third-century BC author Hieronymus of Rhodes. Among his religious functions, we are told that he was a priest of the shrine of the hero Halon, that he welcomed into his house the cult of the healing-god Asclepius while his shrine was under construction, and that for this act he received his own cult as Dexion ('the welcomer') after his death. These anecdotes, as Mary Lefkowitz has demonstrated, are more open to suspicion than the listings of his civic offices; it could be that they are no more than conclusions drawn from details in his plays. The story of his hero-cult, especially, seems likely to be an extrapolation from the plot of his swan-song, *Oedipus at Colonus*, in which Oedipus receives a hero-cult after his mysterious death.

Sophocles certainly was a prolific playwright, producing somewhere in the region of 120 plays and winning some twenty or more victories (out of the approximately 30 sets of plays which he entered). He was said never to have come third (i.e. last) in a competition. Of his tragedies, seven have been preserved, along with substantial fragments of a satyr-play (*Trackers*). Unlike Aeschylus' surviving plays, for the majority of which we have firm dates and placings, the dating of most of Sophocles' extant plays are only rough approximations and their placing in the competition unknown.

Title of play	Date	Placing in competition
Ajax	Early 440s (perhaps 447)	Unknown
Antigone	Late 440s or early 430s	1st place
Women of Trachis	430s	Unknown
Oedipus the King	Early 420s	2nd place
Electra	410s	Unknown
Philoctetes	*409	1st place
Oedipus at Colonus	Composed *c.* 406, performed posthumously in 401 BC	

* Play whose date is secure.

The following entry for Sophocles is given in the *Suda*, a lexicon dating to around the tenth century AD.

7.4   Sophocles, son of Sophilus, from Colonus, an Athenian, tragedian, born during the seventy-third Olympiad [i.e. 488–485 BC], thus being seventeen years older than Socrates. He was the first to use three actors and the so-called tritagonist, and first to bring on a chorus of fifteen young men [previously it was twelve who came on]. He was called the Bee because of his sweetness. He himself began the practice of competing with one play against another **instead of competing with a tetralogy**. He wrote elegy and **paeans** and a work in prose on the chorus; he competed against Thespis and Choerilus. The sons that he had were Iophon, Leosthenes, Ariston, Stephanus, Menecleides. He died after Euripides at ninety years of age. He put on 123 plays – according to some, many more – and won 24 victories.

Particular contributions

Sophocles occupied an intermediate position between Aeschylus and Euripides in the history of the development of tragedy, and this may have played a part in the fact that, while Aeschylus was seen as a trailblazer and Euripides as a rebel, Sophocles was credited with many of the later innovations that became standard practice such as the addition of a third speaking actor, the introduction of scene-painting, and the expansion of the chorus from twelve choreuts to fifteen.

---

instead of competing with a tetralogy   this is a tentative emendation of an apparent corruption in the text. According to this version, Sophocles discontinued the tradition of putting on four thematically related plays.

paeans   hymns performed for a god, especially a god of healing such as Apollo or Asclepius.

Plot

For Aristotle, the plot is the cornerstone of tragedy. When delineating what he considered to be a well-constructed plot, he turned most frequently to Sophocles and in particular to his *Oedipus the King* for illustrations. He appreciated (*Poetics* 1452a) how its recognition (*anagnōrisis*) and reversal (*peripeteia*) were woven from the same thread, with the one resulting in the other. He admired (1452a, 1455a) the way in which its plot evolved organically from events internal to the story line, citing the scene in which Oedipus summons the old servant. This plot development arises from Oedipus' natural impulse to try to dispel his fears about his mother by obtaining proof that they are unfounded, but it has the opposite outcome to the one intended, leading to his discovery of the terrible truth of his incest. All of Sophocles' surviving plays show the same careful attention to plot (see **7.5**), though their structures vary widely and are indeed tailored to the individual play, as can be seen by comparing the plots of two of his plays.

In *Women of Trachis*, the main reversal already occurs in the third episode, when Hyllus announces to his mother Deianeira (739–40): 'Know that this day you have destroyed your husband – yes, my father!' More than five hundred lines follow this climactic moment; they explore the terrible consequences of Deianeira's unwitting act. First, Deianeira's suicide is reported by the Nurse, then we witness the horrendous suffering inflicted on Heracles as he is brought on stage and we watch his once invincible body now writhing in agony. Then another moment of recognition occurs as Heracles discovers that Deianeira received the poison from the centaur Nessus and realizes that this fulfils a prophecy. The final scene focuses on Hyllus' relationship with his father and on the terrible decisions that the son faces when his father asks him to end his agony by burning him alive on his funeral pyre, and charges him to marry Iole, the very woman who stole Heracles' affections from Deianeira and thus was a cause of the whole disaster. Hyllus' intense sorrow as he prepares to carry out his father's requests brings the play to its close long after the initial act that caused so much anguish.

Sophocles' *Electra* has a very different trajectory; its originality becomes all the more apparent when we compare it to Aeschylus' prior treatment of the story in his *Libation Bearers*.

In Aeschylus' play, Orestes overhears Electra lamenting at the tomb of their father in the very opening scene. Convinced by this demonstration of her loyalty, he reveals himself to her at line 212 and together they plot the killing of Aegisthus, which occurs some 650 lines later. Sophocles' play seems to be following the same course. In its opening scene, Orestes overhears Electra weeping. But, just as the recognition scene seems on the point of happening, the Tutor sends Orestes off on a mission to pour libations on his father's tomb (off stage in this play). The reunion is postponed until line 1220!

Sophocles seems to be playing with the audience's expectations; but the delay in the joyful reunion between brother and sister is also crucial to the play, since it gives space for Sophocles to explore the predicament of Electra. Her isolation, grief and unstinting desire for revenge are given full rein in a series of episodes in which her situation seems to deteriorate from bad to worse until her one remaining hope is seemingly dashed by the news of her brother's death. Once the reunion finally takes place, the play draws rapidly to its bloody close. Here too Sophocles shows his characteristic dexterity in the handling of plot: the play ends with Aegisthus led off stage to his execution, though at the end of the play it has not yet occurred. Thus Sophocles projects a continuation of the plot even beyond the end of the play in a manner reminiscent of Aeschylus' *Oresteia* trilogy – in which another play *did* follow.

> The *Life of Sophocles* (20–1), compiled by an anonymous ancient author (date unknown), singles out a number of facets of Sophocles' dramatic skill as worthy of praise, including his sense of *kairos*, a concept that embraces both due proportion and good timing.

7.5 Many others have imitated one of their predecessors or contemporaries, but only Sophocles gleaned the best from each, for which he was called the Bee. He brought together every element: timing [*kairos*], sweetness, daring and variety. He knew how to match timing [*kairos*] and events, so that from a tiny half-line or a single speech he could express a whole character. This is the greatest quality of a poet's art, the ability to reveal character or suffering.

Characterization

Sophocles' characters are generally more fully delineated than those of Aeschylus, though his characters, too, are defined by their actions rather than by personality traits. In fact, conceiving characterization in terms of personality is a modern way of thinking which, when anachronistically applied to Greek tragedy, has resulted in misguided attempts to trace the 'tragic flaw' of characters such as Oedipus.

In his influential study, Bernard Knox described what he termed the 'Sophoclean hero' as being marked by a characteristic passion and uncompromising single-mindedness. It is certainly true that the protagonists of several of his plays (*Ajax*, *Antigone*, *Oedipus the King* and *Electra*) are strong characters who show a certain stubbornness; however, Sophocles' plays offer a wider range of main characters than Knox's study suggests: we have Deianeira, the protagonist of *Women of Trachis*, a tender soul distinguished by her desire to please, and the contemplative and awe-inspiring Oedipus of *Oedipus at Colonus*, who shows nothing of the bravado that characterized the protagonist of *Oedipus the King*.

In several of his plays, Sophocles uses one character as a foil for another. His *Electra*, for example, differs from Aeschylus' and Euripides' treatment of the story by introducing the character of Chrysothemis, Electra's sister, who seeks to dissuade Electra from her extreme stance. Chrysothemis responds to their predicament by playing it safe and adopting the submissive role expected of a woman; Electra's decision to seek vengeance even at risk to her life seems all the more courageous – and rash – after hearing Chrysothemis' impassioned appeals to her sister to reconsider. Ismene plays a similar counterpoint to her sister in *Antigone*, while in *Philoctetes*, the ethical issues that the play explores are all the more complex because they are triangulated among three characters: Philoctetes, Neoptolemus and Odysseus.

Sophoclean irony

Sophocles' plays show a delicious mastery of the use of **irony**. In his *Electra*, the dramatic irony at work when Electra fails to recognize the 'stranger' whom the audience knows to be Orestes heightens the pathos of their encounter (see **5.7**), while the structural irony (see p. 109) of the way in which the Tutor arrives in seeming answer to Clytemnestra's prayer to Apollo intensifies the feeling of suspense as Clytemnestra walks blithely into the trap that has been set. Often irony serves to highlight the deeper concerns of a play: in *Oedipus the King*, the fate of Oedipus reminds us of our human limitations. The hero known for his intellectual acumen (he was the only one able to solve the riddle of the Sphinx) and determined to solve the murder of King Laius is unable to see that the evidence which he is relentlessly tracking points plainly to him as the wrong-doer and will ultimately prove his undoing. And the inherent futility of our efforts to understand and control our destinies is underscored by the verbal irony of Oedipus' name, at the root of which is the Greek verb *oida* ('I know'), a word that occurs frequently throughout the play and is often used to devastating effect to draw attention to the 'knower' who does not know his own identity and whose eventual self-knowledge will lead to his blindness. Furthermore, the verb *oideō* ('to swell') in combination with *pous* ('foot') also bears testimony to his true identity both as a foundling whose ankles were bound and as the answer to the riddle of the Sphinx.

Sophocles' plays are a treasure-trove for those interested in 'semiotics' (the study of signs), since Sophocles himself seems to have taken pleasure in the inherent ambiguity of signs. For example, he frequently exploits the ambiguity of language as a sign-system. Deianeira says in *Women of Trachis* (685–7) that Nessus ordered her 'to always keep this *pharmakon* in a hidden spot, away from fire and untouched by the warm rays of the sun' until such time as she was ready to use it. The word *pharmakon* means both 'medicine' and 'poison'; the ointment that she thinks is a love-potion will prove to be a noxious toxin which will corrode her husband's flesh and destroy him. Other signs, too, such as dreams and oracles, can be ambiguous, and receive differing interpretations by different characters. Even physical objects – such as the urn that Electra takes as clear evidence that Orestes is dead (see **5.7**) – sometimes turn out to be misleading. The audience must negotiate these signs for itself, since the characters and even the chorus can misconstrue them. Paradox and the unexpected are mainstays of Sophocles' outlook. The great superhero Heracles is undone by the weak woman he ignores, and by the monster that he vanquished, Aegisthus is killed by the man that he thought to be dead, while the exiled Oedipus becomes a talisman for the community that welcomes him.

Euripides

Euripides.

Euripides is the subject of an even greater accumulation of speculative and colourful stories than Aeschylus and Sophocles. A number of these can be traced back to jokes made at Euripides' expense by Aristophanes (see **7.7**), which were then taken literally by ancient biographers to 'reconstruct' details of his life; others are details taken from his own plays and applied autobiographically to the playwright; still others are fanciful ideas that contradict other more reliable evidence. What follows is a précis of the evidence that appears most reliable. An example of the more fanciful biographical tradition can be found at **7.6**.

Euripides' birth is placed by most authors in the year 480/79, though one source, an inscription known as the *Marmor Parium* probably dating to the third century BC, gives the date as 485/84. The dating of his death to early 406 is more secure: he died not long before the performance of Aristophanes' *Frogs* in January 405 and just before Sophocles was about to present his actors at the *proagon* for the City Dionysia (see **2.7n**, p. 37) in what must have been March 406.

His hometown was Phyle, near Athens; his father's name is given as Mnesarchus or Mnesarchides and his mother's as Cleito. Some sources describe her as a vegetable-seller (see **7.6** and **7.6n** and **7.7**), but others depict Euripides already as a child moving in the circles of the noble-born and one source, the fourth-century historian Philochorus, explicitly states that Cleito came from a noble family. The fact that his mother is the subject of such interest is perhaps reflective of the limelight enjoyed by female characters in his plays. There is no record of Euripides' involvement in political or religious office or military service, though this does not mean that he was indifferent towards his city – in fact, several of his plays (e.g. *Children of Heracles* and *Suppliant Women*) are unabashed celebrations of Athens' virtues.

Sources connect a number of famous teachers with the education of the young Euripides – these include Anaxagoras (a pre-Socratics philosopher investigating the composition and arrangement of the cosmos), the sophists Prodicus and Protagoras, and Socrates. Such stories are unlikely to be true but do perhaps indicate that Euripides' plays were seen as reflecting the philosophical and rhetorical currents of the time. That he was said to have been a collector of books (a rare practice at that time) also suggests an interest in the ideas of others. In Aristophanes' plays, both Socrates and Euripides are intellectuals on the cutting edge of the latest – and wackiest – ideas. Their unorthodox views might have been the reason why both were accused of atheism.

Euripides' debut as a dramatist is dated to 456/55 (the year in which Aeschylus died); his first victory came in 441. Over the course of half a century he composed somewhere in the region of 90 plays; but of the 22 times he competed at the City Dionysia, he only won four times during his lifetime (and once posthumously when a set of his plays – including *Bacchae* and *Iphigenia at Aulis* – were put on by a son or nephew also called Euripides). Scholars wonder about the reasons for his relatively poor results: were many of his plays simply not as good as those of his competitors, or did they not suit the tastes of the judges? If the latter, then why was he so frequently awarded the right to enter the competition? Perhaps we must content ourselves by assuming that Euripides was composing at a time when the competition was stacked with a very talented field.

- It could be argued that for an avant-garde and challenging dramatist such as Euripides, being awarded the first prize was a somewhat dubious distinction since it would indicate that he had pleased his audience (and the judges in particular) rather than disturbing them. What do you think of this line of reasoning?

Euripides, we are told, lived the last two years of his life in Macedon at the court of King Archelaus at Pella. Macedon was at the time considered the back of beyond, and Archelaus may have been trying to put Macedon on the cultural map by developing a reputation as a patron of the arts (he also apparently played host to the tragic poet Agathon, the dithyrambic poet Timotheus, and the painter Zeuxis). It is certainly plausible that Euripides accepted an invitation to the court of a king (as Aeschylus had done), but it is worth noting that the stories told about this visit (such as his gruesome death ripped apart by the king's hounds or by women) seem suspiciously similar to his *Bacchae*.

Despite his relative lack of success during his lifetime, after his death his plays became wildly popular, and as early as the fourth century his reputation as one of the three great tragedians was secure. Of his plays, eighteen survive, including a satyr-play (*Cyclops*) – a nineteenth play (*Rhesus*) that made it into manuscripts of his plays is unlikely to be his work. Ten of them appear in manuscripts with accompanying scholia (commentary), apparently chosen as an anthology of his best works for study in schools. These are arranged in chronological order, thus providing us with a skeleton of datable plays. The other nine, preserved in a single manuscript, represent a selection of the rest of his plays that were fortuitously preserved. Given that their titles all begin with four letters of the Greek alphabet (epsilon, eta, iota, kappa), it seems that they were part of an edition of the complete works of Euripides that was arranged alphabetically. Their dating is less secure, based on a combination of thematic and stylistic considerations (especially the statistically demonstrable trend of Euripides' iambic metre to become looser over the years). On the opposite page is a full list of surviving works with approximate dates.

Title of play	Date	Placing in competition
Alcestis	*438 BC	2nd place (performed as fourth play instead of a satyr-play)
Medea	*431	3rd place
Children of Heracles	c. 430–29	Unknown
Hippolytus	*428	1st place (revision of an earlier version that did not meet with critical approval)
Andromache	c. 427–25	Unknown
Hecuba	c. 424	Unknown
Suppliant Women	423–20	Unknown
Electra	c. 420–16	Unknown
Madness of Heracles	c. 417–16	Unknown
Trojan Women	*415	2nd place
Iphigenia in Tauris	414–12	Unknown
Ion	c. 413–10	Unknown
Helen	*412	Unknown
Phoenician Women	*c. 410–09	2nd place
Orestes	*408	Unknown
Cyclops (satyr-play)	c. 412–08?	Unknown
Bacchae	*written c. 407	1st place (performed posthumously c. 405 BC)
Iphigenia at Aulis	*written c. 407	1st place (performed posthumously c. 405 BC)
[? *Rhesus*	Unknown	Probably not by Euripides]

* Play whose date is reasonably secure.

The following is the entry for Euripides found in the *Suda*. It serves as a good example of the mix of facts and fiction contained in the biographical tradition.

7.6   Son of Mnesarchus or Mnesarchides and Cleito; his parents **fled to Boeotia** and lived there as *metics* [resident aliens], then lived in Attica. It is, however, not

---

fled to Boeotia   the *Suda* seems to be trying to reconcile two divergent traditions: one that Euripides has Boeotian roots, the other that he is Athenian. The story of his association with Boeotia may have arisen from attempts to connect his name with Euripus, the narrow strait separating Boeotia from the island of Euboea.

true that **his mother was a vegetable-seller**. In fact, she was of very well-born parentage, as Philochorus attests. His mother conceived him while Xerxes was making his crossing and gave birth to him on the very day that **the Greeks defeated the Persians**. He first became a painter, then a pupil of Prodicus in rhetoric and of Socrates in ethics and philosophy. He also studied under Anaxagoras of Clazomenae. He turned to writing tragedy after he saw what dangers Anaxagoras faced because of the teachings he put forward. He had a sullen and gloomy temperament, and avoided company; this is why he was considered a misogynist. Nevertheless, he did get married, first to Choirine, the daughter of Mnesilochus, who bore him Mnesilochus, Mnesarchides and Euripides. He divorced her and remarried, but his second wife also turned out to be unfaithful. **He left Athens** and went to the court of Archelaus, king of Macedon, where he lived and enjoyed the highest honour. He died as the result of a plot by Arrhibaeus of Macedon and Crateuas of Thessaly, poets who were jealous of him. With a bribe of ten minas they persuaded a member of the king's household called Lysimachus, who looked after the royal hounds, to set them loose on him. But some accounts record that he was **ripped apart** not by hounds but by women at night, as he headed in the middle of the night to visit Craterus, the young lover of Archelaus; others state that he was going to visit the wife of Nicodicus of Arethusa. He lived to the age of 75,

---

his mother was a vegetable-seller   the tradition that Euripides' mother was a vegetable-seller is almost certainly derived from comments made in Aristophanes' plays (see **7.7** and **7.8**); these comments may be Aristophanes' comic way of saying that Euripides' tragedies are vulgar because of their preoccupation with ordinary people (and insulting someone's mother is still a mainstay of comedy – just think of all the *yo' mama* jokes).

the Greeks defeated the Persians   according to tradition, Aeschylus fought at the battle of Salamis, the young Sophocles danced in the chorus of youths at the victory celebration, and Euripides was born on the very day of the victory (20 September 480 BC). This is likely to be a fiction, not mere coincidence, created in order to tie together the lives of the three great tragedians and to peg their chronologies to a single, easily remembered date. This kind of contrived synchronism is common in ancient biography. At any rate, Euripides could not have been conceived during Xerxes' crossing to Greece and born on the day of Greek victory at Salamis, since at the most four months separate these two events.

He left Athens   although the connection is not made explicit, the implication is that he left Athens because he was disenchanted at his wife's infidelity. Similarly, Aeschylus' departure for Sicily is explained as resulting from frustration at having been defeated by the young Sophocles (*Life of Aeschylus* 8).

ripped apart   Aeschylus and Sophocles also met unexpected deaths, according to the biographical tradition: the former by being hit on the head by a tortoise dropped by an eagle, the latter by choking on a grape or from overexcitement over a victory. The playwrights, like their tragic characters, seem to experience a sudden reversal at the height of their good fortune, and the manner of the death is suited to the individual playwright: Aeschylus dies from the animals that featured as omens in his plays, while Euripides is killed by the women he supposedly hated (in what is probably a conflation of the plots of Aristophanes' *Women at the Thesmophoria* and Euripides' own *Bacchae*).

and his bones were buried by the king in Pella. Some put the number of his plays at 75, others at 92; 77 plays survive. He won five victories, four while he was alive and one after his death, when his nephew Euripides put on his work. Euripides put on plays **for 22 years in total**, and died during the 93rd Olympiad [i.e. 408–405 BC].

> 1 What kind of details in the *Suda* entry on Euripides are likely to be most reliable, and which would be more open to doubt?
>
> 2 Is it valid to suppose that the personality of a playwright rubs off on his plays and can therefore be deduced from what he writes?
>
> 3 What types of explanation does the biographical tradition tend to offer? What motives, for example, are suggested for his becoming a playwright, for his departure from Athens and for his death?

The following are two of a handful of references in Aristophanes' plays to Euripides' mother as a seller of herbs or vegetables. In *Acharnians*, Dicaeopolis, trying to disguise himself as a pauper in order to win pity, asks Euripides for some rags to wear, for a couple of broken props, then finally for some chervil, a kind of parsley (475–8).

7.7 My sweetest, dearest little Euripides, may I die horribly if I ask you for anything else – just give me this one thing, only this, just this: give me some of that chervil that you get from your mother!

In *Women at the Thesmophoria*, Mica delivers a speech before the assembled women lambasting Euripides for the way he portrays women in his plays (384–7).

7.8 … for a long time now I have had to suffer watching you have mud slung at you by Euripides, that son of a vegetable-seller.

Particular contributions

To Aristophanes, Euripides was a clever innovator who had a fondness for the unorthodox. That he keeps cropping up in his plays suggests that he was a prominent and perhaps controversial figure. Although Aristophanes' portrayal of Euripides, friend of the riff-raff and sworn enemy of women, remains a comic caricature, behind it lie certain characteristics that we can observe for ourselves in the many plays of Euripides that have come down to us. His dramaturgy does show a remarkable creativity and variety along with other qualities that naturally appeal to audiences in modern times.

---

for 22 years in total   it seems that the *Suda* has misunderstood its source, which probably stated that he entered plays in 22 different years rather than that his career spanned this number of years.

Euripides and his milieu

Euripides' plays reflect the times in which they were written. Athens during the second half of the fifth century BC was a hotbed of new ideas and enjoyed an intellectual milieu that could justifiably be described as axial. Architecture, sculpture and wall-painting were being reinvented at a breakneck pace. And Athens was a magnet for rhetoricians and philosophers from all over the Greek-speaking world. These were no bookish scholars sequestered in ivory towers; they offered to teach the young men of Athens knowledge that could be applied in daily life. The rhetorician Gorgias was known for teaching the art of defending the indefensible. Hippias taught a wide range of subjects including mnemonic techniques that could help a speaker memorize a set speech. And the philosopher Protagoras argued that justice is culturally defined, introducing an early form of relativism; his famous saying that 'man is the measure of all things' was seen as axiomatic by later humanists.

Many of these intellectual and cultural trends can be seen in Euripides' plays. They are generally more rhetorical than those of Aeschylus and Sophocles. Although all three playwrights use the formal debate (*agon*) to present an issue from opposing viewpoints, in Euripides' plays the arguments employed are bolder, more succinctly expressed, and sometimes reflect Gorgias' interest in defending the indefensible. Medea's pithy statement 'I would rather fight three times in war than go through childbirth once' (*Medea* 250–1) is justifiably famous; but it is merely one in a salvo of arrows that she lets fly in an extended speech that strikes at the heart of the traditional values of Athenian society and delivers a vitriolic attack on its double-standards and the injustices it perpetrates on women.

> Medea is 'clever' (Greek *sophos*, at the root of 'sophist') in her ability to argue her case; as she herself notes, this can work against her (294–305).

7.9　No sensible man should have his children
Taught to be too clever. 295
They are called idlers, and excite
Resentful envy in their fellow citizens.
Present some clever, new idea to fools –
They'll think it's you who are useless and a fool.
As for those who think they have a subtle intellect, 300
If you are thought superior in the state, they take it hard.
That has been my fate. Because I'm clever,
Some are jealous, to others I'm objectionable.
But I am not really so clever. 305

What makes Medea such an arresting character is that she – a woman, and a foreign woman at that – can outmanoeuvre every man in the play, first Creon, then Jason and finally Aegeus. Even her claim that she is not really as clever as people think is a ruse to disarm her opponent. And yet she is not merely a persuasive speaker; we also experience the emotional turbulence going on in the heart of a mother as she contemplates killing her children, and her effect on her audience is such that we can almost understand why she committed the terrible deed. One can imagine how a figure like Medea could be construed not only as a threat to male hegemony but also as an affront to women in that she acts outside the narrowly prescribed bounds of acceptable female behaviour. Though to many nowadays Euripides is a champion of feminism, to Aristophanes – and no doubt others – he was a woman-hater.

- From what you have read of Euripides' *Medea*, does he portray his female protagonist sympathetically and in a positive light or critically and negatively?

Challenging assumptions

Medea's case is not atypical of Euripides' approach: he often introduces conventions in order to stand them on their head. In *Trojan Women*, it is the Greeks who behave like barbarians (i.e. love luxury and are excessively cruel), while it is the barbarian queen Hecuba who champions the Athenian virtue of due process, urging Menelaus to grant his estranged wife Helen the opportunity to speak in her own defence when he is about to summarily execute her.

The first speech of his *Electra* is delivered by a new character invented by the playwright: a husband for Electra who, we soon discover, is a poor farmer. Euripides' Electra is self-pitying and at times alienating in her lack of feeling, Orestes is cowardly and morally bankrupt, but the farmer is generous, virtuous, and praised by all. Often his 'heroes' are decidedly unglamorous. Euripides seems to be reflecting a current of contemporary Athenian thought that believed that nobility was a function of character not lineage and insisted that privilege should be earned rather than inherited.

Confounding expectations

One of the hallmarks of Euripides' dramaturgy is his tendency to confound expectations often deliberately set by the playwright. Orestes will return and boldly kill his enemies, Electra predicts (277); in fact, he sneaks up on Aegisthus and executes him from behind while his unsuspecting victim is conducting a sacrifice. Medea, the mother who killed her children entirely of her own volition, is at times presented in a sympathetic light, while Orestes, who acted under orders from Apollo and to avenge his father's death, is an unheroic character who ends up regretting his deed and reproaching Apollo.

This fondness for the unexpected sometimes takes his plays in radically new directions. His *Alcestis*, for example, was performed in 438 BC as the fourth play of a set; instead of the usual satyr-play, the audience got a play that has been described as a tragicomedy, but in fact defies categorization. It is in essence a tragedy, but one that, like a number of others (especially among Euripides' plays), has a happy ending. It contains comic elements, such as a blithely ignorant Heracles drinking and singing party songs while Admetus' household is in mourning, and its liberation of Alcestis from the grasp of Death follows the story-pattern of satyr-play; but at its core it explores the issue of human mortality and its characters face the difficult choices typical of tragedy.

Characterization

Sophocles, we are told by Aristotle (*Poetics* 1460b), remarked that he portrayed people as they should be, while Euripides portrayed them as they were, and we can see why he may have said this: Euripides does not shy away from total candour in his character portrayal. His characters are driven by a range of urges and motivations, and they express controversial sentiments with disarming frankness. Scholars often commend Euripides for his masterful psychological portraits, and there is certainly something very compelling about the way in which character traits are revealed and often externalized. In *Alcestis*, for example, Admetus promises his wife Alcestis, who has agreed to die in his place, that he will ease his sorrow and honour her memory by commissioning a sculpture of her which he will take to bed with him – a telling reflection of his self-absorption and objectification of his wife.

Plot

Euripides' plays take a wide range of approaches, making it virtually impossible to represent them all in a single portrait. A number of plays (e.g. *Electra*, *Iphigenia in Tauris*, *Ion*, *Helen*, *Orestes*) revolve around an intrigue – a plot to kill, to escape from a dangerous situation, or both. These plays are marked by an interest in the intricate details that go into engineering a successful plot. Electra pretends that she has just given birth in order to lure Clytemnestra into a private encounter; Iphigenia orchestrates her own escape and that of her brother Orestes, who has been captured by Thoas, king of Tauris, by inventing an elaborate story in which she needs to perform a purification ritual at sea, away from the eyes of the uninitiated.

Surprisingly perhaps, Euripides often uses the *deus ex machina* to bring plays to an end, employing this closing device more frequently than either Aeschylus or Sophocles had done and even using it in some of the plays in which he shows such apparent concern for realism. Though to modern tastes these abrupt endings may seem artificially contrived (a view shared by Aristotle – see **3.10**), it may be that many in his contemporary audience saw them as sensational *coups-de-théâtre* in which his plots succeeded in defying the odds. It is interesting that in Aristophanes' *Frogs*, when Heracles suggests to Dionysus that he would be better off bringing Sophocles back from the Underworld rather than Euripides, Dionysus replies (lines 80–1) that, unlike Sophocles, Euripides is ready for anything, and would even help him make an escape from Hades, probably a back-handed tribute to his ingenuity in pulling off 'great escapes'.

Euripides' plays show certain tendencies that seem to reflect changing tastes. His prologues are usually extensive monologues in which the mythological background and the action of the play are set. Although his characters tend to use language that is closer to everyday speech than the elevated style of Sophocles and especially Aeschylus, there are times – especially during debate scenes and other set speeches – when their speech patterns are highly rhetorical. While the chorus is given fewer odes to sing and their importance to the play declines, the actors start to sing more solo pieces or duets, sometimes in conjunction with the chorus. *Phoenician Women*, for example, closes with a mournful duet in which Antigone and her father Oedipus lament his impending exile. The musical changes discernible in Euripides' later plays have been examined by scholars such as Eric Csapo (1999–2000) and Peter Wilson (1999) in the context of the so-called 'New Music' developing at the end of the fifth century BC.

> 1 In what ways do Euripides' plays seem to differ from those of Aeschylus and Sophocles?
>
> 2 What do you see as Euripides' most lasting contributions to the theatre?

Aristophanes

Aristophanes, son of Philippus, was born in the early 440s. He belonged to the deme of Cydathenaeum, a neighbourhood within the city of Athens. Both Aristophanes' name (literally meaning 'conspicuously the best') and that of his father ('lover of horses') suggest that they came from an aristocratic family. His first play was titled *Banqueters* (now lost); it was apparently performed at the Lenaea in 427 BC and placed second. Ancient sources state that his first two plays were listed and performed not under his own name but under that of Callistratus, someone whom he continued to employ as his producer in later times. In fact Aristophanes' *Clouds* seems to allude to this vicarious arrangement in its parabasis, where the

Aristophanes.

chorus-leader, here describing Aristophanes' earlier drama and speaking as if he were the playwright, says (530–3): 'since I was still a virgin and not yet able to give birth, I exposed my child and it was adopted by another; you all kindly raised it and gave it an education and have ever since given me sworn assurance of your support'. Why he did this is not clear, though ancient commentators found in his young age a ready answer (he would have been in his late teens or early twenties when his first play was performed).

We know virtually nothing about what Aristophanes did outside the world of theatre. An inscription from the early fourth century lists someone by his name (and likely to have been him) as a member of the *boule* (council). He also features in Plato's *Symposium*, a fictionalized account of a banquet held by the tragic poet Agathon at which all the guests are invited to deliver a speech in praise of love. Aristophanes comes across as a witty and creative story-teller; he relates how humans originally had eight limbs but were split by the gods, which he uses to explain the attraction humans feel to their 'opposite half'. Like his plays, this story is far-fetched, but has a serious underlying point.

All but two of his surviving works were written during the Peloponnesian War (fought 431–404). At the start of the war, Athens was at the height of her power and was brimming with confidence, wealth and artistic talent. The chorus-leader in the parabasis of the *Acharnians* (630–41) defends the playwright's practice of making fun of Athens by saying that it helps his audience see through the many superlatives lavished on their city by admiring visitors. And it may be that this sense of superiority allowed Aristophanes to make such public sport of powerful Athenian leaders and cherished Athenian institutions with relative impunity. He outlived most of the figures he parodied and lived through the war and the political turmoil that followed. His line of work must have been particularly dangerous at certain points. In 411 BC oligarchs seized power in a coup and assassinated leading democrats. Although full democracy was restored a year later, another violent oligarchic regime headed by a junta of thirty (dubbed the 'Thirty Tyrants') was set up by the Spartans in 404 following their victory over Athens. The Thirty were ousted the following year, and most of them ended up dead. It is remarkable that someone whose plays were as topical as those of Aristophanes survived all this political turmoil unscathed (Socrates was not so fortunate). In fact, Aristophanes in his plays constantly champions the playwright's right to freedom of expression; the vehemence with which he asserts this privilege may reflect how precarious it really was.

In all he composed roughly 40 plays, of which 11 survive. His total number of victories is not known, but he won at least four times at the Lenaea and twice at the City Dionysia. He was very prolific in his early years, entering at least one play a year at either the Lenaea or the Dionysia or both. Since comic poets entered only one play (in contrast with the tragedians, who competed with sets of four), it was easier for them to pull off back-to-back productions at the Lenaea in January/February and then at the City Dionysia some two months later. He died *c.* 386, having put on his last two plays, we are told, under the name of his son Ararus. Whether those identified as playwrights' sons were actually sons rather than followers is open to question – in Aristophanes' case, a total of four comic playwrights were said to be his sons (Ararus, Nicostratus, Philetaerus and Philippus).

A list of the extant plays is given below. The dates and placings for many of them are given in production notices found in the *hypothesis* (introductory note) accompanying the play.

Title of play	Event	Date	Placing
Acharnians	Lenaea	425	1st place
Knights	Lenaea	424	1st place
Clouds (later partly revised)	City Dionysia	423	3rd place
Wasps	Lenaea	422	2nd place
Peace	City Dionysia	421	2nd place
Birds	City Dionysia	414	2nd place
Lysistrata	Lenaea?	411	Unknown
Women at the Thesmophoria	City Dionysia?	411	Unknown
Frogs	Lenaea	405	1st place
Assembly-Women	Unknown	*c.* 392–91	Unknown
Wealth	Unknown	388	Unknown

Contemporary evidence is hard to come by for all our playwrights; but for Aristophanes, we do not even have the benefit of Aristophanes' plays and their caricatures! Instead, ancient biographies of Aristophanes treated comments made by characters in his plays as if they were the gospel truth, spoken by Aristophanes about himself. And where characters do make mention of the playwright, biographers failed to see the humorous context of their remarks.

A good example of this is their naive interpretation of the parabasis of *Acharnians*. The parabasis is typically a moment in the play in which its plot is temporarily put on hold and the chorus-leader addresses the audience directly and builds a rapport with them; in essence, it is a shameless but humorous plug for the play. In this particular parabasis, the chorus-leader takes the following approach (643–51).

7.10 Because of him [i.e. Aristophanes], the embassies bringing the tribute from our allied cities will keep coming – because they're desperate to see this brilliant poet, who has risked telling the Athenians right from wrong. His reputation for boldness has already spread so far that even the king, when he was debriefing the delegation from Sparta, after asking them which side had the stronger navy, then asked which one the poet more frequently criticized: for they, he added, would have improved the most and would win the war since they had him to advise them.

As Mary Lefkowitz (1981: 111) notes, these remarks reappear in the *Life of Aristophanes* (40–2), compiled by an anonymous ancient biographer.

7.11 The poet became so famous that his reputation spread as far as Persia, and the king enquired of his advisers whose side the comic poet was on.

> • How do you think the chorus-leader's comments should be taken? What mistake does the biographer make in the way he makes use of them?

Particular contributions

Aristophanes arrived on the scene when Athenian comedy was still in its formative phase. Comedies were integrated into the City Dionysia in *c.* 486 but only became part of the Lenaea festival in *c.* 440 BC. The works of other famous poets of Old Comedy that were his forerunners (Cratinus, Crates, Pherecrates, Eupolis) have not survived beyond a few excerpts and papyrus fragments, so it is hard to judge Aristophanes' contribution. It is likely, however, that the distinct strain of humour characteristic of his surviving plays is largely a product of his genius. In fact, his first surviving play (*Acharnians*) shows all the vigour and self-confidence of later works.

Plot

The structure of an Aristophanic play tends to follow a standard pattern, especially in his earlier plays: a long prologue designed to draw in the audience (see **6.5** and **6.19**), then the entry of the large and often rambunctious chorus of 24 in the *parodos*, followed by a string of alternating episodes and choral odes. Quite early on in the play, the chorus-leader usually delivers the parabasis (literally 'stepping forward'), in which he addresses the audience directly, usually on topics irrelevant to the plot: he might sweet-talk them, poke fun at them, cheerlead for the playwright or accuse his rivals of plagiarism, give advice to the city or crack a joke at the expense of someone in the audience. Some plays have two parabases. There are usually also one or more *agon* scenes in which characters square off in a contest of words. Unlike its counterpart in tragedy, mud-slinging and low punches are the order of the day.

Within this basic formal structure, plays go off in many different directions – and, indeed, within a given play the episodes are often much less tightly interconnected than is the case in tragedy. In *Frogs*, for example, Dionysus arrives in Hades and has a series of encounters with Underworld residents who mistake him for Heracles because of his disguise. Aeacus, still angry with Heracles for stealing Cerberus, takes it out on Dionysus, while his maid wants to show 'Heracles' the good times. After several encounters of this type, the plot switches over to the contest between Aeschylus and Euripides. Whereas in the preceding scenes, Dionysus is the butt of the humour as he desperately tries, chameleon-like, to adapt to his constantly changing situation with some wild improvisation, now he assumes the role of judge and pokes fun at the two competing tragedians.

This fluidity is a mainstay of the humour. Not only does the audience not know what will happen next, but even within a given scene the peculiar mix of characters and action can be eye-popping – a farmer flies up to Olympus on a dung-beetle (see **3.11**), or the poet Cinesias shows up at the birds' newly founded colony of Cloudcuckooland looking for a pair of wings. These bizarre and at times surreal scenarios are usually not as random as they first seem; underlying the apparent absurdity is often a serious point. *Birds*, for example, follows two Athenians as they try to get away from Athens, with all its lawsuits and fines. It seems that they have succeeded when they settle with the birds in a fantasy world somewhere up in the clouds. But even this apparent Utopia is invaded by a string of officious Athenians, each trying to assert his claim on this new colony in a way reminiscent of Athenian meddling in the internal affairs of her colonies and allies.

This deliberate disjuncture between fantastical setting and the contemporary realities that intrude into it is typical of Aristophanes' art. In many of his plays, the protagonist encounters a predicament (often reminiscent of a social problem faced by Athens at the time). The play then comes up with an ingenious and often fantastical solution to this problem which takes the plot in a direction often described as an escape fantasy, creating a topsy-turvy world in which the normal world order is suspended. When an Athenian farmer is unable to persuade the assembly to negotiate for peace, he decides to pursue a private peace – to the Greek mind, a contradiction in terms (*Acharnians*). Or the women of Athens, tired of the war, collude with the Spartan womenfolk to bring it to an end by imposing a sex-strike; the men quickly capitulate (*Lysistrata*).

Over the course of a play, the wacky idea is taken to its logical extreme and breeds a whole set of related scenarios and word-play – *Birds*, for example, capitalizes on the many bizarre possibilities that are created when humans start conversing and living with birds, and is permeated by a web of witty bird-related puns and metaphors. The protagonist encounters opposition from certain individuals or factions who attempt to obstruct him – but in the end the parties reconcile and the plot comes to fruition in a grand finale (the **exodos**) that brings the promise of prosperity, feasting and priapic sexual gratification (the fantasy world that Aristophanes' plays inhabit is decidedly male). The celebration that typically ends the plays also mirrors the festival context in which they were performed. The savage ending of *Clouds* is a deliberate inversion of the norm: the torches that light the cast's festive procession out of the theatre are put to destructive use as Strepsiades burns down Socrates' school.

Topics

To a modern audience, Aristophanes' plays often seem reactionary and even politically subversive. But it seems that Aristophanes and his contemporaries believed that the comic poet played an important role in the education of citizens. Certainly his plays deal with a wide range of issues and institutions central to the *polis* – politics, gender, class, education, the lawcourts, assembly and navy. No topic is off limits, and no one is exempt from parody – even the gods. Indeed, Aristophanes delights in making fun of the serious, whether they be characters in tragedy, self-important government officials or reverent initiates of a mystery cult. He is as likely to smear a politician for his sexual tastes as he is to attack him for being corrupt. In fact, sexual innuendo, jokes about bodily functions and graphically crude language pervade his plays, which also delight in slapstick (e.g. slaves are tortured, walk-on characters are beaten and sent packing), gags involving exaggerated physical humour, odd combinations of props, and absurd uses of the *mechane*. But at the heart of his vision is an appreciation that Athens, her institutions and her citizens matter, and that comedy can contribute to the health of the *polis* by alleviating its pain, diagnosing its maladies and offering caustic treatment of its cancers.

1 How political is modern satirical comedy (e.g. magazines like *The Onion* and *Private Eye*, and TV shows such as *The Simpsons* and *Real Time with Bill Maher*)? Do they attack the same kinds of targets as Aristophanes did?

2 Can you think of any modern works that combine the element of fantasy with biting contemporary satire?

3 Modern satire is rarely written in verse form. In what other important ways is modern satire different from the satire of Aristophanes?

4 Do you think that respect should be shown to political leaders?

5 Is it fair to mock people for personal traits (as Aristophanes mocked Cleisthenes for his sexual orientation and Cleonymus for his cowardice)?

Menander

Menander, son of Diopeithes and Hegestrate, was born *c.* 342/41 BC, apparently into a noble and wealthy family from Cephisia, a deme just north-east of Athens. He made his debut *c.* 321 with a play titled *Anger* that hasn't survived; he was apparently still an ephebe (a young man on military service) at the time. Over the course of the next three decades he produced a whopping 108 plays, according to the *Suda*. The actual number is likely to be somewhat lower, since a number of plays had alternative titles that the *Suda* may have mistakenly counted as separate plays. Even so, it is highly likely that some of Menander's plays were composed for events other than the Lenaea and City Dionysia. This is hardly surprising, especially since his plays did not include topical references specific to Athens and so would have appealed to audiences elsewhere. Moreover, by this period, there was a demand for Attic-style drama in other parts of the Greek-speaking world.

Menander died *c.* 291/90 reportedly as a result of a drowning accident while swimming near the Athenian harbour at Piraeus (but see the caveat about such stories in **7.6n**, p. 172). He is said to have won eight victories at Athens, a surprisingly low number. Some scholars account for his lack of popularity by pointing to his political associations. Diogenes Laertius (5.79) informs us that he was a friend of Demetrius of Phalerum. Demetrius had been appointed governor of Athens in 317 by the Macedonians, who exercised a tight control over a debilitated Athens after Philip of Macedon's defeat of Athens and her allies at Chaeronea in 338. Diogenes adds that when Demetrius was ousted (in 307), Menander was almost put on trial because of his association with him. A playwright with such close ties to the Macedonian-backed powers would have been viewed with resentment, it is argued. Such arguments, however, remain speculative.

What is clear is that Menander was already appreciated as one of the greats soon after his death. The third-century BC scholar Aristophanes of Byzantium considered him second only to Homer. Quintilian, writing in the late first century AD, singled out Menander as an example of an author whose work had stood the test of time, and said of his posthumous celebrity (*Institutio Oratoria* 3.7.18): 'For some, like Menander, have been more fairly treated by the opinions of later generations than by their own generation.' And it wasn't only Greek and Roman authors who admired, quoted and imitated him. There was a market in Menander memorabilia among the educated general public too: portrait busts, mosaics with scenes from his plays, and many papyri fragments attest to his popularity.

This makes it all the more surprising that his works then dropped out of circulation in the seventh or eighth century AD. For over a millennium, his work was known only through fragments, quotations and descriptions of his art preserved in other authors, and the Roman comedies of Plautus and Terence, who drew heavily on Greek New Comedy. Then, just as dramatically, his lost works began to resurface as papyri were dug out of the sands of Egypt, many at the site of Oxyrhynchus: first a short section of his *Farmer* in 1897, then a series of more substantial fragments, including one virtually complete play, *Old Cantankerous*, discovered in 1957 and published in 1959. Sizeable sections of a third-century BC papyrus of *The Sicyonian* were even found to have been cut down and reused as cartonnage for wrapping mummies! We now have substantial portions of seven plays, listed in the box in rough order of completeness from *Old Cantankerous* to *Man from Sicyon*, of which perhaps half survives. Only *Old Cantankerous* can be securely dated: an early work, it won first prize at the Lenaea in 316 BC.

Play	Title in Greek	Alternative titles in translation
Old Cantankerous	*Dyskolos*	*Curmudgeon, Grouch, Malcontent, Misanthrope*, etc.
Girl from Samos	*Samia*	*Samia, Woman from Samos, Samian Girl*, etc.
Arbitration	*Epitrepontes*	*Arbitrators*
Shield	*Aspis*	---
Girl with the Cropped Hair	*Perikeiromenē*	*Girl with the Shaven Head, Rape of the Locks, Shorn*, etc.
Hated Man	*Misoumenos*	*Hated, Man She Hated*
Man from Sicyon	*Sikyōnios*	*Sicyonian, Sicyonians*

Also preserved are shorter sections of *Double Deception* (Greek *Dis Exapatōn*), *Hero* (*Hērōs*), *Lyre Player* (*Kitharistēs*), *Farmer* (*Geōrgos*), *Apparition* (*Phasma*), *Flatterer* (*Kolax*), *Spirit-possessed Girl* (*Theophoroumenē*), *Girl from Leucas* (*Leukadia*), *Girl from Perinthus* (*Perinthia*), *Man from Carthage* (*Karchēdonios*), *Women Drinking Hemlock* (*Kōneiazomenai*) as well as snippets of other plays.

The *Suda* includes the following entry on Menander.

7.12   Menander, an Athenian, the son of Diopeithes and Hegestrate, about whom much has been reported by many authors; a poet of New Comedy, he had squinty eyes but a sharp mind, and was completely **mad about women**. He wrote 108 comedies, as well as letters to King **Ptolemy** and many other stories written in prose.

- How might you explain the claim that Menander was crazy for women?

---

mad about women   Athenaeus (*Learned Banqueters* 594d) tells us that he was madly in love with a prostitute named Glycera (her name literally means 'sweet'), but then had a falling out with her. Glycera is the name of the title character of Menander's *Girl with the Cropped Hair*, the courtesan who ends up marrying her young lover, the soldier Polemon.

Ptolemy   Ptolemy I (also known as Ptolemy Soter), who ruled Egypt 323–283 BC. Nothing certain is known of his reported correspondence with Menander.

Particular contributions

Menander's plays (New Comedy) are very different from those of Aristophanes (Old Comedy). Gone are the scathing personal jibes, coarse language, and fantastical plots that so rapidly switch gear. The focus of interest has clearly shifted from the *polis* (the city-state) and its concerns to the *oikos* (the household). The *skene* and its doors now represent two adjacent houses, inhabited by ordinary people who may just as easily be living in Corinth (*Girl with the Cropped Hair*) or Eleusis (*Man from Sicyon*) as in Athens. Social issues prevail over political ones, and topical asides are replaced by more universal themes. In *Old Cantankerous*, the rich young urbanite earns the respect of his prospective father-in-law by digging in the field and developing a farmer's tan. The old grouch learns that no man is an island, is reconciled with his estranged son and agrees to marry off the daughter who had shared his reclusive existence. And the young groom's well-heeled father must come to terms with the fact that his son has married into a family of inferior status and means. Quite apart from their dramatic vitality and the continuing relevance of their themes, Menander's plays offer the social historian valuable access to the details of daily life in the late fourth century – everything from the minutiae of inheritance laws and culinary delicacies to broader issues such as social mobility and class prejudice.

> The third-century BC author Satyrus, in his *Life of Euripides* (fragment 39), makes the following remark about Euripides' influence on New Comedy.

7.13 … scenes of dramatic reversals, rapes of girls, substitutions of children, recognitions by means of rings and necklaces: these things are, for sure, **the cornerstones of later comedy**, which Euripides brought to their peak.

> Satyrus' claims are borne out even among the surviving plays of Euripides. In his *Ion*, for example, we first see Ion sweeping the steps of the sanctuary of Apollo at Delphi, where he has been reared as a foundling by the priestess after having been abandoned there as an infant by his mother Creusa, who was raped by Apollo. Creusa and her husband Xuthus come to Delphi to seek Apollo's help for their childlessness; after an elaborate series of misunderstandings and mistaken identities that almost result in Creusa killing Ion and him killing her, they eventually recognize each other's true identity through the use of tokens (the homemade clothes and necklace which the baby Ion was wearing when he was exposed), and mother and son are happily reunited.

---

the cornerstones of later comedy Satyrus was referring to Greek New Comedy. But these same elements continue to exert their influence on theatre into modern times, showing up in *The Marriage of Figaro* and many a Gilbert and Sullivan opera.

Menander's plays also show evidence of Euripides' influence on them: they include direct quotations of lines from his works as well as clear thematic and philosophical affinities.

> The *Life of Aristophanes* (1.4–6, 46–51), however, credits Aristophanes with these very same influences.

7.14 He was the first to exhibit the style of New Comedy in his *Cocalus*, from which Menander and **Philemon** took their lead in their dramatic compositions.

He was a source of inspiration for the poets of New Comedy, namely Philemon and Menander. For when **the decree on *choregoi* had been passed** that made it illegal to make fun of anyone by name, and also the *choregoi* did not have the necessary means to perform their choregic duties, and because of these things there was no comic material left – since the point of comedy is to make fun of people – he wrote a comedy called *Cocalus*, in which he introduced rape, recognition, and all the other elements that Menander imitated.

> • At first these two extracts (7.13 and 7.14) seem to make mutually exclusive claims; but can you see a way in which both authors may be right? (Think about what you know about Aristophanes' plays and his use of tragedy.)

Plot

Like Aristophanes, Menander frequently builds his plays around a problem that needs resolution, but now the problems are of a domestic nature. In *Shield*, a greedy uncle wants to marry his niece in order to inherit the booty that her brother acquired while on campaign in Lycia before apparently dying on the battlefield. Her family, through the services of their artful slave, tries to outwit the uncle by pretending that his younger brother is on his deathbed, hoping that this will make him decide to marry his daughter instead of the original niece and thereby get his hands on her far larger inheritance. The scheme works, and the whole plot ends

---

Cocalus   a lost comedy of Aristophanes, apparently one of his last works.

Philemon   a prominent poet of New Comedy of whose works only fragments and extracts survive.

the decree on *choregoi* had been passed   Platonius (date unknown) in his *On Differences between the Comedies* also gives a political explanation – he ascribes the change to intimidation rather than legislation. It is not clear, however, whether these authors, writing centuries later, are drawing on concrete evidence that no longer survives or whether their comments are nothing more than speculations invented to explain the shift away from invective.

happily when the young soldier suddenly shows up (he was captured, not killed) and he and his sister both marry their chosen sweethearts.

This plot has all the hallmarks of a Menandrean play. 'There is not a plot by playful Menander that lacks love' (i.e. a love affair), remarks Ovid (*Tristia* 3.7.18) as he enumerates the long line of distinguished poets who applied their talent to love poetry. Indeed, love affairs are often the main thread in Menander's wonderfully contorted plots, though in each play the pattern is woven quite differently. In *Arbitration* (*Epitrepontes*) the young man discovers that his fiancée is pregnant and is about to disown her, only then to discover that the child is in fact his; in *Hated Man* (*Misoumenos*) a young girl captured in war hates the soldier who acquired her and refuses to marry him, since she thinks that he killed her brother – until her brother shows up alive and she happily relents.

Such summaries cannot do justice to the intricacy of the plots of these pioneering situational comedies. Mistaken identities, misunderstandings, subterfuges, antagonisms and delightful coincidences conspire to create a seemingly intractable knot, which is then just as cleverly unravelled. The anecdote found in Plutarch (see **7.15**) that Menander thought out his plot and then let the rest of the play develop from there certainly rings true. Structurally, the plays consist of five acts (Menander's five-act division later becomes standard practice in western theatre) punctuated by choral interludes.

> Plutarch in his *Moralia* (347e) tells the following story about Menander. It is part of a broader essay arguing that deeds (and the men who perform them) are more important than words (and the men who write about deeds).

7.15   It is told that one of Menander's friends said to him: 'The Dionysia is almost here, and you haven't yet composed your comedy?' Menander replied: 'By the gods, I certainly *have* composed the comedy: the plot has been laid out – now there's just the small matter of adding the lines to accompany it.'

Characterization

Menander's plays include many of the stock characters already present in Middle Comedy (see pp. 17–18). However, his characters often surprise us by proving more complex than initially anticipated; in *Hated Man* (*Misoumenos*), for example, the soldier (who as a stock character is normally self-serving, boastful and aggressive) shows self-restraint and compassion for the woman he bought as a prisoner of war. Some of the instances in which the playwright challenges the audience's preconceptions seem to have a philosophical purpose to them. Although Menander's characters have a certain degree of comic exaggeration, they are nevertheless credible, 'realistic' and fully rounded. Similarly, their conversations, though written in verse-form like all Greek drama, mimic the language of ordinary dialogue in other respects: they talk in half-sentences, use colloquial expressions and everyday proverbs and speak in contemporary Greek (i.e. early *koinē* or 'standard' Greek instead of the 'classical' Attic dialect of the fifth century).

---

1 Menander was known for his ability to accurately represent human nature. How true to life are the characters in modern situation comedy (e.g. a TV soap opera)? Does the exaggeration that usually goes along with comic caricaturing detract from the believability of characters?

2 Compare modern comedy (e.g. comedy shows on television, comic films and live comedy routines) to Athenian Old and New Comedy. Which is it closer to in spirit and subject-matter?

3 What types of plot strike you as more amusing: those of Aristophanes or those of Menander?

In his *Amores* (1.15), the Roman poet Ovid (writing in the first century BC) celebrates the immortality of art. This is what he writes about Menander.

7.16   As long as the tricky slave, the stern father, the wicked pimp and the sweet courtesan endure, Menander will live on.

Ovid singles out the stock characters of Menander's plays as the most notable aspect of his art.

He implies that Menander is guaranteed immortality because the characters in his plays are true to real life – as long as tricky slaves and stern fathers exist, his plays will continue to be popular.

Menander's plays are frequently praised for their verisimilitude (i.e. trueness to real life). Perhaps the most famous expression of this is the following saying attributed to the third-century BC Alexandrian scholar Aristophanes of Byzantium (found in Syrianus' *Commentary On Hermogenes* 2.23).

7.17   O Life, O Menander, which of you imitated the other?

Ancient literary critics and philosophers often make comparisons between reality and its representation in art. According to the Platonic theory of forms, artistic representations were a pale imitation of real-life objects, which were themselves replicas of an ideal form. Thus to describe Menander's plays as being so true to life that it was impossible to tell whether they were the original or the copy is a powerful compliment. A similar testimony to the artistic genius of the Italian Renaissance painter Raphael can be found on his marble sarcophagus in the Pantheon in Rome. A translation of the Latin inscription reads: 'Here lies Raffaello. While he lived, Nature feared that he would defeat her. When he died, she wanted to die too.'

In the following essay from Plutarch's *Moralia*, a later compiler records Plutarch's effusive praise for Menander. After critiquing Aristophanes for not differentiating his character types (a king should speak with gravity, the ordinary guy in the market-place should use vulgarities – but not the other way around), Plutarch goes on to say the following about Menander (853d–f).

7.18　But Menander's language is so polished and blends together so cohesively that, although it brings together many emotions and character types and adapts itself to **people** of all kinds, it still comes across as a single whole that preserves its uniformity in its use of ordinary words in common circulation. But if the plot calls for something more bewitching or bombastic, he will open, as it were, all the stops of his *aulos*, then quickly close them again in a way that is believable, returning to his natural tone. And although there have been many celebrated artisans, no craftsman has ever fashioned a single shoe, no mask-maker a mask, nor anyone a cloak capable of equally fitting a man, woman, youth, old man and a household slave. But Menander blended his language so successfully that it fits every nature, disposition and age. And he accomplished this even though he began his career while still young and died while at his peak as a **poet and director**.

- Can Aristophanes be defended against Plutarch's criticism? From what you know of Aristophanes' approach, can you think of a good reason why he might refuse to observe differences in tone and have a king use vulgarities or have the man on the street speak with gravity?

---

people　the word translated as 'people' can also mean 'masks'; Plutarch is using language drawn from the theatre.

poet and director　distinguishing between the two main aspects of the ancient playwright's role: that of *poiētēs* or composer of plays (literally 'maker') and that of *didaskalos* or director (literally 'teacher').

The sculptural relief in **7.19** is one of several later copies of what appears to be an original dating to the Hellenistic period (*c.* third century BC). It shows a young Menander, represented in heroic nudity from the waist up, contemplating the mask of a young man. Two more masks – those of a young girl and old man – rest on a nearby table.

7.19

1 What do you think the sculptor is trying to communicate about the playwright in the way he has chosen to depict him?

2 Do you see any connection between the representation of Menander in this relief and the descriptions of him in the preceding literary sources (7.14–7.18)?

3 From what you have read, which playwright do you think presents more credible and well-rounded female characters, Aristophanes or Menander, and what makes you think this?

Recommended reading

The best short general introduction is **Erika Simon**, *The Ancient Theatre* (Methuen, 1982). Another readable introduction to Greek theatre is **J. Michael Walton**, *Greek Theatre Practice* (Greenwood, 1980). A comprehensive and very useful introduction is **Ian Storey** and **Arlene Allan**, *A Guide to Ancient Greek Drama* (Blackwell, 2005).

The ancient evidence for Athenian drama is collected in **A. W. Pickard-Cambridge**, *The Dramatic Festivals of Athens* (Oxford University Press, revised edn 1968); it includes many of the primary texts under discussion (in the Greek or Latin original). A comprehensive collection of ancient sources with accompanying commentary is provided in **Eric Csapo** and **William Slater**, *The Context of Ancient Drama* (University of Michigan Press, 1994); it is more accessible than Pickard-Cambridge, especially since the sources are given in English translation.

The most comprehensive treatment of the physical evidence for ancient theatre, both Greek and Roman, is still **Margarete Bieber**, *The History of the Greek and Roman Theatre* (Princeton University Press, revised edn 1961). It examines the development of the theatre building as well as evidence from vase-paintings and other visual evidence, and contains a staggering 866 illustrations! A shorter and beautifully illustrated exploration of a selection of artefacts is **Richard Green** and **Eric Handley**'s *Images of the Greek Theatre* (University of Texas Press, 1995). A recent reappraisal of the theatre at Athens is **David Wiles**, *Tragedy in Athens: Performance Space and Theatrical Meaning* (Cambridge University Press, 1997). For acting, see **Pat Easterling** and **Edith Hall** (eds.), *Greek and Roman Actors: Aspects of an Ancient Profession* (Cambridge University Press, 2002). For the biographies of the playwrights, see **Mary Lefkowitz**, *The Lives of the Greek Poets* (Johns Hopkins University Press, 1981).

For Greek tragedy, **Oliver Taplin**, *Greek Tragedy in Action* (University of California Press, 1978) remains a most stimulating investigation of aspects of performance. An engaging discussion of issues relating to modern performance is provided by **Simon Goldhill**, *How to Stage Greek Tragedy Today* (University of Chicago Press, 2007). **Peter Arnott**, *Public and Performance in Greek Theatre* (Routledge, 1989) offers an accessible study of scenes from tragedy and comedy, investigating what they tell us about actors and audience. A wide range of topics is covered in the essays collected in **P. E. Easterling** (ed.), *The Cambridge Companion to Greek Tragedy* (Cambridge University Press, 1997), **Justina Gregory** (ed.), *A Companion to Greek Tragedy* (Blackwell, 2005) and **Marianne McDonald** and **J. Michael Walton** (eds.), *The Cambridge Companion to Greek and Roman Theatre* (Cambridge University Press, 2007). For satyr-play, Dana Sutton's overview in **P. E. Easterling** and **B. Knox** (eds.), *The Cambridge History of Classical Literature,*

Vol. I, Part 2, *Greek Drama* (Cambridge University Press, 1989) offers an excellent introduction. For New Comedy, excellent thematic treatment can be found in **Richard Hunter**, *The New Comedy of Greece and Rome* (Cambridge University Press, 1985).

A sensible introduction to Aeschylus is **John Herington**, *Aeschylus* (Yale University Press, 1986). Helpful analyses of Sophocles' plays are found in **A. F. Garvie**, *The Plays of Sophocles* (Bristol Classical Press, 2005) and **James Morwood**, *The Tragedies of Sophocles* (Bristol Phoenix Press, 2008). Two studies of all the extant plays of Euripides are **D. J. Connacher**, *Euripidean Drama: Myth, Theme, and Structure* (University of Toronto Press, 1967) and **James Morwood**, *The Plays of Euripides* (Duckworth, 2002).

Good general introductions to Aristophanes are **Kenneth McLeish**, *The Theatre of Aristophanes* (Taplinger, 1980) and **Douglas MacDowell**, *Aristophanes and Athens* (Oxford University Press, 1995). A lively and wide-ranging treatment of his plays is provided by **Kenneth Reckford**, *Aristophanes' Old-and-New Comedy* (University of North Carolina Press, 1987). For Menander, an engaging introduction is provided by **J. Michael Walton** and **Peter Arnott**, *Menander and the Making of Comedy* (Greenwood, 1996).

The Cambridge Translations from Greek Drama series (edited by **Judith Affleck** and **John Harrison**) offers accessible new translations with facing notes of many of the plays. I have used its translations for extracts where indicated in the introduction. Inexpensive translations of the plays and other primary texts are available in the Oxford World Classics series.

Authors referred to in the text but not mentioned above

Csapo, Eric, 'Later Euripidean music', in M. J. Cropp, Kevin Lee and David Sansone (eds.), *Euripides and Tragic Theatre in the Late Fifth Century, Illinois Classical Studies 24–25* (1999–2000), pp. 397–426.

Goldhill, Simon, 'The audience of Athenian tragedy', in P. E. Easterling (ed.), *The Cambridge Companion to Greek Tragedy* (Cambridge University Press, 1997), pp. 54–68.

Green, Richard, 'Art and theatre in the ancient world', in Marianne McDonald and J. Michael Walton (eds.), *The Cambridge Companion to Greek and Roman Theatre* (Cambridge University Press, 2007), pp. 163–83.

Halliwell, Stephen, 'Comic satire and freedom of speech in classical Athens', *Journal of Hellenic Studies*, 111 (1991), pp. 48–70.

Henderson, Jeffrey, 'Women and the Athenian dramatic festivals', *Transactions of the American Philological Association*, 121 (1991), pp. 133–47.

Hughes, Alan, 'The "Perseus Dance" Vase revisited', *Oxford Journal of Archaeology*, 25:4 (2006), pp. 413–33.

Knox, Bernard, *The Heroic Temper: Studies in Sophoclean Tragedy* (University of California Press, 1964).

Pomeroy, Sarah B., Burstein, Stanley M., Donlan, Walter and Roberts, Jennifer Tolbert, *A Brief History of Ancient Greece* (Oxford University Press, 2004).

Taplin, Oliver, *Comic Angels and Other Approaches to Greek Drama through Vase-paintings* (Oxford University Press, 1993).

Trendall, A. D., in A. D. Trendall and A. Cambitoglou, *Second Supplement to the Red-figured Vases of Apulia* (London, Institute of Classical Studies, 1991).

Wiles, David, *Greek Theatre Performance: An Introduction* (Cambridge University Press, 2000).

Wilson, Peter, 'The *aulos* in Athens', in Simon Goldhill and Robin Osborne (eds.), *Performance Culture and Athenian Democracy* (Cambridge University Press, 1999), pp. 58–96.

Inscriptions

Inscriptions are referenced by giving their citation in the multi-volume IG (*Inscriptiones Graecae*) or *SEG* (*Supplementum Epigraphicum Graecum*).

Glossary

Words in italics are transliterations of Greek words; those without italics are in common use in English. A mark over a vowel (e.g. ō) indicates that the Greek vowel is long and should be extended.

agōn literally 'contest'; used of competitions (athletic, musical, dramatic), of formal debates (in lawcourt and political assembly) and also of contests between two antagonists in drama

agōnothetēs official appointed to organize the festivals from the fourth century BC onwards; also used of a judge in the competitions

anagnōrisis literally 'recognition'; the moment in drama when a character discovers his or someone else's true identity, or realizes the true nature of his or her situation

Anthesteria festival of Dionysus at Athens in late February

antistrophe *see under* 'strophe'

archaic term used to describe the period of Greek history from 776 BC (traditional date for the first Olympic Games) to 479 BC (end of the Persian Wars)

architektōn theatre manager; he leased a theatre and paid its operating expenses

archōn annually appointed official; at Athens, the chief *archon* gave his name to the year

Artists of Dionysus guild of actors, securing for its members special privileges

Attic belonging to Attica, the region of Greece of which Athens was the *polis*

aulētēs piper or player of the *aulos*, a reed instrument accompanying dithyrambic and dramatic performances

boulē chief executive council at Athens composed of 500 members, fifty from each tribe

chitōn tunic worn by men and women (knee-length for men, ankle-length for women)

chlamys cloak, often worn by soldiers and messengers, fastened with a brooch

chorēgos rich citizen who funded and organized a chorus (*see* 'liturgy')

choreut member of a chorus, usually a young man

chorodidaskalos professional chorus-trainer

City Dionysia (also referred to as the **Great Dionysia** or simply the **Dionysia**) festival of Dionysus at Athens in March / early April; most important occasion for drama

classical term used to describe the period of Greek history from 479 BC (Greek victory over the Persians) to 323 BC (death of Alexander the Great)

demarch chief official of a deme

deme a village or township of Attica; the word refers to the settlement, its inhabitants and the surrounding land

deus ex machina Latin meaning 'god from the machine'; a god who flies in on the *mēchanē* and contrives a solution to a seemingly impossible situation

diazōma horizontal passage-way dividing audience seating into upper and lower sections

didaskalos director and producer of a play, often the playwright

dithyramb hymn sung and danced by a chorus in honour of Dionysus

eisagōgē procession escorting the statue of Dionysus into the city for the City Dionysia

eisodos (also called *parodos*) side-entrance of theatre leading into the *orchestra*; these side passageways separated the *theatron* from the *skene* on either side

ekklēsia political assembly of Athenian male citizens

ekkyklēma wheeled platform rolled out into the theatre to display indoor scenes

episkēnion upper storey of Hellenistic theatre-building

episode section of play spoken by actors (and sometimes chorus) between choral odes

epode *see under* 'strophe'

exarchos leader of dithyrambic chorus

exodos final section of a play, performed as chorus is leaving the theatre

Hellenistic term used to describe the period of Greek history from 323 BC (death of Alexander the Great) to 30 BC (death of Cleopatra, queen of Egypt)

himation cloak worn by men and women, usually worn draped over the tunic

hypokritēs Greek word for actor

hypothesis introductory note accompanying the text of a play, usually giving plot summary and details of original performance

ikria temporary wooden seating in *theatron*

irony discrepancy between apparent and intended meaning or between appearance and reality; in *dramatic irony*, the words or actions of a character have a deeper meaning for the audience than the character realizes

katharsis term used by Aristotle to describe the 'purification' or 'purging' of the emotions of pity and fear aroused in the viewer of a tragedy

kerkis wedge-shaped section of audience seating bounded by vertical staircases

kōmos literally 'revel'; drunken and bawdy procession characterized by singing and dancing; participants are termed komasts or 'revellers'

kordax dance of comedy; characterized as coarse

koryphaios leader of tragic chorus; engaged in dialogue with actors

kothornos (usually in plural, **kothornoi**) high-laced leather boot with soft, flat sole worn by actors in tragedy (also referred to as 'buskin')

Lenaea festival of Dionysus at Athens in January / early February, especially important for the performance of comedies

liturgy public work such as the funding of a chorus or of a trireme imposed on the wealthiest Athenian citizens

logeion literally the 'talking place': probably the roof of the *proskēnion* that functioned as a raised stage for actors in the Hellenistic period

Magna Graecia Latin term used to describe the region of southern Italy colonized by Greeks, especially along its coastline

mēchanē crane used to raise a character aloft in simulated flight

metatheatre term used to describe drama when it makes deliberate reference to itself as an act of performance (i.e. drawing attention to its artifice or theatricality instead of concealing the fact that it is make-believe)

Middle Comedy term used for comedy composed *c.* 386–321 BC, the period between Aristophanes and Menander

mimēsis 'imitation' or 'representation' of the real world through literature or art

New Comedy term used for comedy composed *c.* 321–263 BC; its main playwright was Menander

odeon roofed auditorium used for recitations, musical performances, lectures etc.

Old Comedy term used for comedy composed *c.* 486–386 BC; the most famous playwright of this period was Aristophanes

orchēstra literally the 'dancing place'; the main performance space in a Greek theatre, often circular in shape

parabasis section of Old Comedy in which a character (often the chorus-leader) addressed the audience directly, speaking on behalf of the playwright

paraskēnion projecting wing of the theatre building

parodos song sung by the chorus while entering the orchestra near the beginning of a play; term also used to describe the side-entrance (the *eisodos*) by which they entered

peripeteia literally 'reversal'; sudden change of fortune in tragedy, usually from good to bad

phallus leather appendage attached to the costumes of male actors in Old Comedy to represent a penis; also appears in other contexts as a symbol of fertility

phlyax genre of farcical drama found in southern Italy and Sicily

phorbeia head-strap worn by the *aulētēs* (piper)

pilos conical traveller's hat

pinax painted panel inserted in openings in both the *proskēnion* and *episkēnion* of the Hellenistic theatre-building to provide temporary scene-setting

polis a city-state (of which demes are subdivisions); the word refers to the state, its main city and the inhabitants

pompē procession of festival participants

proagōn event presenting the playwrights and their casts ahead of the competition proper

prohedria right to a front-row seat enjoyed by certain priests, officials etc.; also used to refer to the seats themselves

proskēnion literally 'before the *skēnē*'; front section of the Hellenistic theatre, a colonnaded porch from whose roof actors performed (*see* '*logeion*')

Rural Dionysia (also known as **Lesser Dionysia**) festivals of Dionysus put on by individual demes (mostly in December/ January)

scholiast ancient commentator

scholion (often in plural, **scholia**) ancient commentator's note written in the margin of a manuscript

sikinnis   dance of satyr-plays, characterized as highly energetic

skēnē   stage-building that provided the backdrop for the action and offered a central doorway and later two side-doorways through which actors could make their entrance

skēnographia   scene-painting

stasimon   choral song (also referred to as 'ode')

strophe   a choral ode was divided into shorter units: a strophe was followed by an antistrophe, whose metrical pattern was identical to that of the strophe; the closing section, known as the epode, was metrically independent from the preceding strophe(s) and antistrophe(s)

tetralogy   set of three tragedies and one satyr-play entered by a playwright and performed consecutively on one day

theātron   literally the 'viewing place'; the audience seating area, later used of the whole theatre

theologeion   literally the 'talking place for gods': an elevated vantage-point (most probably the flat roof of the *skēnē*) from which gods could appear

theōrikon   festival fund given to Athenian citizens

thymelē   originally used to refer to the altar in the centre of the *orchestra*, later to the area around the altar

thyrsus   sacred fennel-staff carried by worshippers of Dionysus, usually wreathed in ivy and often topped by a pine-cone

Index

abuse poetry 11, 12
actors: Aeschylus 5, 7, 162;
    emergence of 131–2; number
    of 5, 7, 12–13, 101, 162, 165;
    pronunciation mistake 141n;
    Sophocles 131, 165; *see also*
    masks
Aeschines 27; *Against Ctesiphon*
    2, 40; *Against Timarchus* 97,
    141–2
Aeschylus 56, 158–63, 172n; actors
    5, 7, 162; *Agamemnon* 82–4,
    105–6, 110, 116, 117, 160, 161,
    162; choral dance 75–6; as
    didaskalos 45; *Edonians* 92n,
    98; *Eumenides* 84–5, 147, 148,
    162; *Libation Bearers* 86, 145n,
    161, 162, 163, 166; *Oresteia*
    trilogy 45, 49, 70, 162; *Persians*
    4, 20, 46, 65, 78n, 86, 110, 124,
    158, 162; *Phrygians* 76; *Proteus*
    45; *Seven against Thebes* 76,
    161, 162; *Suppliants* 162;
    Women of Aetna 20, 158
Agathon 23, 40, 69, 77, 134n, 178
agōn 23, 154, 194
agōnothetēs 35, 194
Agora 49, 50, 121n
anagnōrisis 151, 166, 194
anapaests 6, 100
animal choruses 11, 12, 94–5, 119
Anthesteria festival 8, 23, 25, 194
Antiphon 39
antistrophe 80, 81, 194
Archelaus 170
Archilochus 2, 74
architektōn 142n, 194
archōn 26, 29, 31, 141, 145, 194
Arion 19
Aristides, Publius Aelius 78
Aristocles 76
Aristophanes 11, 177–82;
    Acharnians 54, 68, 130, 143–5,
    173, 178, 180, 181; on Aeschylus
    14, 15, 76, 92n, 103–5, 160;
    Assembly-Women 42; *Birds*
    12, 91–3, 95, 99–100, 135,
    150n, 181, 182; *Clouds* 12, 43,

119, 131, 145–6, 177–9, 182;
    Cocalus 186; directly addressing
    audience 134, 139–40; on
    Euripides 12, 14, 15, 70, 78,
    103–5, 169, 173; *Frogs* 12, 14,
    15, 65, 103–5, 110, 124, 126n,
    140–1, 160, 162, 169, 177,
    181; *Knights* 12, 23, 119, 120;
    Lysistrata 113, 181; Middle
    Comedy 16–17; opposite-half
    concept 178; *Peace* 12, 136–7,
    146; *Plays* 14; plot 180–2; *Pre-
    contest* 14; on Socrates 12; on
    Sophocles 164; *Wasps* 12, 145n,
    149, 150; *Wealth* 16; *Women at
    the Thesmophoria* 12, 50, 69, 72,
    126–30, 135–6, 173
Aristophanes of Byzantium 183,
    188–9
Aristotle: *Athenian Constitution*
    28–9; on comedy 11, 23;
    improvisation 22; *Nicomachean
    Ethics* 149n; plot 166; *Poetics*
    4–5, 6n, 21, 71, 76n, 77, 92n,
    106, 108, 150n, 151, 153, 160;
    scene-painting 64; spectacle
    92n
Artists of Dionysus 131–2, 194
assembly: *see ekklēsia*
Athenaeus 2, 16, 75, 79–80, 87, 97,
    134n, 138, 184n
Athenian Constitution 28–9
Athens 2, 16, 19–21, 34, 133, 153–4
Atilius Fortunatianus 80
Attic drama 21, 61–2, 183, 194
audience: emotion in 152; and
    judges 43; playing to 145–8;
    response of 149–55; seating
    133; size of 134–43; ticket
    fee 133; vase painting 61–2;
    women 133, 134, 135–6
aulētēs (piper) 75, 96–100, 194
aulos (pipe) 2, 3, 96–100, 194

bacchants *see* maenads
Bacchylides 1
benches 49, 50, 59; *see also ikria*
boulē 41, 135n, 143, 178, 194

Chamaeleon 76
characterization 167–8, 187–8
characters 17, 104, 110, 133, 139–
    40; *see also* stock characters
chitōn 9, 114, 115, 123, 127, 194
chlamys 13, 114, 194
choral dance 2–3, 74, 75–6, 79–80,
    84–7, 164
choral odes 4, 16, 75, 82n, 100n,
    161, 180–1
choregic monuments 33
chorēgos 62, 138n, 194; and
    archōn 29; costs 34, 35, 74;
    decree on 186; end of 46;
    influencing judges 41; liturgy
    26; rewards 30–1, 34; vase
    paintings 13, 15
Choregos Vase 13–15, 16, 120
choreuts (chorus-members) 8, 74,
    76, 79, 194
chorodidaskalos 38, 74, 194
chorus: circular 2; civic
    performance 84n; as idealized
    spectator 77; New Comedy
    95; Old Comedy 12–13, 91–5;
    orchēstra 79; plot development
    81n; satyr-play 87–91; spectacle
    92n; tragedy 75–87; training
    of 74
chorus-leader: *see exarchos;*
    koryphaios
City Dionysia 1, 24, 25–8, 194;
    comedy 11; *Didaskaliai* 46;
    as international event 143–5;
    processions 138n; protagonist
    131; satyr-plays 8; state
    involvement 41; tragedy 4;
    tripods 10; winners 44
Cleisthenes 129n
Cleon 144, 146, 150
Cleonymus 93
coincidence, in New Comedy 95n
comedy 11–19; costume 13;
    ekkyklēma 68–9; extant 1;
    iambic poetry 23; masks 13,
    119–24; Megara 19; processions
    148; sacred 129–30; taboos
    130; vase paintings 11,